ESSENTIALS OF
STAGE SCENERY

ESSENTIALS
OF
STAGE SCENERY

SAMUEL SELDEN AND TOM REZZUTO

University of North Carolina
at Chapel Hill

APPLETON-CENTURY-CROFTS
Educational Division
MEREDITH CORPORATION *New York*

10-5-73 Boston 10.06

Youngken

CONTENTS

ILLUSTRATIONS

FIGURES

PREFACE

Stage Scenery and Lighting appeared as a collaboration between Hunton D. Sellman and me in the summer of 1930, with Hunton Sellman as author of the second part and me the first. The collaboration continued through three revised editions, issued in 1939, 1946, and 1959.

Through the long period since the first appearance of the scenic manual the center of my work in the theatre has gradually shifted to other areas—administration, directing, and playwriting. Although I have strongly continued my interest in the technical field, I have become unable to give it the close, undivided attention that I applied to it originally, and when Appleton-Century-Crofts proposed in time that Hunton Sellman and I divide the treatments of scenery and lighting and develop them separately, I realized how difficult it would be for me then to do a really thorough updating of my section on scenery.

Fortunately, I have been able to enlist the collaboration of a long-time associate, Tom Rezzuto, whom I regard as an outstanding technician and designer. He is a veteran of both the professional and academic theatre with extensive experience in working under many different conditions. Since he has been at times an actor, scene designer, director, and playwright, he has acquired a practical knowledge of the problems that must be faced by the other artists and craftsmen in the playhouse—both indoors and outdoors.

Mr. Rezzuto has revised and extended much of the text taken from the original volume for this one, added a large number of new drawings, and incorporated a chapter on the planning and construction of stage properties.

SAMUEL SELDEN

1972

xv

ESSENTIALS OF
STAGE SCENERY

Figure 1-1

Setting for *Macbeth,* designed by Robert Edmond Jones. Courtesy of The Theatre Collection, The New York Public Library at Lincoln Center; Aster, Lenox, and Tilden Foundations.

SCENERY AS AN INTERPRETIVE AND COLLABORATIVE ART

CHAPTER 1

1 THE ORGANIC PRODUCTION

The *process* of the theatre, as it is generally understood, consists of two parts: the writing of a play and the presenting of it to an audience. An author conceives a pattern of physical and vocal images that he puts down in words on paper. A group of fellow artists, following the words they find in the play's text, translate the written images into patterns of movement, sound, light, and

3

color. They embody the author's words with visible and audible life before an audience.

Words in a script, however, only stand for or symbolize an interplay of ideas and emotions, and symbols may be translated in a number of different and plausible ways. An expert in the art of acting, music, dancing, costume, scenery, or lighting design can read a script and assess its dramatic values for his medium in ways that are opposite to, or at least in conflict with, those of his fellow artists. If several of these dissimilar translations are placed on the stage simultaneously, only confusion can result. The effect produced will be that of a symphony orchestra composed of many excellent musicians but lacking a conductor. Re-created or translated imagery, if it is to be meaningful to an audience and remain faithful to the author's intentions, must be unified in all its elements. In other words, all aspects of a performance must conspire to produce upon its audience a single coherent set of effects.

The *art* of the theatre is a single body of principles and practices to the extent that its component parts—playwriting, acting, dancing, music, costumes, scenery, and lighting—all converge and reinforce each other. Orchestrated and rehearsed, then presented as an ensemble before an audience, skillful applications of the several components of theatrical art can lead the audience to the emotional and intellectual awareness that an author originally plotted in his script. The unseen conductor of this symphony is the play's director. He attempts to make the same thought and spirit govern his translated image as governed the author's original image.

The most important element of this translated image is *action*, that is, the vital flow or life force that is inherent in a play, not simply physical movement and speech. This flow or life force, which constitutes the *dramatic action* of the play, is illuminated through the media of movement and speech by the actor as he brings the play to life on the stage. Since the actor is the special instrument of dramatic action, all other interpretive arts of the theatre—music, scenery, lighting, and the rest—must be complementary and contributive to the actor's central art.

"As an artist painting my first sketch for a setting," says Jo Mielziner in *Designing for the Theatre*, "I am master of that expression, but its value to the final result comes from submitting myself and my talents to the collaborative effort." An eminent designer of stage scenery, he insists that the life of a stage set, however striking its pictorial values, "consists in its continuing development in relation to the movement of the play."

The study of scenery is, then, the study of one interpretive art that moves conjointly with other interpretive arts to reveal and enrich the dramatic action created by the author and translated into a living presence by the actor and director. All the various talents involved in a production fuse their expressions into one expression that reaches the audience as an organic whole.

2   SCENERY, THE ENVIRONMENT OF ACTION

How can scenery reveal and enrich action? Looking at the written thoughts of some founders of modern stagecraft, one finds interesting clues for an answer. Scenery, said Gordon Craig, should be the visual expression of the dynamic spirit of a play "in all that comes before the eye." Adolphe Appia felt that scenery, in its best sense, should be a pattern of light and form surrounding and supporting a living and active presence on the stage and adding to its validity. Lee Simonson held much the same view. Scenic art, he believed, is "the creation of plastic forms and spaces that are an integral part of acting and project its meaning." Kenneth Mac-Gowan offered a similar view when he said that scenery should function as "an emotional envelope appropriate to the dramatic mood of the author, a visualization in color, line and light of the dominant emotions to be pictured by the actors." Robert Edmond Jones, regarded by many as the father of modern American scene design, said simply that scenery should be the "environment" of a dramatic action.

Gathering from these giants of theatre, we might answer the question, "What should scenery contribute to dramatic action?" simply as follows: In an organic production of a play, scenery contributes a helpful environment to the play's dramatic action.

To produce this environment, the scenic designer must understand the full meaning of such concepts as "plastic," "surrounding," and "emotional envelope." To understand these terms clearly and distinctly is to realize that dramatic action is enriched when it occurs *in* a setting, not merely *in front of* a setting. In other words, the actor is helped to illuminate the dramatic action *in* an environment to which he can relate his character, rather than *in front of* a setting that merely furnishes a background for his performance.

3   FUNCTIONS OF THE ENVIRONMENT: PLACING THE ACTION

The first function of scenery is to place or locate the action—to give it a home. Many authors very specifically locate the action of their plays with explicit stage directions and scene descriptions. Others do not. Even when provided with a detailed description

Figure 1-2 Realistic setting for *Long Day's Journey into Night,* designed by Tom Rezzuto, The University of North Carolina at Chapel Hill.

from the author, the designer may find that the director wishes to emphasize certain elements in the environment that the playwright did not emphasize. The director and designer may arrive at a plan for an environment that, at first glance, seems foreign to the playwright's intent but that on further examination is found to emphasize certain values in the dramatic action more effectively than the playwright's prescription. There is, of course, no limit to the approaches a director and designer may take to the planning of a particular production. Finally, the only limit to the type of environment they provide exists in their creativity and unique vision. The final style of the production will depend on those elements of the environment that they choose to emphasize or minimize.

Following are indications of various approaches to the planning of sets. These approaches can be roughly categorized by the elements each consistently emphasizes. Each type locates the action in a distinctive environment.

The Fully Realistic Setting

A realistic setting attempts to present a lifelike portrayal of the locality in which the action takes place. Such a setting attempts to make the spectator feel he is gazing into a real place that actual people, not the characters in a play, might use. The designer, through the careful selection and arrangement of details, builds the environment out of seemingly real walls, real doors, real moldings.

The Suggestively Realistic Setting

Just as the fully realistic setting depends on the choice of detail, so does the suggestively realistic setting. The difference, however, is that suggestive realism does not attempt to produce a completely delineated locality. It attempts, rather, to localize through suggestion, through the use of a few indicative details. In a setting of this sort, each item functions as a symbol for a cluster of associated details called up in the spectator's mind by the limited details he actually sees. A Gothic bench and a chest, for example, set in front of a medieval tapestry or a massive, rough column can, with appropriate lighting, create the illusion of a complete room in an early English castle.

Many types of plays, among them classic as well as modern works that require considerable scene shifting, are set very effectively in environments of this sort. Plays such as *Summer and Smoke* or *Death of a Salesman*, which require several locations at once, or simultaneous areas—also are handled effectively through the use of suggestive realism.

The Nonrealistic Setting

The nonrealistic setting attempts to picture an underlying idea, emotion, or mood of a play. The designer attempts to create a psychological rather than a naturalistic environment, to imply by its outward form some inner characteristic of the play. By taking an abstract idea at the heart of the play and by using form, color, line, or proportion, he translates that idea into material objects that he arranges as the environment. If violence, for example, is inherent in a script, the designer might translate the abstract idea "violence" into a setting based on jagged diagonal lines and paint of strong, jarring colors. If the play is a farce, the designer might choose to use a rollicking line with active, laughing colors.

The Architectural or Formalistic Setting

The architectural or formalistic setting, although it provides an acting area for the play, makes no attempt to represent a particular

Figure 1-3 Three examples of suggestive realism:
(Left, above): Summer and Smoke, designed by John Stockard, The University of North Carolina at Chapel Hill.
(Left, below): West Side Story, designed by John Sneden, East Carolina University, and reproduced with his permission.
(Above): Blood Wedding, designed by George W. McKinney, University of Illinois, and reproduced with his permission.

locality. In addition, the setting usually does not change during the performance except possibly for furniture or fabrics. Architectural elements such as steps, platforms, columns, and walls indicate the mood and period of the play. Because a given area of the setting may serve as several different localities during the course of the action, lines and colors are frequently neutral or unassertive. For example, a particular area of the setting might be used for a bedroom scene one moment and a waiting room the next. If that area had been made to look too specifically like a bedroom it could not, of course, be used for the waiting room later.

Changes in properties as well as the lighting can denote different locales, changes of mood, or gaps in time. Indeed, lighting here plays a key role in achieving variety in locale, mood, and pictorial composition. Because the same physical elements cast under different lighting can change character markedly, the designer should

10

Figure 1-4 Three examples of nonrealistic settings:
> *(Left, above): The Tempest,* designed by D. W. Powell, San Diego State College.
> *(Left, below): Tiger Rag,* designed by George W. McKinney, University of Illinois, and reproduced with his permission.
> *(Above): Mother Courage,* designed by Barrett Van Loo; lighting by H. D. Sellman, San Diego State College.

make use of such changes to bring variety and interest to his set. The audience, asked to accept the environment as a theatrical structure in which the dramatic action takes place, is freed to focus its attention on the play rather than being distracted by elaborate scenery. The tragedies and comedies of ancient Greece and Elizabethan England were originally written for this type of staging. Certain modern, poetic works, for example those by Samuel Beckett and Eugène Ionesco, can also be very effective in this type of environment.

In recent years, several theatre companies have incorporated

Figure 1-5 Formalistic setting for *Becket,* designed by Tom Rezzuto, The University of North Carolina at Chapel Hill.

formalistic settings as basic elements of their theatre buildings. Notable among them is The Stratford Festival Theatre in Ontario and The Tyrone Guthrie Theatre in Minneapolis. A wide range of plays can be presented on architectural stages of this type to audiences who increasingly understand and appreciate their dramatic conventions.

The Unit Setting

By combining some elements of the formalistic type of setting with elements of the suggestively realistic type, the designer can create a unit set. In this type of setting, shifts from scene to scene are accomplished by changing indicative details or rearranging minor portions of the setting within a major, fixed framework.

Its advantages for certain kinds of plays are obvious. In addition to saving space and simplifying scene shifts, the cost of constructing scenery is reduced because certain parts are repeated. A danger, however, is inherent in this type of design. If it becomes too clever or ingenious, it is apt to degenerate into a plaything, and the audience is likely to take on the designer's role: "Let's see where the tall, pointed arch and the three little windows will appear next."

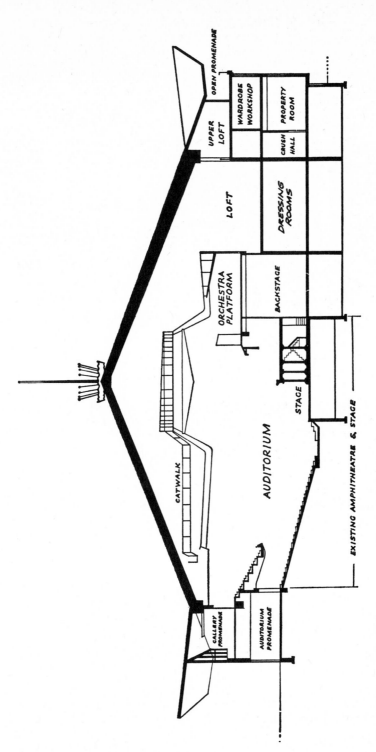

Figure 1-6 Stratford Shakespearean Theatre at Stratford, Ontario.

14

Figure 1-7 Three views of a unit setting for *Volpone,* designed by Tom Rezzuto, The University of North Carolina at Chapel Hill.

The actors will then work under a needless handicap, and the audience itself may become distracted from experiencing the production's total dramatic values.

4 FUNCTIONS OF THE ENVIRONMENT: REINFORCING THE ACTION

The second general function of scenery as environment, which might be called reinforcing the action, is to help explain and to give significance to the action of a play.

Surroundings may reveal the thought and explain the behavior of the characters. They can reflect the character's interest, tastes, fears, and so on, directly, or they can stand in polar opposition to the character's total personality. Both these functions can be seen at work in Kaufman and Hart's play *You Can't Take It With You.*

Each member of the Sycamore family has a special and passionate interest: Ed studies printing, the father and Mr. DiPinna make firecrackers, Penny writes and paints, Grandpa collects snakes. The confusion that results from the interaction of these diverse characters and their pursuits is the center of the play's action. The setting can visually reinforce the characterizations by providing an environment in which the confusion seems natural: Ed's printing press in the livingroom, Penny's loaded-down desk and boxes of manuscripts, Grandpa's snake aquarium, a motley collection of furniture and wall dressing. The family's character is illuminated by how well it fits into this eccentric but comfortable environment. Late in the play, however, Tony Kirby's staid, proper parents appear in the room. The contrast established between their neat, formal demeanor and the mass confusion in the room points up the differences between the two families vividly. One group of characters, then, is explained by its association with the environment. Another group is explained by its contrast to the environment.

Scenery may explain action also by symbolizing it in such forms as the rock and mist of Gordon Craig's conception of a set for *Macbeth:* "I see two things. I see a lofty and steep rock, and I see a moist cloud which envelops the head of this rock. That is to say, a place for fierce and warlike men to inhabit, a place for phantoms to nest in. Ultimately the moisture will destroy the rock; ultimately these spirits will destroy the men." In his interpretation of the

Figure 1-8 The Kirby family's entrance in *You Can't Take It With You.*

same play, Robert Edmond Jones hung three large masks above the stage in several scenes to remind the audience of the ever-present influence of the three witches.

Scenery helps to describe conditions surrounding the action. It creates atmosphere for the action. By the use of appropriate lighting and inclusion of certain objects, such as lamps and fireplace ablaze, muted, or dead, or coatracks empty or full, scenery can describe the time of day, the season, and even the weather. By the shape, color, and physical condition of the scenery—walls, furniture, clothes, and so on—the economic and social status of the characters can be indicated.

An atmospheric set helps attune the audience's emotional response to a play. In a setting for the scene in the convent park in the last act of *Cyrano de Bergerac*, for example, the soft fall of leaves, the quiet movement of the black-gowned nuns, and the light slowly fading through the trees all help the audience to understand how the old soldier's poetical life is finally drawing to a close.

5 FUNCTIONS OF THE ENVIRONMENT: DRESSING THE ACTION

The third (and by no means least important) function of scenery is to help make the action of the play visually interesting. This function might be termed dressing the action.

The designer supplies the director with a setting that provides for effective placement of the actors onstage and allows for flexible and evocative arrangements of the stage picture. Even the setting for a play that demands drab surroundings must be designed with visual excitement in its elements. There are times when the designer and director may wish the scenic effects to dominate the action pictorially. During transitions of the dramatic action, for example, they may depend on the sets, costumes, lights, and so on, to sustain the audience's interest.

6 THE FOUR ELEMENTS OF THE ENVIRONMENT

Designing an environment for dramatic action involves the planning and coordinating of four related elements: (*a*) *scenery* (forms that represent walls, archways, the sky, trees, fences, and the like); (*b*) *properties* (furniture and incidental objects); (*c*) *costumes* (clothes worn by the actors); and (*d*) *lighting* (specialized illumination).

a Scenery supplies the physical and psychological location for the action.

b Properties make the scene intimate by relating it directly to human action. As the objects that the characters handle, as those upon which they sit or lie, and as those about which they talk, properties can frequently place the action quite specifically. Also, by entering into the mass and line composition of the scene, they become an integral part of the total set design. A bookcase, cupboard, or mirror in an interior setting, for instance, may be as important a feature in a wall arrangement as a door. A long, low table or couch may be employed to give the right line of contrast to a tall, narrow panel—and so on. Properties also enter very obviously into the choice and disposition of colors in a scene. With the present tendency to keep the larger areas of the background fairly neutral and to accent primarily the smaller objects placed in the foreground, a set generally looks very bare until it has been dressed up with furniture, window hangings, table covers, books, or flowers.

c Costumes, too, play a vital part in the composition of a stage design. Color here, if properly handled, has the same value as color in properties—often more, because it has the added advantage of motion. Costumes, which have been termed very appropriately "scenery worn by actors," have often the most pronounced accents in the total scene.

d Light, one of the artist's most valuable media, is placed first by some designers. By the manipulation of color, highlights, and shadows, light helps powerfully to compose the tone, mass, and line elements of the scene and thus to intensify its dramatic values.

Ideally, from the point of view of a coherent artistic vision informing the entire production, a single designer should control the environment. He should conceive the scenery and supervise its creation, select the properties and see to their placement, sketch the costumes and choose their fabrics, and design the lighting and supervise its installation. Usually, however, one man finds it impossible to do all the detailed, creative planning in each of the four departments of building the framework in which the actor and director will create the living world of the play. Yet, if the final expression is to be unified, a single artistic vision, in which many persons share, must infuse a production from its initial conception to its final realization.

Although our primary concern here is with constructing, painting, and assembling scenery, we cannot disregard, from the moment we begin to define a play's scenic values, the consideration of properties, costumes, and lighting. These three complementary elements will always be involved, at least indirectly, in our discussions of the principles of scenic design and their applications.

7   THE PRACTICABLE SETTING

A set must be capable of being efficiently constructed, assembled, and handled. In other words, it must fulfill the general technical requirements of scenery construction, and it must meet the specific technical demands of a particular stage (or class of stages, if the scenery is planned for touring).

To make the set of scenery fulfill the general construction requirements it must be designed so that it can be

a   Easily and rapidly constructed.

b   Economically constructed.

c   Quickly and silently shifted.

d   Protected against strain and wear.

e   Well assembled.

f   Packed or stored away after the performance. This means that the artist must plan his scenery so that it can be constructed, as nearly as possible, in accordance with the standard methods outlined in Chapter 5.

To make the set of scenery meet the specific technical demands of a particular stage (or group of stages), the artist must consider the shape and amount of space (Chapter 2) and the shifting facilities (Chapter 8) available.

The set must be capable of being placed on a particular stage in such a way that

a   The sight lines are good.

b   The wings, the flies, and all other parts of the stage or scenery that are not supposed to be seen are properly masked.

c   There is space for packing the scenery that is not in use in a given act.

d   There is space for the manipulation of properties, lighting apparatus, and the off- and onstage movements of actors.

Before starting to design his set, then, the artist must thoroughly familiarize himself with the size and shape of the stage on which his scenery is to function.

8   A SUMMARY

In this chapter we have analyzed the objectives of scenery in the theatre and shown that the whole process of play presentation must be considered as a unit made up of such elements as acting, dancing, music, scenery, costumes, and lighting—all cooperating under the guidance of the director to produce a single emotional effect upon the audience. At the heart of the design is dramatic action. It is the purpose of scenery, one of the contributive arts, to place the action, to reinforce the action, and to dress the action. The artist who designs a set of scenery is successful when he makes it locative, expressive, attractive, clear, simple, utilitarian, practicable, and organic, in a style appropriate to the thought and feeling of the play.

To meet the varying demands of an ever-changing theatre, the designer and his scenic collaborators must be imaginative, resourceful, cooperative, and flexible. Much as they may be tempted to make their work central in the playhouse, they must remember that the dominant figure is the actor. Scenery exists not to give him competition but to explain and support his performance.

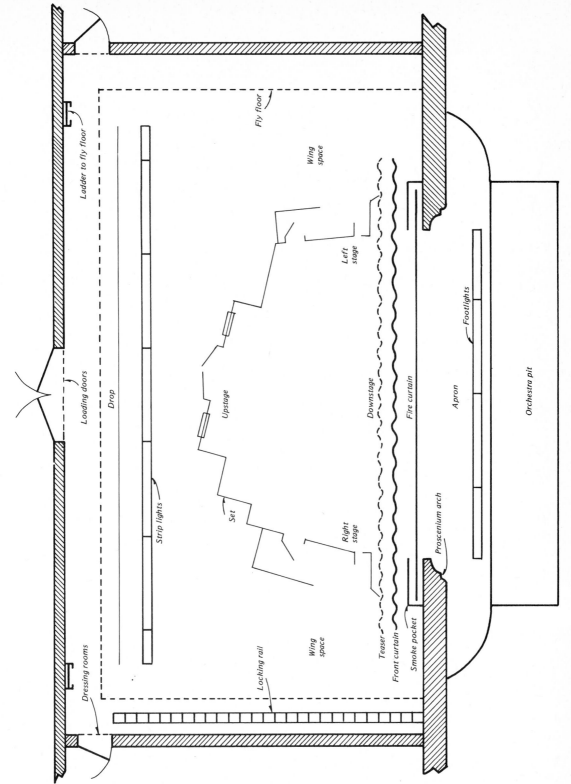

Figure 2-1 Plan of a typical proscenium stage.

SCENERY AND THE PERFORMANCE AREA

CHAPTER 2

1 INTRODUCTION

Before beginning to plan a setting for a production, the designer must acquaint himself thoroughly with the performance area in which the production is to be staged. He will find that modern theatre offers him several types of performance area, with each of them making particular demands.

The designer always aims at an "organic" production, no matter

23

which type of area he is using. He finds, however, that performance areas differ primarily in the actor–audience relationship and this relationship necessarily affects the nature of the scenery he provides. For example, a production of Chekhov's *The Three Sisters* on a proscenium stage might require complete walls, doors, windows, and many pieces of furniture for the interior scenes—and trees, a painted drop, and garden walls for the exterior scene. A production of the same play on an arena stage could not, of course, make use of the complete walls or the painted drop. It would probably have to depend on the furniture and a few indicative set pieces to establish its environment.

2 THE PROSCENIUM THEATRE

The most common type of performance area is the proscenium theatre. This traditional form seats the audience on one side of a raised stage that has been placed behind a frame, or proscenium arch.

The Topography of a Typical Proscenium Stage

The transverse wall dividing the auditorium from the stage is the *proscenium*. The opening in this wall, through which one sees the stage, is the *proscenium opening*. The architecture of the opening is the *proscenium arch*. In older theatres, this arch is quite ornate and establishes a definite visual separation of stage and audience. Newer theatres have attempted to minimize this separation by making the arch very simple and unobtrusive. Behind the proscenium wall, the spaces offstage, right and left, are the *wings*. Usually located here are the exit to the dressing rooms, the loading doors, the counterweight system—if the equipment includes one, scenery waiting to go on stage, properties, lighting apparatus, shifting devices, safety devices, a clock, and the stage manager's desk. The floor of the stage is of softwood boarding, usually unwaxed fir or yellow pine, laid parallel to the proscenium. It is frequently pierced by *traps* that open into the basement to permit the use of sunken staircases, for example, and is usually covered for a performance by a large piece of heavy waterproof canvas called a *ground cloth*. If included, the *footlight trough* is set into the floor along the edge of the stage nearest the audience.

One should remember that in all references to positions on the stage floor, *downstage* means toward the audience and *upstage* means away from the audience. *Onstage* is toward the center of

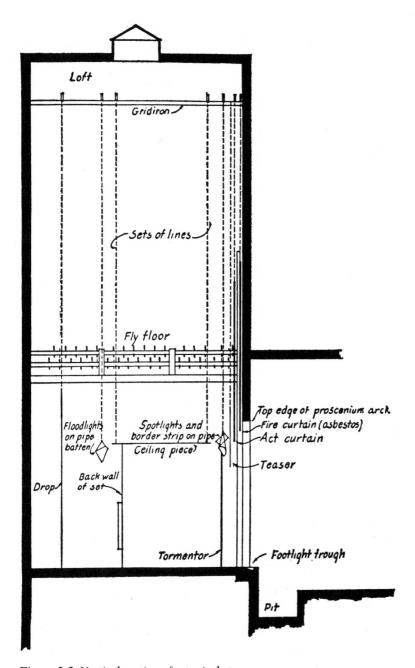

Figure 2-2 Vertical section of a typical stage.

the stage, *offstage* is toward the wings or the rear wall. *Right* and *left* are determined from the point of view not of the audience but of the actor facing the audience.

At the top of the space above the proscenium, known as the *flies*, is the *gridiron* or *grid*, a steel or wooden framework of open beams placed 5 to 10 feet below the roof, 40 to 100 or more feet above the stage, and extending over the entire working area. From this frame is suspended all the hanging scenery, such as drops, borders, and tree trunks, as well as certain lighting units. *Sets of lines* are attached to each hanging piece, passed over pulley blocks in the grid, carried to the side, brought down, and tied off on a double row of belaying pins, called the *pinrail*, on the *fly floor*. The fly floor is a shelf, or narrow gallery, extending along the wall of one of the wings some distance above the main floor. A more detailed description of the gridiron and the fly floor will be found in Chapter 3. In many of the newer theatres the fly floor, with its pinrail, has been omitted and all hanging scenery is handled with a *counterweight system* operated from the floor. This method also is described in Chapter 3. Under the general subject of flies, mention might be made also of the occasional *bridges* found in some theatres. These are light, narrow, steel frames which, extending across the stage, may be fixed, moved on tracks, or suspended from the grid some distance above the floor; they are now used principally for mounting overhead lighting units.

3   THE PROBLEM OF SIGHT LINES

One of the very first requirements of any arrangement of scenery is that it have good sight lines. A sight line is the line of vision from the spectator to the stage. A setting with good sight lines is one that is so shaped and so placed in relation to the proscenium opening that the vision is good from all positions in the audience. If not the whole set of scenery, at least every feature that is important dramatically or pictorially should be well in view from every seat— the seat in the first row, the last row, and at the extreme side in the orchestra, and the seat in the first row, the last row, and at the extreme side (if the theatre is reasonably constructed) of the balcony, as well as the seat in the ideal center of the auditorium. This means that the setting must not be so wide or so tall that a part of it is hidden behind the edge of the proscenium; and it must not be so deep that the features at the back of the set are cut off from the view of the spectators at the sides or above. On the other hand, the setting must not be so narrow or so low that, to mask the

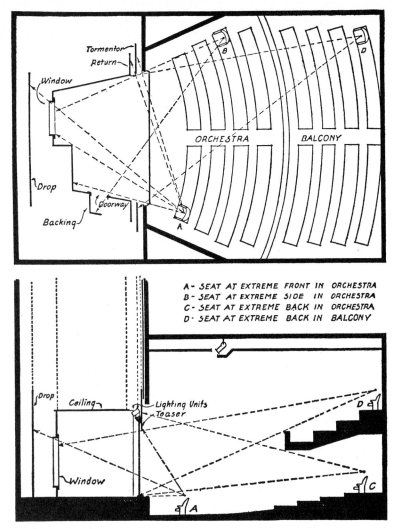

A - SEAT AT EXTREME FRONT IN ORCHESTRA
B - SEAT AT EXTREME SIDE IN ORCHESTRA
C - SEAT AT EXTREME BACK IN ORCHESTRA
D - SEAT AT EXTREME BACK IN BALCONY

Figure 2-3

Sight lines. Good lines of vision to the stage from the auditorium require (1) the full visibility of the acting area and the chief features of its setting, and (2) the adequate backing of door, window, and fireplace openings in the setting, and the complete masking of lighting units and stage machinery for every position in the house (except, occasionally, a few of the first-row seats, if very close to the stage).

downstage edges of the scenery, the two tormentors and the teaser have to be set in a position where they shield the view of the back parts of the setting from these same spectators.

When the artist works out the problems of good sight lines for various positions in the auditorium, he considers not only how he may bring into view all that the audience should see but also how he may hide all that they should not see—that is, the nonscenic part of backstage. When he is dealing with the conventional enclosed interior he seldom has much trouble with the latter phase of the problem; the side walls of the set mask the wings and the ceiling masks the flies quite naturally. All that he must see to is that the teaser and tormentors are trimmed to hide the downstage edge of the set all the way around, that the sky drop (if one is used), or other scenic pieces, is in a position to back up all exterior views of the scene itself, and that wall backings are in position to back up all interior views through doorways and other openings.

One point that the artist must never forget in the matter of arranging the downstage masking of the top edge of an interior is the necessity for taking into account room for the lighting instruments—borderlights and spotlights—hanging just behind the teaser. As these lights must be placed just below the edge of the ceiling, and the teaser, in turn, must be dropped down far enough to hide completely the lights from persons sitting in the first few rows of the orchestra, it is clear that the height of the set must be 18 inches to 3 feet more than that of the final trimming of the teaser.

When the artist is dealing with an exterior scene he is likely to run into considerably more difficulty than when he is dealing with an interior one; he cannot use in the exterior set the natural masking offered by interior walls and a ceiling. If the scene represents a street, a courtyard, or a garden set between houses, he has at his disposal some exterior walls, and his problem may be narrowed down to concealing the flies. In this case he will probably carry the walls and the sky (if one is used) so far up into the flies that with the help of a plan of illumination that keeps all light out of this part of the stage, the tops of the pieces of scenery will not be visible even to people seated in the first row. If this arrangement involves making the flats and drop too tall for practical construction and handling, the artist may have to hang a couple of black borders in the flies (as much out of the range of the lights as possible)—frankly theatrical masking pieces.

If, on the other hand, the exterior scene represents an open country landscape or a grove of trees, the artist may have to arrange his maskings without the help of walls at all. If there is enough room on the floor of the stage and the gridiron is sufficiently high, the artist will probably back the hanging or set pieces of his scene with a large sky cyclorama, or a plaster dome (see Chapter 3, Section 8), which extends all the way around and downstage out of sight in the wings and away up out of sight in the flies. In front of this he can set anything he pleases—trees, fences, sides or corners of buildings, or distant mountains—with the comforting knowledge that from whatever angle the spectator may view the scene he will see sky beyond. If, because of limited space, however, the artist cannot count on the use of a cyclorama (or dome) and must limit himself to a flat sky drop, he must do some ingenious designing to cover the view into the stage wings. If he can possibly do so, he brings into his picture the side wall, or walls, of buildings—sheds, cottages, and the like—and supplies whatever deficiencies there still may be in maskings at the side by using closely packed tree trunks, green gauze tabs, rocks, banks of earth, or other scenic pieces. The flies he generally masks by means of cut foliage borders.

4 ALTERNATIVES TO THE PROSCENIUM STAGE

The majority of theatre workers still seem to prefer the proscenium type of stage, since for them it is the most flexible in the long run. On it they can construct settings covering the wide range from illusional realism to theatrical formalism in a variety of forms impossible to set up in other types of performance area.

Still, there clearly are disadvantages to be met with on the proscenium stage. One exists in the hard line of the arch, which

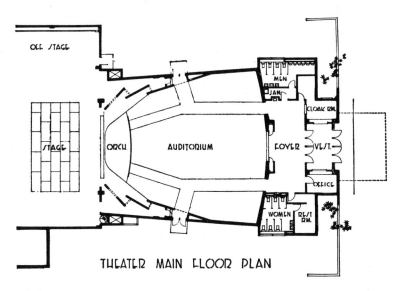

Figure 2-4

University Theatre at the University of Oregon. The main stage with a con-cave-curved front is supplemented by two side stages, which continue the curve into the sidewalls of the auditorium. Entrances at the side are made from behind the louvers.

limits the sides of the acting area. Another is in the elaborate, expensively equipped stagehouse, which frequently requires for the operation of all its machinery a crew of technicians as large as the whole acting company put together.

One solution that has been offered for the first difficulty is a plan that extends the frontal acting area right and left out beyond the edges of the proscenium frame onto two small side stages. Sometimes these side spaces take the form of plain little nooks, with no access except through the main opening or by steps from the side aisles of the auditorium. More often they have special doors of their own opening through the proscenium wall to backstage. The University Theatre at the University of Oregon runs the front of its stage in a concave curve beyond the right and left edges of the proscenium arch to provide two side spaces for action. Entrances and exits to these small supplementary stages are made behind louvers, two on each side. The upstage louvers have door openings.

Arch Lauterer and some of his associates tried to solve the mechanical problem of scene changing by eliminating the conventional flies and suspending all hanging pieces, such as drops, drapes, and the rear walls of sets, from trolleys running on tracks attached to a low ceiling. The scenic units can be shifted laterally, instead of vertically, by a minimum crew.

5   THE APRON, OR OPEN, STAGE

A form that has had considerable promotion in the United States in the last several years, though it is by no means new to Europe, is the *apron,* or *open,* stage. Its principal feature is a raised promontory that sticks out into the auditorium much like the forestage of the old Elizabethan playhouse; but it also has a transverse, conventional stage at the back. Scenery hangs or is set up behind this.

The apron stage combines certain features of both the horseshoe and proscenium forms. The audience, sitting in a wide curve around the three sides of the big apron, can see action on both this front platform and the transverse part of the stage behind it (see Figure 2-5). Actors make their entrances and exits through portals right and left at the ends of the transverse portion of the stage, behind tormentor screens framing the central façade, or through some part of the scenery in the middle. This scenic element may be quite flat or it may have depth.

James Hull Miller, a principal proponent of the apron stage in

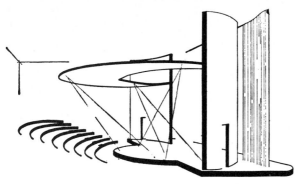

Figure 2-5

Apron stage: The Roundup Theatre in Dallas, planned by James Hull Miller. In some forms of this type of stage, the apron protrudes farther into the audience and the slotted hanging ceiling extends over the whole interior—the seats as well as the platform—making the auditorium and stage one room.

this country, describes some of its characteristics as follows: "Not as radical as central [arena] staging, nor as conservative and illusory as the picture frame [proscenium arch] setting, it depends more on a free-style theatricality and flair which has been the mainstay of production style over the ages. . . . The apron stage supplies the intimacy of arena while retaining a portion of the visual spectacle" ["Initial Factors in Theatre Planning," *Educational Theatre Journal*, 8 (May, 1956), page 91].

The development of the modern apron stage has moved in two directions: one toward a kind of compromise with the old proscenium stage which exploits the thrust-out apron but retains something of the conventional arch and a modified stagehouse behind it, and one toward what its promoters call a purer, more historical form, with no arch and no fly space. In this development the slotted ceiling (for lighting) is continuous from front to back, over both the spectators' seats and the actors' platform, making the whole space in effect one room.

Miller has arrived at three general forms of open staging: (*a*) the forward-thrust platform; (*b*) the reverse-curve caliper; and (*c*) the arcade. The forward-thrust platform projects a platform or apron stage out into the house with the audience sitting around three sides of it. The caliper stage projects out into the house along the sides and partially encircles a portion of the audience. The arcade provides facilities similar to the Elizabethan "inner above and below." It encloses an acting area upstage at floor level and provides support for another acting area above floor level.

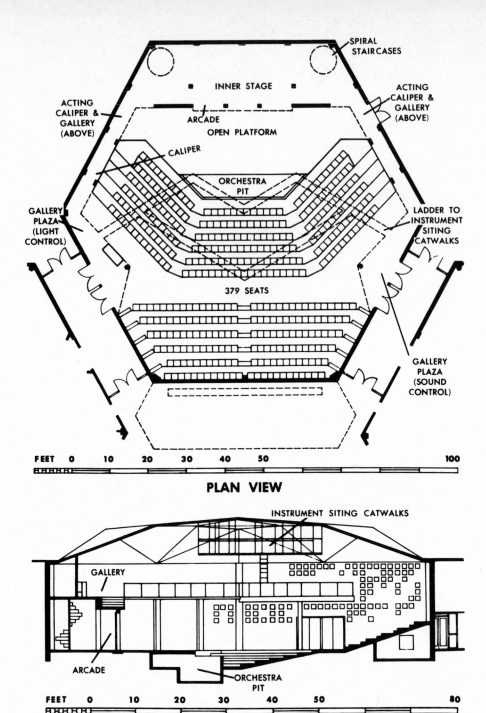

PLAN VIEW

SECTION

Figure 2-6

Plan and section views of the combination forethrust and caliper stage at the senior high school, La Junta, Colorado. Shaver and Company, Architects. Reproduced by permission of Hub Electric Company, Inc., Elmhurst, Ill.

These forms can be used singly or in combination. The theatre of La Junta High School in Colorado demonstrates a synthesis of all three of Miller's open stage techniques.

The scene designer preparing a set for an open stage can, says Miller, "cut right to the heart of an environment and select highly characteristic details which will trigger a chain of imagery in the mind of the audience" ["The Language of Vision," *The Open Stage* (Chicago, Hub Electric Company, 1965), page 3]. Since much of the scenery in an open-stage production is set in the midst of the action with the audience on several sides, conventions of design have been developed. The use of free-standing screens, projected backgrounds, platforms, simultaneous acting areas, highly selected details, and great dependence on lighting are characteristic features of open staging.

6 THE ARENA THEATRE

In arena theatre or "theatre-in-the-round" the acting area, usually square or rectangular, is placed in the center, and the spectators encircle it. Players' entrances and exits are made down aisles between sections of the audience. Sometimes the acting is done on a level with the lowest seats, sometimes it is raised a foot or two. Ideally, the surrounding audience chairs are banked (sloped up) to give the spectators better vision. There are only two definite rules about the size and shape of the arena space and the relation between the acting and audience areas: The front seats should be close enough to the playing area to keep the feeling intimate but not so near as to inhibit the actors' freedom of movement; and the rear seats should be so arranged that people sitting in them can hear and see easily every part of the performance, including the entrances and exits.

Generally speaking, arena staging uses no scenery. Occasionally, directors staging plays with multiple locales have found it advantageous to mark off one part of the playing space as a sitting room, another as an office, another as a street corner, and to erect one or two low scenic set pieces to help the spectators visualize the different places. One device that has been used is to give areas in the different spaces different colors by means of rugs or painted pieces of canvas. Since, however, this kind of arrangement tends inevitably to corner the action during each of the several scenes, it is usually frowned upon. In arena theatre, the actors are supposed to play equally to every part of the audience, and this cannot be done if their actions are restricted to specific areas.

Sometimes, of course, the whole play may be set outdoors. In this case, the use of a scenic rock or one or two tree trunks (not so large as to interfere with lighting or sight lines) may help to create a sense of locale. Generally, however, the responsibility for creating a feeling of surroundings rests with the actors, assisted by the lighting director. This does not mean that there is consequently nothing for a designer to do. There is much for him to do in the selection and construction of properties—pieces of furniture, utensils, bits of machinery, and various portable objects, which will *suggest* by their form and style the kind of surroundings that would naturally go with them. Thus the properties help the actors create an illusion of scenery.

And, of course, there are always present the problems of texture and color, and of the composition of the various blocks, lines, and contours of physical objects in relation to the costumes and the movements of the players. All these details are especially impor-

Figure 2-7 Arena theatre, or "theatre-in-the-round": The Penthouse Theatre, University of Washington, planned by John Ashby Conway.

Figure 2-8 Production of *On Borrowed Time*, designed by Richard Wilcox. Theatre 170, Department of Theater Arts, University of California at Los Angeles.

tant in arena staging, and the designer will find himself busy attending to them.

7   THE HORSESHOE THEATRE

A modification of the arena is the *horseshoe*, or *three-quarter-round*, theatre in which the audience sits not on four but on three sides of the central acting area. The fourth side is reserved for a simple scenic façade whose form suggests an environment for the performers working in front of it. Perhaps what is selected for this pictorial plane is a prominent window, door, or fireplace, with some of the surrounding wall attached to it, or, if the place of action is outdoors, a tree or a rock. In the horeshoe theatre, like the arena,

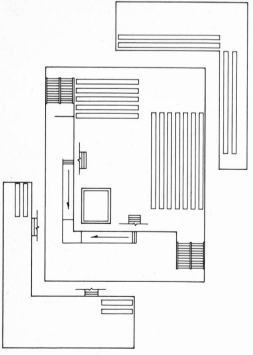

Figure 2-9

Flexible 299-seat theatre, designed by David
    Hays and Peter Blake. The design is
    based on a system of levels, which may be
    used as seating areas, acting areas, or light-
    ing areas, depending on the plan of a par-
    ticular production. Reprinted by permis-
    sion of The American Federation of Arts.

(Above): The theatre arranged for a pro-
    duction of *Macbeth*.

(Left): Plan view of the *Macbeth* arrange-
    ment. Notice how the designer altered the
    plans in developing the models.

(Right, above): The theatre arranged for
    arena staging.

(Right, below): Plan view of the arena ar-
    rangement.

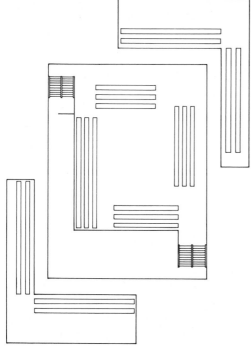

*(figure continued
on next page)*

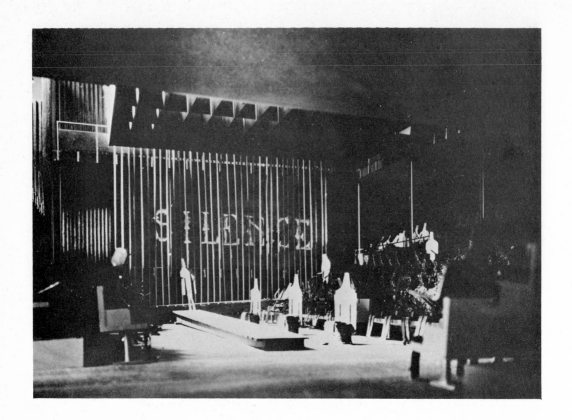

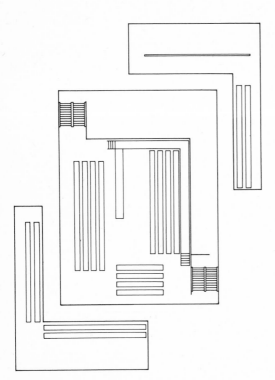

Figure 2-9 *(continued)*

(Above): The theatre arranged for a production of *The Quare Fellow*.

(Left): Plan view of *The Quare Fellow* arrangement.

(Right, above): The theatre arranged for lateral seating. Some of the galleries have been closed off with panels.

(Right, below): Plan view of the lateral seating arrangement.

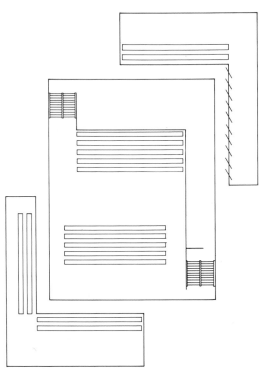

39

players can make their entrances down aisles through the audience; commonly, however, they make their exits through the scenic façade or around its edges in order to seem to carry with them some of the environmental image.

The designer's problems in the horseshoe are similar to the ones he has in the arena, except that to these he now must add special consideration for the design of the scenic background. Into this one screen or three-dimensional shape (or group of shapes) he must concentrate much of the planning that he would distribute throughout the three planes—plus through-door or through-window vistas—if he were working on a conventional proscenium stage. This does not mean, of course, that he will try to crowd into one wall all the forms that would ordinarily be found on the three walls, but he will have to capture and place in the one wall as much as he can of the sense of place and mood desired for the scene as a whole.

8   OTHER EXPERIMENTAL FORMS OF INDOOR STAGING

The theatre is always growing and growth means change. Playwrights experiment with new forms of drama, actors vary their approach, directors and designers try out new ways of staging—all working to make drama more evocative, more stimulating, more expressive.

The principal problem (in which all people in the theatre are interested) is the relationship of audience to performer. Driven by a desire to build a more and more exciting place for action and response, many minds have labored toward the evolution of a "perfect stage" and a "perfect auditorium," each considered as a separate area of planning, and for nearly 300 years very little was done about the link between the two. It was generally assumed that the connecting link between acting area and spectator's chair was the proscenium arch. Early in this century, however, a few revolutionaries challenged that assumption. In recent years the voice of protest has become stronger. Now the desire for trying new arrangements is clearly evident in this country.

The Ford Foundation Program for Theatre Design of a few years back, for instance, illustrated vividly how leading architects and theatre designers continue their search for an ideal theatre that can diminish "the inhibition on the drama produced by fixed and frozen staging" [The American Federation of Arts, *The Ideal Theatre: Eight Concepts* (New York, The American Federation of Arts, 1962), page 7].

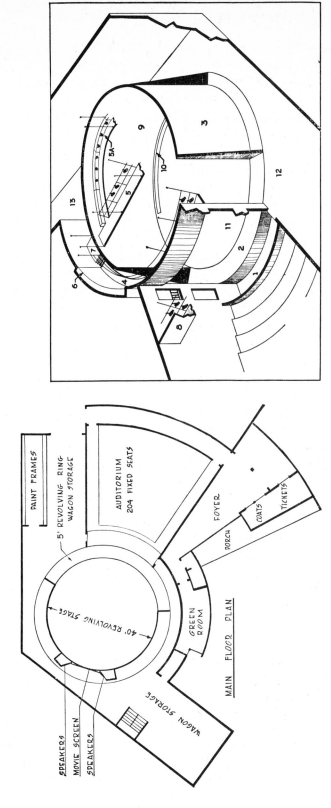

Figure 2-10 Proposed theatre for the University of Washington in Seattle, designed by John Ashby Conway. The circular shell mounted on the revolving ring serves as a cyclorama when the front is open. When it revolves a quarter turn, it closes the opening. (1) Hydraulic lift, which can be used as an elevator, orchestra pit, forestage, or which will carry extra rows of seats. (2) Revolving ring which operates independently, carries the cyclorama, motion-picture screen, and two side stages. (3) Side stage. When used in conjunction with the forestage, it will allow a set 11 feet deep. Two proscenium doors and balconies are available if needed. (4) First lighting bridge. Conway suggests that the switchboard and sound control be placed up on this bridge. (5) Second lighting bridge, connected with (4) via (7). (5a) Connecting lighting bridge for cyc lighting. (6) Top of switchboard. (7) Connecting platform, connects (4) to (5). (8) Beam, entered through door in wall from wagon storage (12). (9) Plaster cyc. Revolves on its ring, making a sight barrier between forestage and main stage. (10) Light pit. (11) Revolving stage, 40 feet in diameter. (12 and 13) Wagon storage. By permission of the designer.

One variable theatre plan designed by Peter Blake and David Hays for this program is based on a system of levels that can be adapted to accommodate various forms, ranging from proscenium staging to arena staging. This theatre does not depend on scenery to establish environment; rather, it attempts to use the spaces created by the relationship of the acting area to the audience as its primary environmental element.

John Ashby Conway's proposed theatre for the University of Washington goes back to the use of the proscenium frame. However, what he has put behind the frame is quite novel (Figure 2-10). The principal parts are an inner revolving disc, and an outer revolving ring on the inner edge of which is mounted a circular cyclorama wall. The wall has one break in it, which may be oriented to the proscenium opening. When the ring is given a partial turn, the wall seals the opening. Since there is a shallow space on the ring in front of the wall, actors can deliver before-the-curtain speeches or play transitional scenes here. In fact, since the ring has considerable circumference, a whole series of short scenes can be given in front of the wall, one after another, with the ring taking a quarter turn—forward, or forward then backward—for each shift. (One segment of the wall is reserved for a motion-picture screen.) A forestage in front of the ring gives additional depth, when needed, to the front scenes.

On the main part of the stage—that is, on the central disk—the scenic artist can create one permanent setting that will not move or a number of temporary settings back to back that will be revolved into view as they are needed. The circular wall behind the scenery serves as a sky backing in every scene opening to the outdoors. Reserve elements may be mounted on wagons stored in the rooms set aside for their use on stage right and left. With the use of the two revolving sections and the wagons, the artist and his technical associates can handle easily and swiftly an almost unlimited number of scenes in one play, or present one show in the afternoon and change to a completely different one in the evening.

The forestage is movable by means of an hydraulic lift. If the front space is not needed, it can be dropped all the way down to provide a pit for an orchestra or halfway down for a level area for additional auditorium seats. Heavy properties, usually kept in the basement, can be brought up to the stage on the elevator and later returned to storage the same way.

One of the principal advantages of this theatre design is that it places practically no restriction on the width of the auditorium.

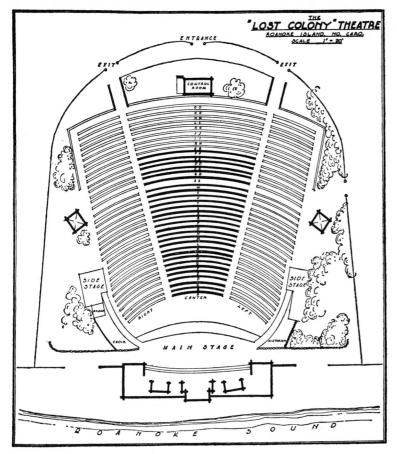

Figure 2-11

Ground plan of the Waterside Theatre on Roanoke Island, N.C., home of the presentation of Paul Green's outdoor drama, *The Lost Colony*. Designed and constructed by Albert Q. Bell.

The sight lines would be good even if the boundary of this segment were increased almost to a semicircle.

9 OUTDOOR THEATRES

The recent development of outdoor historical drama, more usually referred to as "symphonic drama" in several parts of the United States, has necessitated considerable revision in amphitheatre forms. Open-air plays are typically composed of varied elements: dramatic episodes, both mass and intimate; choral and dance groups; and general visual spectacle. There is much physical movement and the story moves swiftly; no waiting at any point can be tolerated once the action starts. Since the presentation takes place in the open, where there can be no proscenium arch on which to hang a traveler track, the changes from scene to scene have to be effected without the help of any front curtain.

The solution for this problem is the use of a main stage, on which the big scenes are played, and two flanking side stages, on which are put the smaller transitional scenes. Lighting (the instruments for which are mounted both behind the proscenium walls of the main stage and, for the most part, in two tall towers on each side of the auditorium) controls the visibility for the audience. It directs attention away from the action on one stage to the action on another, thus permitting scenery to be shifted on the darkened stage without any pause in the continuity of the performance.

The treatment of the scenic factors varies from drama to drama. For Paul Green's *The Lost Colony,* on Roanoke Island, North Carolina, there is a three-dimensional setting, depicting the settlement in the New World, placed toward the rear on the big main stage. This is not revealed, however, until the beginning of the second act. For the first-act settings tall screens are set up in three layers in front of the settlement to suggest, in turn, the reed fence of an Indian village, the stone outer walls of an English garden, and the brick and plaster walls of a tavern courtyard.

The right side stage, on which the natural island shrubbery has been preserved, is retained chiefly for wilderness scenes, while the left stage, a little more bare, can be set up easily with interior scenes.

The main stage of Matoaka Lake Amphitheatre at Williamsburg, Virginia, where Green's *The Common Glory* is performed, reveals the lake at the rear. Here there is no permanent setting of any kind. All the scenic elements are mounted on wagons, which roll in from the wings to make a variety of interiors and exteriors. The side stages in this theatre are quite small and are placed close down against the proscenium walls. There is no effort to set realistically the scenes presented in these little areas. The backgrounds are simply suggestive vignettes.

The modern outdoor theatre, when it is skillfully and sensitively lighted, is a wonderfully flexible instrument for those who enjoy epic imagery. A piece of action can be held for a moment in the tight grip of one small spot of light, then, with the lift of a dimmer handle, suddenly be given freedom to sweep 300 feet from one bank of the theatre down to the central stage and up to the other side, with no limits except the deep surrounding woods and the lofty stars.

Figure 2-12

Two outdoor theatres for historical "symphonic" dramas:

(Above): The Mountainside Theatre, Cherokee, N.C., setting for Kermit Hunter's *Unto These Hills.* Courtesy of the Cherokee Historical Association, Inc.

(Below): Lake Matoaka Amphitheatre, Williamsburg, Va., where Paul Green's *The Common Glory* is presented. Courtesy of The Jamestown Corporation. Photo: Roger D. Sherman.

45

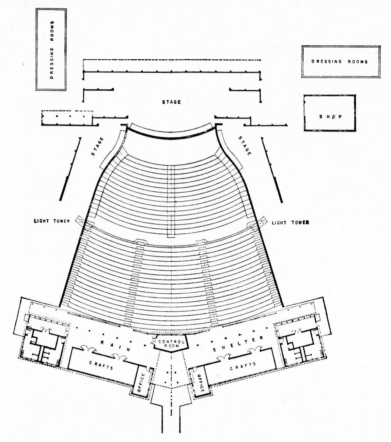

Figure 2-13 Indian Fort Theater at Berea, Kentucky, home of Paul Green's outdoor drama *Wilderness Road*. Designed by John B. Lippard, landscape architect.

10 CONCLUSION

This one brief chapter cannot include all the various performance areas available to the designer in modern theatre. We have attempted, however, to include the major types in order to show the high degree of flexibility available to the designer. We have also emphasized the necessity of the designer's analyzing carefully all the factors in the particular situations in which he works, then attempting to find the best solutions to his problems considered as a whole.

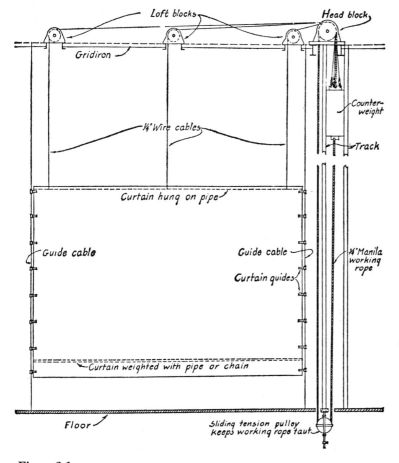

Figure 3-1

Working principles of the drop curtain. (The scale of the rigging parts in relationship to the curtain in this picture has been exaggerated somewhat in order to make clear the way in which the parts work.)

STANDARD STAGE EQUIPMENT

CHAPTER 3

1 INTRODUCTION

In Chapter 2 we saw the great variety of staging possibilities open
to the designer in modern theatre. A scenic artist preparing to work
with experimental factors, however, would be wise to become
thoroughly familiar first with conventional staging. In the theatre,
much of the new is derived from the old—not only its form but
also its materials and dramatic devices. This chapter, therefore,

will examine briefly the standard equipment to be found on most conventional proscenium-type stages.

2 THE FRONT CURTAIN

The front curtain—sometimes called the act curtain or the house curtain—hangs just upstage of the proscenium arch and is used to close the acting area from the audience's view when the acting area is not supposed to be seen. There are several types of front curtains. The *drop curtain* is suspended from the gridiron and is operated by being pulled up, or "raised," to expose the stage, and lowered, or "dropped," to close the stage. The *draw curtain* is composed of two sections of fabric attached to small wheels called *carriers*, which run in a suspended track called a *traveler track*; the two sections of curtain, which part in the middle, are pulled off into the wings right and left. The *tab curtain* gathers the two sections of fabric up and to the sides and usually forms a draped effect when it is opened. The *roll curtain*, while rarely seen as the front curtain in theatres today, is an effective addition to the productions of certain period plays. A long roller at the bottom of the curtain rolls the curtain up and out of sight.

Downstage of the front curtain—between the front curtain and the proscenium wall—there is usually a steel or asbestos *fire curtain*. This curtain is required by fire regulations in most cities and, when dropped, seals off the stage area from the auditorium in case of fire. It usually works on the same principle as the drop curtain.

3 THE TEASER AND THE TORMENTORS

Often the designer needs to adjust the size of the proscenium opening. Since the opening is usually architecturally permanent, he must make his adjustments with movable equipment. To adjust the height of the opening, he makes use of the *teaser*, which is a long horizontal masking piece hung just upstage of the front curtain. The height of the opening can be altered by raising or lowering the teaser. The teaser is often made of the same fabric as the front curtain and is hung in folds or pleats. It can also be made by the stretching of a neutral-colored fabric on a frame so that it presents a flat, smooth surface and a straight edge. Many designers prefer to have the teaser made of black velour no matter what color the front curtain happens to be.

To adjust the width of the proscenium opening, the designer

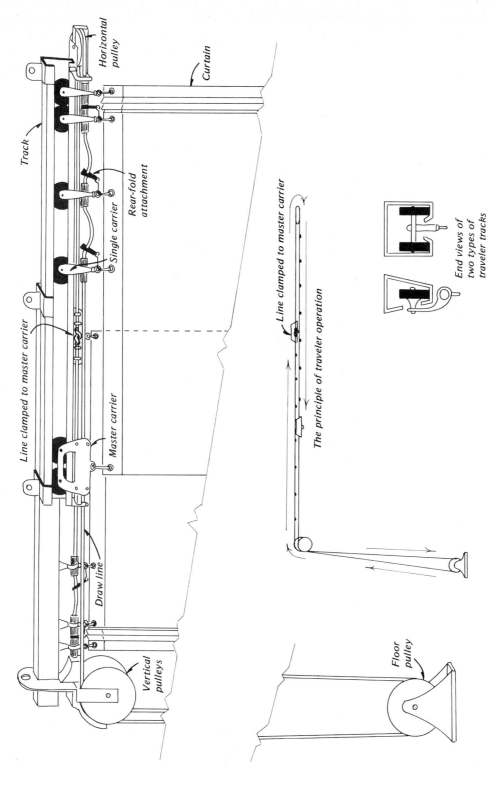

Horizontal pulley

Track

Curtain

Rear-fold attachment

Single carrier

Line clamped to master carrier

Master carrier

Line clamped to master carrier

The principle of traveler operation

Draw line

Vertical pulleys

End views of two types of traveler tracks

Floor pulley

Figure 3-2 Draw curtain. The figure shows a traveler track with rear-fold attachments. These attachments cause all the carriers to move at once, which fold the curtain offstage instead of onstage.

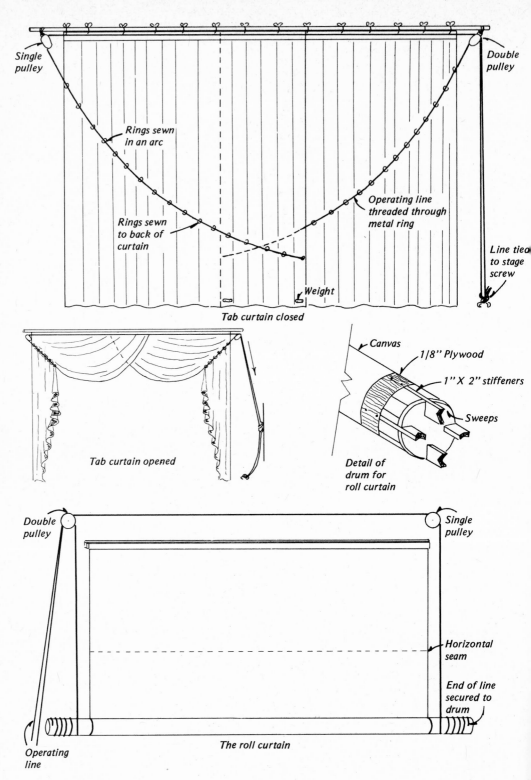

Single
pulley

Double
pulley

Rings sewn
in an arc

Rings sewn
to back of
curtain

Operating line
threaded through
metal ring

Line tied
to stage
screw

Weight

Tab curtain closed

Canvas

1/8" Plywood

1" X 2" stiffeners

Sweeps

Tab curtain opened

*Detail of
drum for
roll curtain*

Double
pulley

Single
pulley

Horizontal
seam

End of line
secured to
drum

Operating
line

The roll curtain

Figure 3-3

Tab curtain and roll curtain. Notice that the rings sewn on the back of the tab curtain are placed in an arced line rather than in a straight line. If they were in a straight line, they would bind and the curtain would not open.

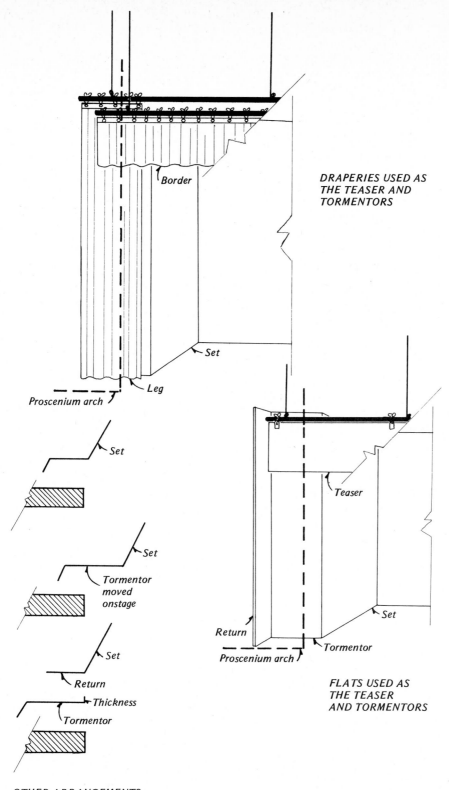

Border

DRAPERIES USED AS
THE TEASER AND
TORMENTORS

Set

Leg

Proscenium arch

Set

Set
Tormentor
moved
onstage

Set
Return
Thickness
Tormentor

Teaser

Return

Proscenium arch

Set

Tormentor

FLATS USED AS
THE TEASER
AND TORMENTORS

OTHER ARRANGEMENTS

Figure 3-4

Teaser and tormentors. They may be made from draperies of a neutral color
or from flats painted a neutral color.

makes use of the *tormentors*. These are vertical masking pieces—either hanging curtains or frames standing on the stage floor right and left—covered with a fabric to match the teaser. In combination with the teaser, they form an inner frame upstage of the front curtain. This inner frame "finishes off" the downstage and upper limits of a setting.

4 THE GRIDIRON AND THE FLY FLOOR

To fly scenery it is necessary to have some arrangement for hanging ropes from above. Every well-equipped stage has a gridiron that extends over the entire working space and is built high enough to permit drops to be lifted completely out of view of the audience. The fly space on some professional stages reaches over 100 feet above the floor. The grid itself is constructed as a skeleton framework of steel I beams, or wood beams, which is supported by the side walls and often vertical hangers from the roof. It is covered with an open latticework of steel strips, and it is slotted from front to back at regular intervals to accommodate the fly ropes. The slots are commonly placed about 15 feet apart. A narrow stage will have four slots, a wider one six or more. Above each of these slots, except one, are bolted large steel protected sheaves called *loft blocks*, while above the last slot, situated directly over the fly gallery, are set up multiple-sheave frames called *head blocks*.

Each set of blocks on an average-sized stage (with a proscenium opening 20 to 30 feet wide) generally consists of three loft blocks and one head block arranged in a row at right angles to the slots and parallel to the proscenium wall. A *set of lines*, made up of three or four ½- to ⅝-inch Manila ropes (depending on the load), is attached to the center and to the two ends of a hanging piece of scenery, passed over the three loft blocks directly above and the common head block at the side, then brought down and tied off on the row of belaying pins (the *pinrail*) on the fly floor.

The fly floor, from which all the fly ropes are controlled, is a narrow floor, sturdily constructed, placed along one of the side walls of the stage between the proscenium wall and the rear wall, some distance from the floor. It is situated high enough to clear all standing scenery—frequently 20 to 30 feet in the air. The pinrail, to which the fly lines are attached, is a double row of 17- to 21-inch hickory or iron belaying pins—commonly just short pieces of 1-inch pipe—stuck through about 8-inch wooden beams or 5-inch iron pipes running the length of the gallery and supported by heavy wood or channel iron posts. The two rows of pins, set on the onstage side of the gallery, are arranged one above the other.

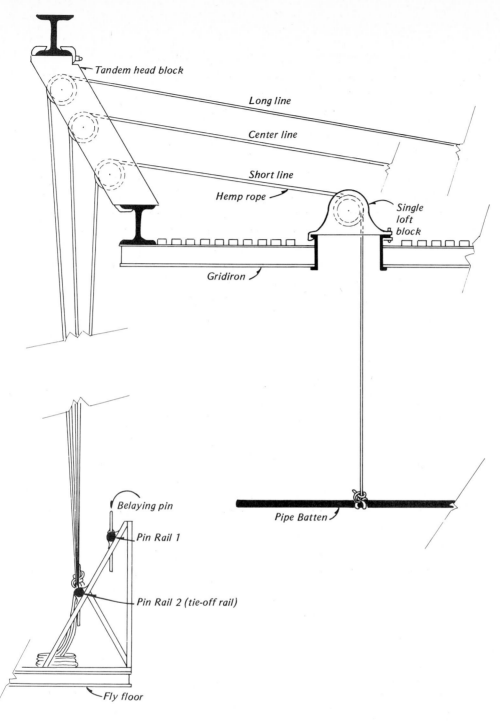

Figure 3-5

Hemp-rope flying system. The line hanging closest to the fly floor is called the *short line;* the line center stage, the *center line;* the line farthest from the fly floor, the *long line*. When the pipe batten is hanging perfectly parallel to the stage floor, it is considered to be *in trim*. Trimming the batten is accomplished by the adjustment of the lengths of the lines from the fly floor.

A well-equipped stage has fifteen to thirty or more sets of lines, with corresponding pins, placed about 9 inches apart and numbered from the proscenium back. The complete system of ropes, blocks, and belaying pins is termed the *rigging*.

5   THE COUNTERWEIGHT SYSTEM

In many theatres the fly gallery has been omitted and all flying is handled with a *counterweight system* operated from the stage floor (Figure 3-6). In the unit form, a pipe batten parallel to the proscenium wall and to the floor is attached to small steel cables, which pass over loft blocks in the grid—in the same arrangement as the Manila-rope flying system—over a common head block at the side, and down to a metal carriage with adjustable weights, which slides up and down the wall in a vertical track. The three or more sheaves (pulley wheels) for the cables and the one for

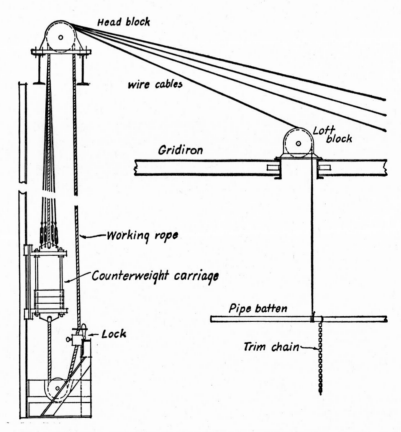

Figure 3-6 Counterweight system. By means of this system, scenery is handled from the floor of the stage instead of from the fly floor.

a Manila rope, which compose the head block, revolve side by side on a common shaft. The Manila operating rope is fastened to the top of the sliding carriage, passed up and over its sheave in the head block in the grid, down and under a single block near the stage floor, and up again to the bottom of the carriage. The latter, pulled up or down by this "endless" rope, in turn lifts or lowers the pipe batten it counterbalances. Scenery is attached to the pipe by means of trim chains. When a piece is flied to the proper height, the operating rope is fastened with a patent clamp lock. The balance weights are usually placed on the carriage from a narrow loading platform under the grid.

Some stages today are equipped with both a counterweight system and the older rope system. The combination permits a flexibility of control impossible with one system alone.

6 ELECTRICAL FLYING SYSTEMS

Various attempts over the years to develop an electrical system for flying scenery have run into several difficulties: slow speed, inflexibility, ineffective braking devices, and a lack of trimming control.

The most successful of these attempts has been George Izenour's synchronous-winch system which, while falling short of its initial proposal of synchronized control of the various winches, does contribute a far more flexible arrangement of the gridiron. His use of swivel loft blocks mounted in channel beams above the gridiron, the greater number of grid openings, and the smaller blocks and steel cable provide a neater, more flexible gridiron system than has been previously available. In addition, it has led to the development of the electric spot-line system, which can provide counterweighted, motor-driven sets of lines anywhere in the stage area. This spot-line system, while not intended to be a complete rigging system, has proved valuable in combination with an underhung pin-and-rail system and a counterweighted system.

7 STAGE DRAPERIES

Every well-equipped stage has a set of dark draperies that defines the perimeter of the acting area when a setting is not in place on the stage or when a minimal set that does not provide complete masking is being used. These draperies can be made from a variety of material: flannel, duvetyn, cotton rep, monk's cloth, corduroy, or velour. Whatever the material, it should be neutral in color and have a surface that will not reflect light a great deal. Velour is considered the ideal fabric because of its deep nap. This kind of nap casts shadows on itself and absorbs light extremely well. Black velour is probably the most flexible of all fabrics for stage draperies, because any color in scenery and costumes may be used in front of it, it is durable, it hangs well, and visually it recedes to create an impression of space. Flannel is a fair substitute for velour. So, also, is corduroy. One must be careful, however, with any of these deep-napped fabrics. If the nap is not running in the same direction throughout the set of draperies, some panels will appear to be darker than others. In such a case, the darker panels have the nap pointed up. It is a good idea, therefore, to construct the complete set of draperies with the nap pointed up in order to get a darker, less reflective surface.

Standard Drapery Construction and Arrangement

Stage draperies are constructed by the sewing of widths of fabric into panels with vertical seams and then sewing the panels at the top onto a strip of 3- or 4-inch webbing. Vertical seams are used because they hang well and bear the weight of the heavy drapery better than horizontal seams do. Webbing, a strip of heavy jute fabric used by upholsterers, strengthens the top edge of the panel and furnishes a base for metal grommets. These grommets are set every 6 to 12 inches through the fabric and webbing with a grommet press. The grommets form a strong hole through which tie lines are threaded. At the bottom of each panel—through the hem or through an additional pocket at the back—a chain is threaded to provide weight for keeping the panel hanging straight.

The panels of fabric may be sewn to the webbing at the top either flat or in pleats. If the fabric has little nap or texture, it is better to sew it in pleats. If it has a deep nap, however, a more flexible panel can be achieved by sewing it flat. This flat panel can then be hung in fullness or flat, as needed.

A word of caution is helpful at this point. While it is possible to construct these draperies in one's own shop, it is advisable, if the budget permits, to order them made by a professional company that specializes in stage-drapery construction. The size and weight of the panels, the heavy-duty sewing machine necessary, the insertion of the grommets, keeping seams and hems straight, and keeping the nap running in the proper direction are all difficult problems for most producing groups. Lightweight drops, draperies, and curtains that are easily constructed will be discussed later.

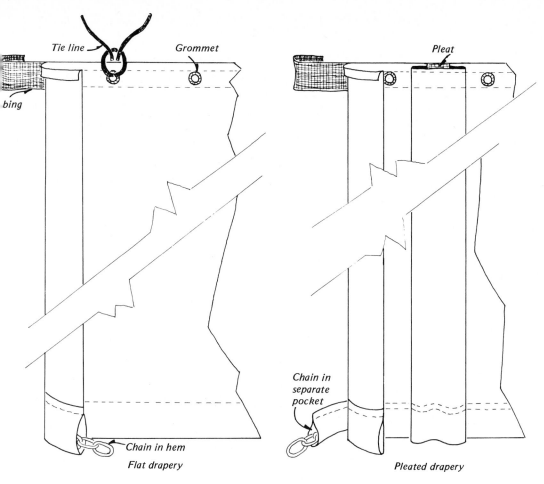

Figure 3-7 Standard drapery construction.

After the draperies have been made and equipped with tie lines, they are tied with bow knots to pipe battens or double wooden battens suspended from the grid. Various arrangements of the battens and draperies are possible.

Figure 3-7 shows standard drapery construction methods, and Figure 3-8 shows various arrangements of complete sets of stage draperies.

8 THE SKY

Representing the sky effectively on stage has always been a problem for the scene designer. The attempt to capture an impression of the sky's great expanse and its luminous quality has led to the development of certain equipment with which it is possible to suggest the sky in exterior sets or to create an impression of space around abstract sets. Three standard methods have been devised.

a The plaster dome: Sometimes called the "horizont," the plaster dome is a permanent concave wall of plaster or concrete placed at the back of the stage—with its sides projecting downstage into the wings and its top arching slightly over the playing area. While the dome provides an excellent surface for reflecting light and is wrinkle-proof and durable, it does pose many problems that limit its use. Because it must be permanently mounted on the

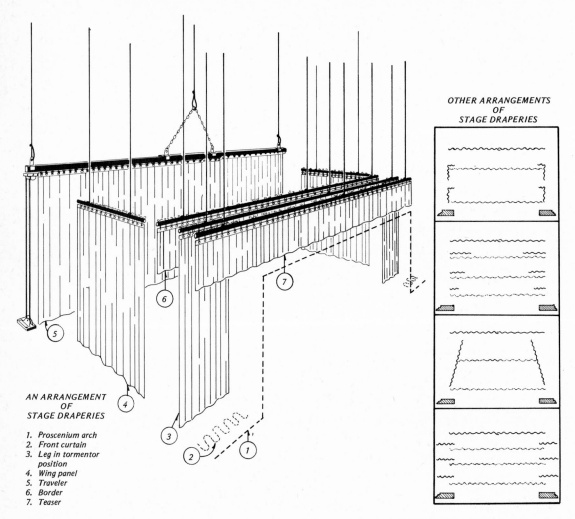

OTHER ARRANGEMENTS
OF
STAGE DRAPERIES

AN ARRANGEMENT
OF
STAGE DRAPERIES

1. Proscenium arch
2. Front curtain
3. Leg in tormentor position
4. Wing panel
5. Traveler
6. Border
7. Teaser

Figure 3-8 Typical arrangements of stage draperies. The drapery panels are tied to pipe battens suspended from the gridiron.

stage floor, requires a great deal of space to be effective, and is expensive to build, it is no longer in general use. In fact, domes originally built into many stages have been removed to allow for greater flexibility of scenery placement and shifting, both of which the domes were restricting.

b   The cyclorama: Commonly referred to as a cyc, this sky piece is made of canvas and offers the advantage of flexibility. In addition, if properly colored, stretched, and lighted, it produces an effect of open sky nearly as good as that of the plaster dome. The cyc is constructed by the sewing together of widths of canvas to form a large, smooth drop. The drop is then equipped with webbing and grommets on both its top and bottom edges. The top edge is laced to a U-shaped pipe batten that is suspended from the grid by two or more sets of lines. The bottom edge of the drop is laced to another U-shaped pipe batten that stretches the drop and prevents it from moving about. If the gridiron is high enough, the cyc may be flied up and out of the way when it is not needed.

Since cycs are necessarily tall and are in an upstage position, most gridirons are not high enough to allow flying them out unfolded. If this is the case, the height of the cyc may be reduced for flying by tripping it. The height of the cyc may be reduced by half if a set of lines is attached—at the back of the cyc—to the bottom pipe batten. When this batten is raised, the cyc will fold up until it is half its original height. Another method makes use of a third U-shaped batten that runs around the back of the cyc halfway between the top and bottom battens. This third batten is attached to grommeted webbing sewn to the back of the cyc or is inserted through a pocket at the back of the cyc. When the batten is raised, the top half of the cyc folds as the bottom half is lifted.

Special consideration must be given to the type of seam used in constructing a cyc. Horizontal seams provide a smooth surface but usually distort the curves of the cyc in turning the corners of the U-shaped battens. Vertical seams turn the corners easily but do not usually provide a smooth surface. If the curve distortion offers no problem, horizontal seams are better. If, for some reason, the curve distortion presents a problem, vertical seams should be used; it may be necessary, however, to hang a seamless scrim cyc directly in front of the canvas cyc to obscure the vertical seams.

Coloring the cyc also presents special problems. It is advisable to keep the cyc material as soft as possible so that it will not wrinkle easily. Cycs, therefore, are usually dyed instead of being

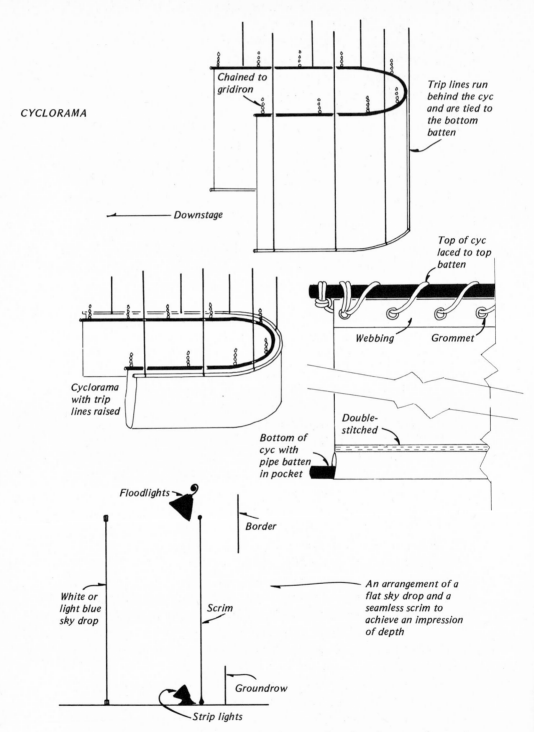

CYCLORAMA

Chained to gridiron

Trip lines run behind the cyc and are tied to the bottom batten

Downstage

Top of cyc laced to top batten

Cyclorama with trip lines raised

Webbing   Grommet

Double-stitched

Bottom of cyc with pipe batten in pocket

Floodlights

Border

White or light blue sky drop

Scrim

An arrangement of a flat sky drop and a seamless scrim to achieve an impression of depth

Groundrow

Strip lights

Figure 3-9 Tripped cyclorama and sky drop combined with a seamless scrim.

painted with scene paint. The dye will provide the desired color without adding stiffening to the fabric. If a scrim is used in conjunction with a canvas cyc, the canvas cyc may remain white with the scrim dyed the desired color.

c *The sky drop:* By far the simplest to construct, to rig, and to shift, the sky drop does not offer the same effect of depth as does either the dome or cyc. It is, however, effective if properly painted, stretched, and lighted. Its great flexibility makes it invaluable on restricted stages and, indeed, remains the solution to many problems on well-equipped stages.

To heighten the impression of depth in a sky drop, many designers have discovered that the use of a seamless scrim in conjunction with the sky drop helps enormously. If a scrim is hung 3 or 4 feet downstage of the drop, and the drop, but not the scrim, is lighted, a great deal of depth impression may be achieved. In this case, the drop may remain white to add to its reflective power and the scrim dyed a light blue to provide color.

Figure 4-1 Design by Mordecai Gorelik for *Desire Under the Elms*.

PLANNING THE SCENERY

CHAPTER 4

1 INTRODUCTION

If all the elements of a production are to work well together and are to present a unified impression to an audience, a considerable amount of planning must be done in advance of the performance. To facilitate this planning, directors, actors, and designers find it necessary to begin visualizing all the elements of a production as early in the production period as possible.

65

The scene designer, to communicate his concept of the set to the director, prepares various graphic representations for him. The representations may take the form of a pencil, ink, or colored sketch with a floor plan, or a dimensional model. In some cases, the designer will find it necessary to present a director with all three.

The evolution of these plans has no prescribed sequence. Some designers prefer to begin with a sketch and then evolve a floor plan from it; others develop the floor plan first and then, from it, evolve a sketch and/or model.

Whatever sequence he chooses, the designer's responsibility is to produce some visualization of his ideas and feelings about the play expressed in scenic terms. The director then checks this visualization to see if it seems to be compatible with his scheme for the overall production of the play.

After a set design has been agreed upon by the designer and the director, the designer produces working drawings from which the various pieces of scenery can be built.

The techniques for producing the representations of a design and the methods for converting these representations into working drawings for the carpenters, who convert the drawings into wood and canvas, are outlined in the following pages.

2   THE SKETCH

In the sketch, the designer attempts to capture the dimensional qualities, the color, and the dominant mood of a particular moment of the play. Through the use of a perspective drawing, he attempts to picture the three-dimensional nature of a set as it might be seen by a member of the audience seated in the center of the auditorium. It is also in the sketch that the designer shows the effect that lighting might have on the particular moment of the play he has chosen to represent.

The designer must be certain that his representation does not mislead by promising more than can be attained in execution. The sketch must not be considered an end in itself. It must be thought of as a plan for visual effects that can be realized fully only in performance.

To make sure that his sketch presents as practical a plan as possible, the designer must pay careful attention to proportion, color, and light in his drawing.

To ensure that proportions are reasonably accurate in the sketch, the designer must be constantly aware of exactly how much space the performance area affords and of how much of that space each scenic unit and each actor will eventually occupy. It is a good

Figure 4-2 Ink-and-wash sketch of the setting for *You Can't Take It With You.*
Figure 1-8 is a photograph of the completed set.

idea always to include at least one figure in the sketch to check proportions in scale with the human body.

If the designer does a completely colored sketch of the set, he must realize that the colors in the sketch are not usually the colors with which the set will actually be painted. In the sketch, they represent the effect of the actual color under stage lighting viewed from a distance. Usually the color on a scenic unit would be more intense than it appears to be in the sketch.

Since a great deal of the visual mood of a design depends on the placement of light and shadow, the designer must be certain that his placement of light and shadow in the sketch not only supplies the desired mood but, when it is actually reproduced on stage, supplies sufficient illumination for the audience to see the actor clearly.

The sketch, then, should be considered primarily as a means for communicating ideas during the preparation of a production. It is not its function to be a work of art in itself but merely a plan for the final effect a design will produce with actors in front of an audience.

3 PERSPECTIVE DRAWING

The designer finds that there are many methods for producing a perspective drawing of a proposed set. If he goes to a regular architectural manual for guidance in preparing such a drawing, however, he will find that the standard methods recommended there are elaborate, complicated, and require the use of more drawing space than he probably has available on his single drafting board. Since, generally speaking, the precise details of a stage setting are fixed in the plan and elevation drawings, the perspective can usually be reserved for just checking the effects. Hence the perspective drawing for the stage does not have to be quite so exact in all its parts as does its architectural counterpart. The theatre man can take a few judicious shortcuts.

The method of making the perspective proposed here has three advantages over the regular architectural methods referred to: it does not require a station point, it employs only two vanishing points, and its rules of work are very simple. Following is the way the linear apparatus is set up and the method put into action.

Draft the rectangular outline for your perspective drawing down far enough on your sheet to allow you to place a plan of your set just above it. The rectangle, drawn to some convenient scale (usually ½ inch = 1 foot), is presumably of the same shape and size as the proscenium opening of the stage on which your scenery will be mounted. The side lines represent the edges of the proscenium arch, or of the tormentors; the top line marks the position of the teaser; and the bottom line the floor.

In Figure 4-3 the teaser line is designated by TL and the floor line by FL. Extend the first line a little to the left to T' and the second line in the same direction to F'. Now drop a center line. Find a point on this line about 5 feet from the bottom and draw a horizontal line, carrying it from the left border of your perspective drawing well over to the right. Since this is the horizon line for your perspective, it is marked HL.

Find a point on HL, to the right of the center line, that has a distance from the center line equal to the width of the proscenium opening. That is, if the width of your opening is 25 feet (according to your scale), put the point on HL to the right 25 feet from the center line; if the width of the opening is 30 feet, place the point on HL 30 feet from the center line. The intersection of the center line and horizon line will be recognized as the center vanishing point (CVP) of the drawing, and the mark to the right, the right vanishing point (RVP).

Above TL will now be the area that will be occupied with reference details of your plan. You are looking straight ahead at the perspective, but down from above at your plan. In the plan, TL will represent the downstage curtain line, and the points T and L the right and left edges of the proscenium opening.

To establish on the floor of the perspective drawing a spot that

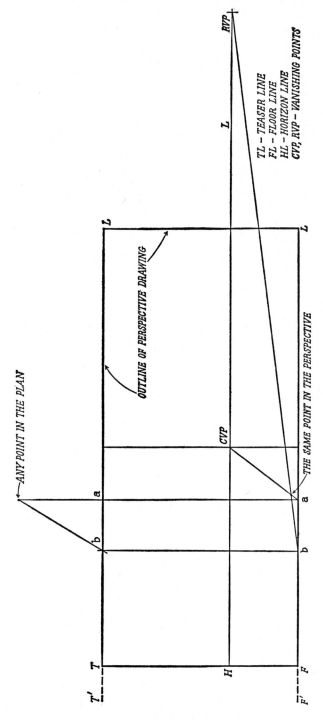

Figure 4-3 Locating a spot on the floor of a perspective drawing of a setting.

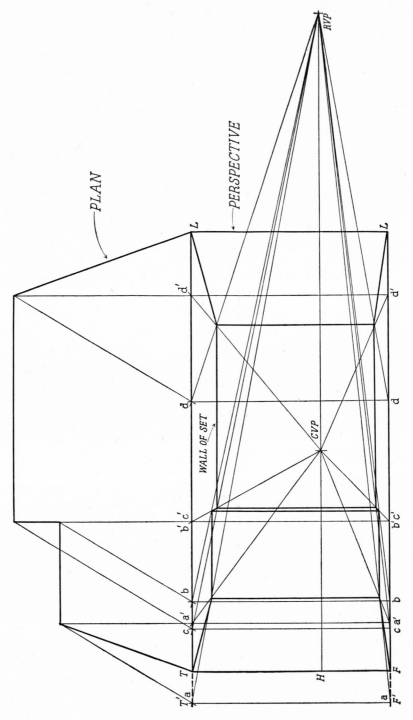

Figure 4-4 Drawing the walls of the perspective.

corresponds to a point in the plan above, plot two sets of lines (Figure 4-3). From the point in the plan drop a vertical line, *a*, across *TL* to meet *FL*, and from here draw another line to *CVP*. Now from the point in the plan draw a second line, *b*, this time to the left at a 30-degree angle to the vertical (use your 30- to 60-degree drafting triangle). From the point where this crosses *TL*, drop a vertical to *FL*; and from the meeting of these two draw a line to *RVP*. The point where the lines to *CVP* and *RVP* intersect each other is the one desired.

Figure 4-4 shows how the method for finding one spot on the floor of the perspective can be applied to the plotting of all the bottom corners of a set of scenery. The upper corners of the various planes also can be found by drawing a second set of diagonals to the two vanishing points (from the intersections of the vertical lines with *TL* to *CVP*, and from the intersections of the 30-degree lines with *TL* to *RVP*). The point where, in each case, the lines to the two vanishing points cross in the space above *HL* is the upper corner of a piece of scenery (just as each corresponding intersection below marks the lower corner). By drawing a line from the upper corner to the one under it you are marking the line along which two sections of the wall are meeting. Now connect all the floor points and all the ceiling points together and you have the perspective of the walls of your set.

Figure 4-5 illustrates a way to mark off a grid on the floor of the perspective.

The wall and the grid should serve as sufficient guides to the approximate location and scaling of other objects in the setting to make the drafting of additional plot lines unnecessary. If, however, you wish to be a little more exact about these objects, you can follow the plotting diagramed in Figure 4-6. To determine precisely the place and size of a perspective window, for example, begin by extending the sides of the window in the plan straight down to *FL* by means of the lines *a* and *b*. All points on a plane parallel to *FL*, if the plane is moved toward the rear, finally vanish at *CVP*. You know now that the window in the flat would have the same proportions if it were drawn downstage at *FL* as it would have upstage in its desired position. So construct on *FL*, to the established scale, an outline of your window, putting it at the right height from the floor. Draw four lines from the corners of the window outline back to *CVP*. Now, from the point where line *a* intersects *FL*, draw a line back to *CVP*; where this line crosses the bottom of the perspective wall, erect a vertical. The segment of this line that occupies the space between the two

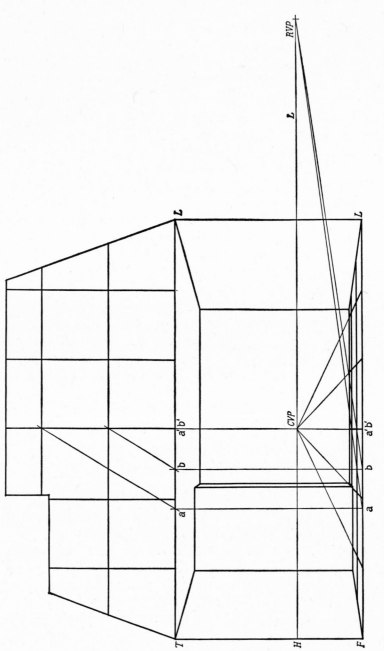

Figure 4-5 Marking off the floor of the perspective in squares.

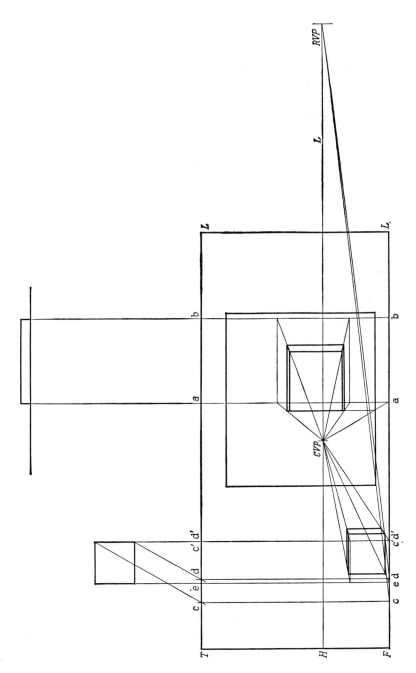

Figure 4-6 Drawing a window and a stage object in perspective.

lines on the left to *CVP* is the left edge of the perspective window. All you have to do now is to connect the ends of this segment of the vertical line to the other two lines going back to *CVP*, add another short vertical on the right, and you have your completed outline for your perspective window.

To ascertain the size and place of an object that does not happen to be touching the back wall, use the same method as that suggested for the window, but start with two corner points on the floor (one downstage, one upstage) so that you will know just where to erect the object's front and back edges.

Other vanishing points can be added, if they should be desired, for objects set on lines not parallel to *FL* (Figure 4-7). All one has to do to diminish a rectangular object set on any angle is to establish three corner points on the floor of the perspective (here designated as *a*, *b*, and *c*), then draw lines in turn from the front point to the two rear points. These two lines will point directly to the special vanishing points (VP 1 and VP 2 on *HL*) for the two upstage planes of the object. Now the draftsman will extend one of the lines down to *FL* and there (*a'*) construct the true elevation of one corner, then draw a line from the top of this back to the same vanishing point as that to which the line below leads. With these lines, plus the three original dots, one has enough guides for the completion of the object. (If one of these supplementary vanishing points threatens to go off the edge of the board, don't hesitate to bring it back. A little forcing of perspective in the drawing of details will do no serious harm.)

The positions of the two vanishing points, *CVP* and *RVP*, illustrated in this section, are not fixed by any rule. If one wants to show more or less of the floor in the perspective, he can raise or lower the line HL with *CVP* and *RVP*. If one wishes to sharpen the pitch of the perspective's angles, he can move *RVP* toward the center line; if one wants to soften the angles, he will move the point farther out to the right.

4 THE FLOOR PLAN

In many ways, the floor plan is the most important drawing a designer will produce. This plan should be a completely accurate scaled diagram depicting the set as if it were being viewed from directly overhead and showing, simply, the lines that every piece of scenery and furniture would make on the floor of the playing area. It is from this carefully scaled diagram that the designer discovers whether his design will fit into the playing area, whether

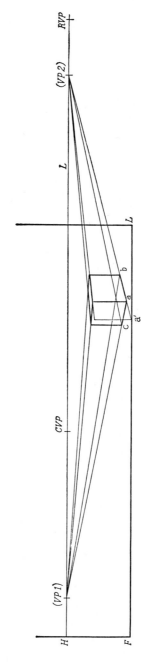

Figure 4-7 Drawing an object on an angle.

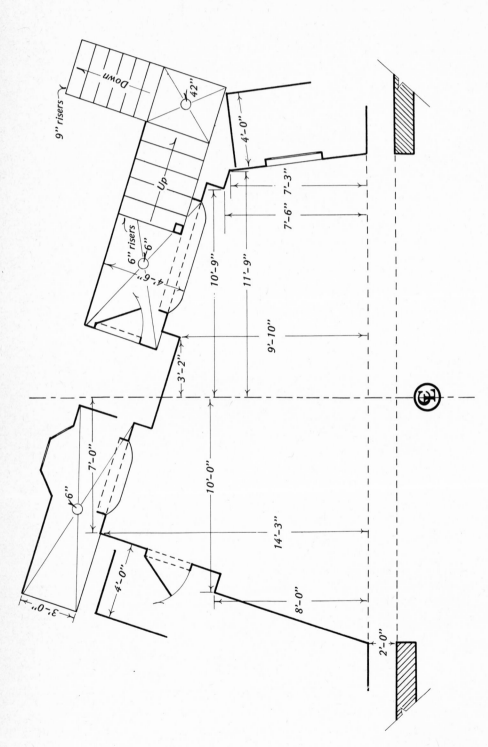

Figure 4-8 Floor plan. Notice that each important point in the set is located by two dimension lines. One dimension line is drawn from the downstage limit of the set and one dimension line is drawn from the center line. The various drafting conventions used to produce a floor plan are discussed in Section 7 of this chapter. The above floor plan is of the setting for *You Can't Take It With You*; Figure 1-8 is a sketch of the setting; and Figure 1-8 is a photograph of the completed setting.

there is room to shift sets, whether all important elements are in proper sight lines, and whether the set affords proper facility for the action of the play. Not only is this drawing important to the scene designer, it is important to the director, the lighting designer, and the building crews as well.

The director will use this diagram to plan the movements of the actors and to set up special effects in the action. He will use it throughout the rehearsal period to make certain that he is containing the action within the set and that his actors are not "walking through the walls" that will eventually be onstage when the set is completed. From this scaled-down diagram, the floor plan is marked off in actual size on the floor of the rehearsal area with masking tape to ensure that the director and the actors are certain of the location of all elements of the set throughout the rehearsal period.

The lighting designer, also, can do much of his preliminary planning using the floor plan. He can plan the hanging of instruments and the placement of light to cover various areas within the limitations of the set.

During the construction of a set, the carpenters will often refer to the floor plan to determine how various pieces of scenery should fit together to form the set. They will use the floor plan also as a guide for setting up the set when it is finished.

While the floor plan is a purely mechanical drawing and represents none of the aesthetic values of a design, except with respect to the placement of various elements, it is of extreme importance in assuring a production staff that the aesthetic values of a design can, in fact, be realized in practical terms.

5 THE MODEL

A model is a three-dimensional miniature of a set built carefully to scale out of wood, cardboard, clay, or other materials. Many designers who develop their ideas in sketch form make use of a miniature to demonstrate their plans to other members of the production staff. From the model, the director is able to get a clear idea of space relationships, and the technical director is able to check scene shifts and construction requirements. A model usually presents a setting much more clearly than does a flat sketch.

The model does not have to be completed down to minute details or painted to be of use to the production staff. An accurately scaled, unpainted, cardboard model will convey enough information to be useful.

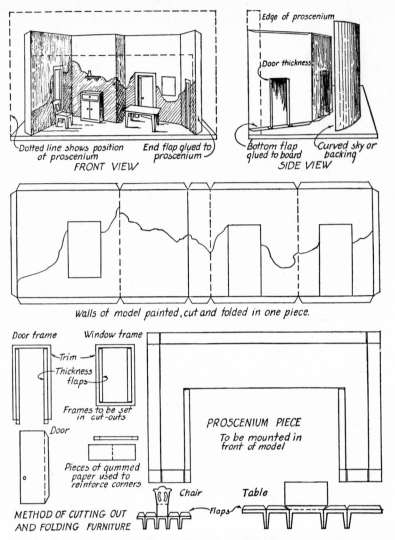

Figure 4-9 Construction of a cardboard model. The various pieces are cut out and folded forward on the dotted lines and backward on the heavy black lines.

The nature of the set will usually determine the materials used in building the model. A model of a simple interior set may best be built with Bristol board. A model of a platformed set is easily built with Upson board. Clay is useful for modeling very irregular shapes, such as rocks. The designer's ingenuity will lead him to employ various materials in his models to achieve interesting shapes and textures. The most important consideration in choosing material, however, is that of scale. The texture of some materials may be so heavy as to be out of proportion with the model. Fabric is particularly difficult in this regard. In a model built to a ½-inch scale, for example, the weave of most fabric is too coarse to appear in scale. Fine-woven, thin fabric, or even paper, would give a better effect. Figure 4-9 illustrates the construction of a simple Bristol-board model for an interior set. The walls are first drawn out carefully to some definite scale such as ¼ inch = 1 foot or ½ inch = 1 foot. When completely outlined, including door and window openings, the walls are cut out. This is done in one piece, if possible, because cardboard can be folded more easily than it can be fastened together. In cutting out the piece, or pieces, leave ¼- or ½-inch flaps along all edges that must be joined with glue to other edges. Now, with the back of a knife or razor blade, score all lines along which folds are to be made. In each case score the cardboard on the side opposite to that of the crease. Fold the wall up and mount it on edge, by means of the ¼- or ½-inch flaps, on a piece of heavy cardboard or a wooden panel. If the glue does not hold very well, the joints may be temporarily held in place by means of thumbtacks or paper clips.

Usually the walls of the model are decorated before they are folded. Common watercolor or show card paints may be used for this purpose. Door and window openings can be made to look more real by inserting paper thicknesses into them to represent their door and window frames, then fastening small door shutters or window sashes to the back edges of the thicknesses. Bits of furniture, folded out of paper and painted, add considerably to the effectiveness of the little set.

When the interior of the miniature has been finished, cut out a small proscenium to the same scale, paint it black or gray, and mount it in front of the set as a frame for it. Place a light-blue sky piece at the back and add any foliage cutouts or mountain rows called for in the final plan. If the walls of the model are made a little higher than the proscenium opening, no ceiling need be used. In fact, it is a good plan in any case to leave at least part of the top open for lighting.

6   THE WORKING DRAWINGS

The working drawings of a set of scenery are the building plans drafted for the carpenter. Laid out to some selected scale—usually ½ inch = 1 foot, or 1 inch = 1 foot—they show the exact dimensions and construction of each unit, and include indications of materials to be used (if that is not apparent) and written explanations of all points that cannot be made clear by lines and figures

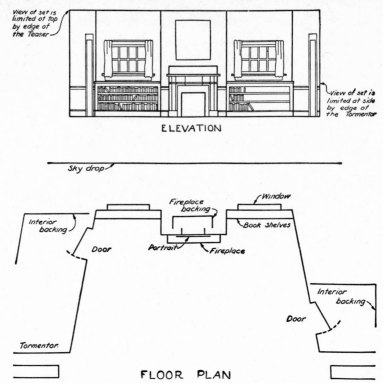

View of set is
limited ot top
by edge of
the Teaser

View of set is
limited at side
by edge of
the Tormentor

ELEVATION

Sky drop

Fireplace
backing

Window

Interior
backing

Book Shelves

Door

Portrait

Fireplace

Interior
backing

Door

Tormentor.

FLOOR   PLAN

Figure 4-10

Elevation and floor plan of an interior set. This drawing illustrates how standard scenery units are assembled to form a typical realistic interior setting. Included in this group are two plain flats, two door flats, two window flats, two jogs, one fireplace flat, two door-frame units, two window-frame units, one fireplace unit, two backing wings (behind the doorways), one fireplace backing, and one sky drop. The drawing also suggests how the designer may work out the elevation and the floor plan of a set together. By placing the plan directly below the elevation, he enables himself, as he draws, to visualize the whole and the parts of his setting in three dimensions, and to check carefully his arrangement of the different units.

alone. Details, such as the plan of a difficult joint, an arrangement of molding, or a special placing of hardware, are shown separately in enlarged detail drawings. Three-dimensional units, such as stairs and platforms, are laid out both in plan and elevation. Cross sections of units are added wherever they are necessary for clarity. As building principles on the stage are seldom complicated, it is usually unnecessary to make drawings elaborate.

If the carpenter who is superintending the building of the scenery is a man of experience in the ways and means of the stage, it is, of course, a waste of effort to include in the working drawings all such details as the standard arrangement of parts in steps and parallels, of frame supports for columns and trees, or of joints and hardware on simple flats. Usually mere outlines of such units, with their widths and heights and the positions and sizes of any special features, such as door or window openings, are all that are required.

A point in drawing flats should be noted. As the frames for

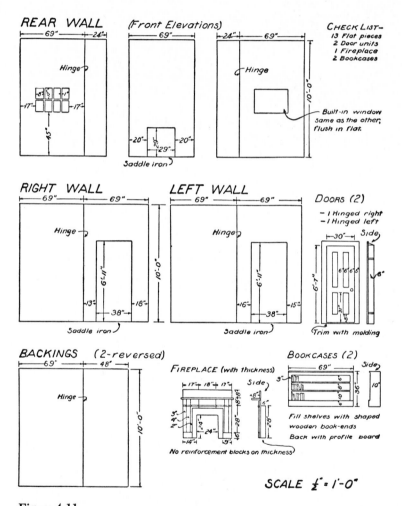

Figure 4-11

Sheet of working drawings for the set of scenery pictured and diagramed in Figure 4-10. Each unit, or combination of units, is drawn separately. Because the two backings are similar (though reversed), only one is drawn. If the carpenter is familiar with standard building methods, simple front elevations are generally sufficient.

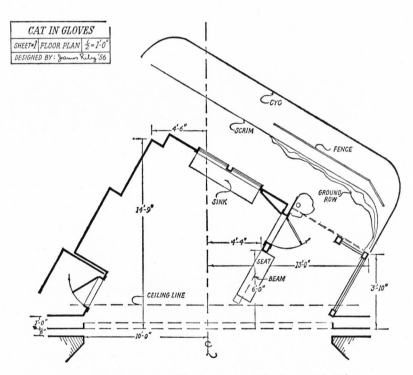

Figure 4-12 Setting for *Cat in Gloves,* designed by James M. Riley:
(*Above*): The finished set.
(*Below*): Floor plan.

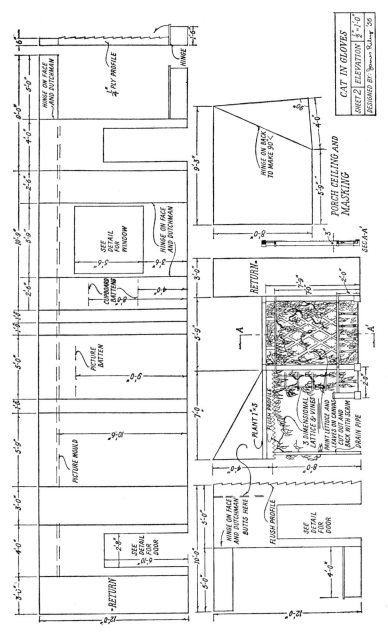

Figure 4-13 Working drawings for *Cat in Gloves:* the walls.

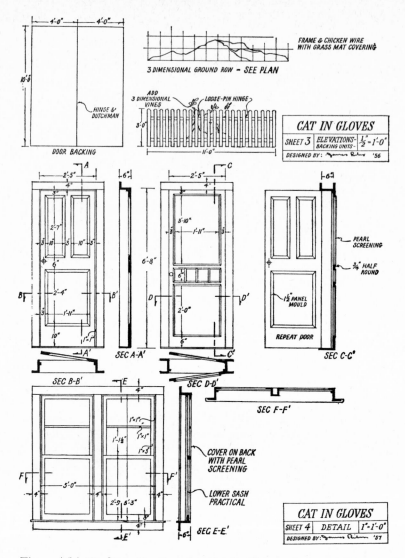

Figure 4-14 Working drawings for *Cat in Gloves*: doors, windows, and a section of fence.

these are constructed face downward, the drawings are frequently done in reverse of the normal front view, for the convenience of the carpenter. To save confusion it is wise to indicate which view of the flats is shown.

In general, make the complete drawing accurate to one scale. For this purpose the use of a scale ruler, such as that employed by architectural and mechanical draftsmen, is essential. By accuracy we mean that a line on the paper 6 inches long should not vary from 6 inches by more than ⅟₃₂ inch. If an enlarged detail is shown, write the scale immediately under it. The scale for the whole drawing should be placed in the lower right-hand corner of the page. Check dimensions carefully several times and be sure that the sum of the dimensions of parts equals the overall dimensions. If there is a discrepancy, the carpenter will probably toss a coin to decide which is correct. Small errors of less than an inch in the completed set will make it very difficult or impossible to put the set together. Use a 2H pencil well sharpened on a sandpad for your light lines, and a 2B pencil for your heavier lines.

Do not overcrowd a drawing with repeated dimensions or with a mass of notes that obscure the outlines. If the drawing is clearly and completely drawn with all the views and dimensions necessary, few notes are needed. Such a drawing will be easy to read.

7   DRAFTING CONVENTIONS

To produce the clearest floor plan and working drawings possible, the designer must be familiar with several conventions of drafting that have been developed to facilitate the drafting of plans and the reading of them. A great deal of time is saved, and even more confusion avoided, if everyone on a production staff is familiar with these conventions and can understand a drawing quickly and correctly.

Elevations, Sections, Plans

There are three types of conventional drawings used to represent objects on paper in flat planes. These types of drawings, called *elevations, sections,* and *plans,* do not involve perspective but, rather, depict a flattened view of an object with no consideration of depth or thickness. By depicting a flattened view of an object, these drawings enable the craftsman to take accurate measurements from any part of the drawing without having to take into account any effect of perspective or distance.

The Elevation: The elevation is a vertical view of an object taken from the front, sides, or rear, in which every element is drawn as if the object were directly in front of the viewer. No perspective whatsoever is employed. A perspective drawing of a simple box (Figure 4-15) compared to the elevation drawings of the same box will clarify the difference between the two types of drawings.

Figure 4-15 gives a good picture of the box but is useless for

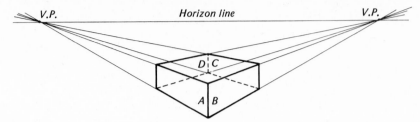

Figure 4-15 Perspective view of a box.

depicting true dimensions, because the sides of the box diminish in size as they approach the vanishing points.

If, however, as in Figure 4-16, we turn the box so that one side is directly facing us and "take the box apart" by flattening all sides and lining them up facing us (ignoring the top for the moment), we can produce a nonpictorial representation of all sides of the box from which accurate measurements could be taken.

Elevations are drawn with a solid, medium-weight line that describes the outline of the surface being viewed.

The Section: There are two types of section drawings: vertical sections and horizontal sections. These drawings are produced by passing an imaginary plane through an object in either a vertical direction or a horizontal direction and then depicting the cut edge of the object.

Various weights of line are used to clarify section drawings. The part, or parts, of the object cut by the imaginary plane are outlined with a heavy line and filled in with cross-hatching. Everything beyond the cutting plane is drawn with a light line. On the elevation drawing of the object to be sectioned (Figure 4-17), a heavy, broken line with arrows indicates the position of the cutting plane on which the section will be shown. The arrows point toward the portion to be shown and are labeled consecutively on a page beginning with A–A′.

The Plan: The plan of an object is either an external view looking directly down on the top of the object or the horizontal section of the object. The external plan, like elevations, is drawn with a medium-weight line. By combining a plan view of the top of the

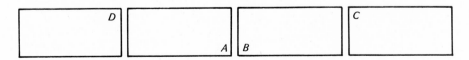

Figure 4-16 Elevations of the box.

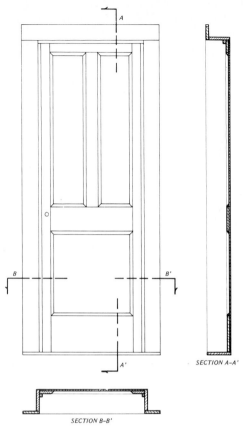

SECTION A–A'

SECTION B–B'

Figure 4-17 Elevation, horizontal section, and vertical section of a door unit.

box in Figure 4-18 with elevations of the sides, we can give a nonpictorial, but clear description of the shape and size of the box.

When one studies the floor plan in Figure 4-8, he discovers that

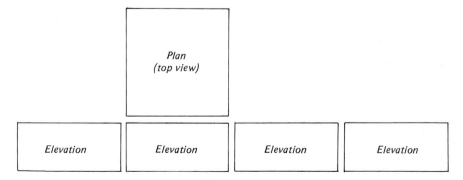

Figure 4-18 Plan and elevations of the box.

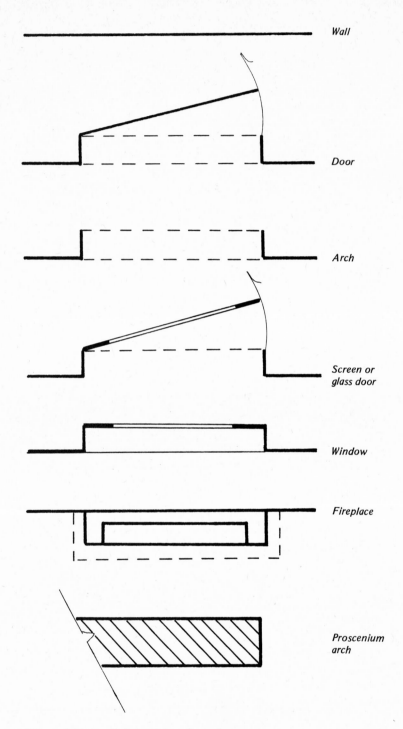

Wall

Door

Arch

Screen or
glass door

Window

Fireplace

Proscenium
arch

Figure 4-19 Symbols used in a floor plan.

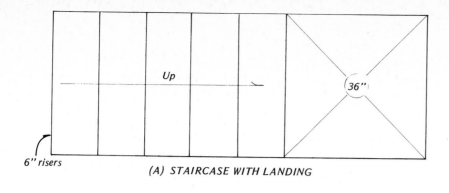

6" risers

(A) STAIRCASE WITH LANDING

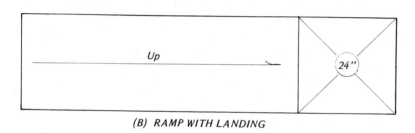

(B) RAMP WITH LANDING

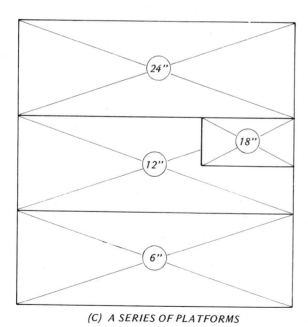

(C) A SERIES OF PLATFORMS

Figure 4-20 Plan views of stairs, a ramp, and a series of platforms.

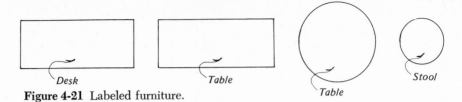

Figure 4-21 Labeled furniture.

it is a combination of horizontal sections and of external plans similar to the box top. The walls and doors are shown in simplified horizontal sections and are drawn with heavy lines. The platforms, steps, and furniture are shown in external plans and are drawn with medium lines. The section drawings of a floor plan need not be as intricate as section drawings used for construction purposes. In fact, because of the relatively small scale of a floor plan, standard simplified symbols have been developed to represent various parts of a set.

In order not to complicate the drawing, objects such as staircases and furniture are shown in external plan. These plans often require labels to clarify them.

The note "6″ risers" indicates that each step is 6 inches higher than the preceding one. The "up" arrow indicates the direction of rise of the staircase. The light diagonal lines on the landing indicate that it is above floor level. The "36″ " notation indicates that the landing is 36 inches above floor level.

These same conventions are applied to other objects in the floor plan, as shown in Figure 4-21.

Labels on furniture are necessary if the plan view is not distinctive enough to identify the object. A label is noted by a lightweight line with a one-sided arrow pointing to the designated object (Figure 4-21). As shown in Figure 4-22, however, other, more distinctive

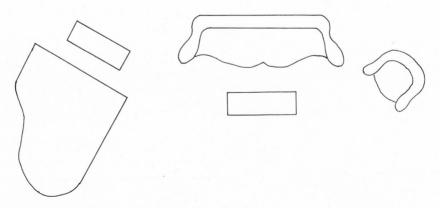

Figure 4-22 Nonlabeled furniture.

objects may not need labels. A good rule-of-thumb to follow is to supply enough labels to make the drawing perfectly clear, but not so many as to clutter it and make it confusing.

Pictorial Drawings

The designer will find that some objects in a design might be explained more clearly in the working drawings by depicting several planes of the object simultaneously. The conventional drawings for accomplishing this are the isometric projection and the oblique drawing. These drawings do not involve perspective either and yet, while having a distorted pictorial quality, do present an accurate representation from which accurate measurements of several planes of an object may be taken.

To produce an isometric projection, the draftsman draws one vertical edge of the object to scale. This vertical edge is set on a horizontal line, which serves as the base for the drawing. The sides of the object are represented as planes slanted to the right and left of the vertical edge at an angle of 30 degrees to the horizontal line. These side planes also are drawn to scale and present accurate measurements of the sides of the object.

Isometric projections are drawn with a medium-weight line except when it is necessary to show hidden outlines of the object. These hidden outlines are drawn with medium-weight dotted lines.

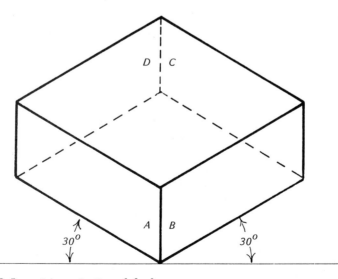

Figure 4-23 Isometric projection of the box.

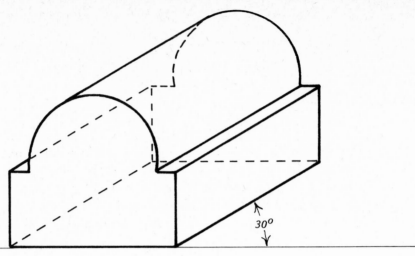

Figure 4-24 Oblique drawing.

Oblique Drawings

If the object to be drawn includes curves or irregular edges, an isometric projection will not present a clear picture of it, because such irregularities become distorted in projection and true measurements cannot be taken from the drawing. By turning the object, however, so that the irregular plane is facing the viewer and then projecting the sides of the object at a 30- or 45-degree angle from the horizontal, an oblique drawing is produced. The oblique drawing is more pictorially distorted than the isometric projection but does give a good shape description from which accurate measurements may be taken.

Dimensions

Even though all the working drawings, no matter what type they happen to be, are drawn to scale and dimensions could be read from them with a scale ruler, the designer should supply enough dimensions to clarify the drawings.

Dimensions are indicated by dimension figures set in the center

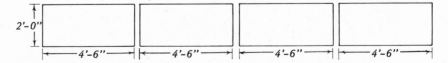

Figure 4-25 Dimensioned elevations of the box.

of a broken lightweight line with an arrow at each end. The arrowed line is placed between, and touching, two short lightweight lines called extension lines, which limit the measurement and set the arrowed line and the figure slightly apart from the line being dimensioned. Dimensioned front elevations of the box are shown in Figure 4-25.

In the isometric projection and the oblique drawing, the extension lines and dimensions are placed in the same plane as the line being dimensioned. A dimensioned isometric projection is shown in Figure 4-26.

In certain cases, there will not be enough space to contain both the arrows and the dimension figure between the extension lines of a small object. In such cases, the draftsman places the figure between the extension lines and places two short arrows outside the extension lines.

In the floor plans in Figure 4-8, it will be noticed that only the dimensions necessary to place crucial corners of the set are given. It is usually necessary to give two dimensions to place any one point in the floor plan—one dimension from the downstage limit of the set, which is designated by a lightweight dotted line, and one dimension from the center line, which is designated by a labeled lightweight line of alternating long and short dashes.

In summary, see Figure 4-27 for a schematic drawing comparing various types of drawings and drawing-line characteristics.

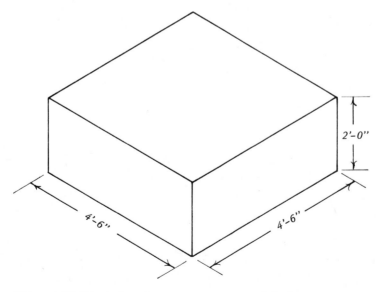

Figure 4-26 Dimensioned isometric projection of the box.

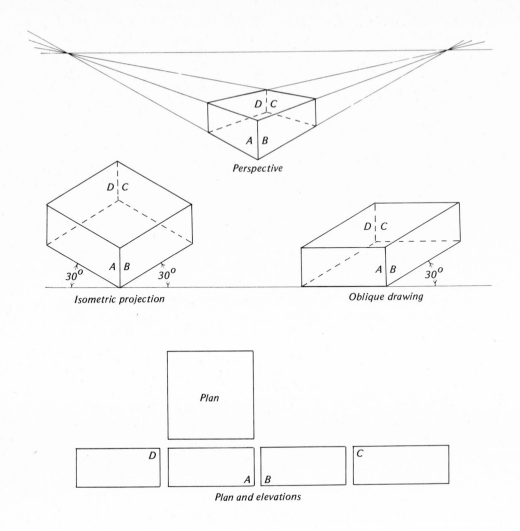

Perspective

Isometric projection

Oblique drawing

Plan

Plan and elevations

LINE WEIGHTS USED IN DRAFTING

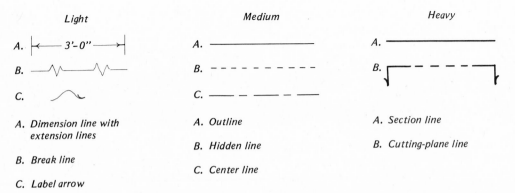

Light

A. |← — 3'-0" —→|

B.

C.

A. Dimension line with
   extension lines

B. Break line

C. Label arrow

Medium

A. ————————

B. - - - - - - - - -

C. —— — —— —

A. Outline

B. Hidden line

C. Center line

Heavy

A. ————————

B.

A. Section line

B. Cutting-plane line

Figure 4-27 Line weights used to produce the various types of drawings.

8 DRAFTING EQUIPMENT

The designer will find it necessary to have available to him certain basic drafting instruments and materials in order to produce neat and accurate mechanical drawings. Since the list of equipment used in drafting for the stage is not as extensive as that employed in regular architectural drafting, the scene designer would be wise to equip himself with the best equipment possible. Inferior equipment is usually more of a hindrance than a help to the draftsman and proves to be completely useless after a short time. The few pieces of drafting equipment necessary to produce a good drawing are discussed next.

Drawing Board: The drawing board is made of a soft, ungrained lumber such as clear white pine or poplar. It is cleated at both ends to prevent splitting and warping. Some boards are also equipped with metal strips at each end to facilitate the sliding of the T square along the edge of the board. Drawing boards come in various sizes, but one approximately 24 × 36 inches will suffice for most basic drafting projects.

T Square: The T square, made of hardwood with transparent plastic edges on the blade, is used for drawing all horizontal lines in the drawing. The blade of the T square should be as long as the larger dimension of the drawing board.

The head of the T square is placed over the left edge of the drawing board with the blade resting on the paper. It is extremely important to keep the head of the T square firmly seated against the edge of the drawing board with the left hand. If this is not

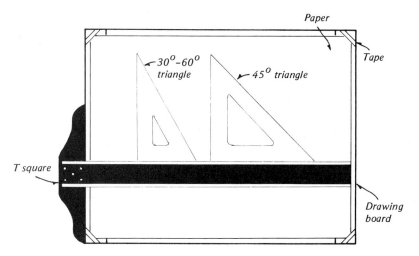

Figure 4-28 Drawing board, T square, and triangles.

done, it is impossible to draw a completely accurate horizontal line. The draftsman draws a line by guiding a pencil, with the right hand, along the edge of the blade from left to right. The left hand is used to hold the head of the T square against the edge of the drawing board and to move the T square to various horizontal locations.

Triangles: Triangles are used in combination with the T square to produce vertical lines and angled lines in the drawing. The transparent triangles may be purchased in various sizes, but the most useful combination for the theatre draftsman would be one 8-inch 45-degree triangle and one 10-inch 30- to 60-degree triangle.

Vertical lines are produced by placing one straight edge of the triangle perpendicular to the edge of the T-square blade and guiding the pencil along the edge of the triangle. The triangle, held perpendicular to the T-square blade, can be guided along the edge of the T square to produce vertical lines anywhere in the drawing.

Again, it must be emphasized that the draftsman must make certain that the head of the T square is firmly held against the edge of the drawing board and the triangle held squarely against the T-square blade if he hopes to produce an accurate drawing.

Compasses: A compass is necessary for drawing circles and arcs. A lengthening arm is a useful piece of additional equipment. Fitted into one arm of the compass, it makes it possible to draw circles and arcs of large diameter. Another useful tool is an inking tip, which fits into the compass arm or lengthening arm for inking circles and arcs.

Very small circles and arcs are best drawn with a bow compass, which locks in position and ensures holding minute dimensions correctly.

Dividers: Dividers are similar to compasses, but, instead of having a lead point or inking tip on one arm, they have a sharp metal point on each arm. Dividers are used to divide a line into equal segments or for transferring dimensions from one part of the drawing to another and from the scale rule.

Scale Rule: Since, of course, floor plans, elevations, sections, and so on, cannot be drawn full size on a piece of paper, it is necessary to draw them in reduced size. While reducing the size the draftsman must also retain the correct proportions of the various elements in the drawing. To accomplish both requirements, the draftsman makes use of the scale rule, which presents the linear foot proportionately reduced in size to various scales. With a scale rule, the draftsman can produce a drawing in which $\frac{1}{2}$ inch in the drawing, for example, represents 1 linear foot of actual size.

Using the same scale throughout the drawing assures that all elements remain in correct proportion. The architect's scale rule presents the linear foot proportionately reduced to ten different scales from which the draftsman may choose, depending on how large a drawing he wishes to produce.

It will be noticed that one edge of the triangular scale rule has a full-sized foot measurement with each inch divided into sixteen segments. On each of the remaining five edges of the rule are represented two different scales. Looking at the edge that presents the 1-inch scale and the ½-inch scale, one will notice that each scale "reads" from different ends of the rule. Usually the 1-inch scale "reads" from left to right, and the ½-inch scale, from right to left.

At the beginning of each scale is a section of rule divided into twelve even segments and these segments are further divided into quarters. These sections represent the scaled foot divided into scaled inches. It is possible, therefore, to represent not only full-foot measurements but also inch fractions of a scaled foot.

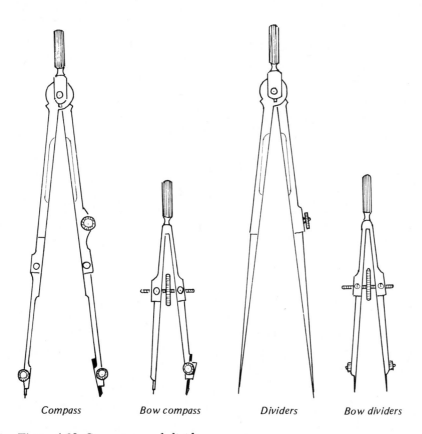

Compass   Bow compass   Dividers   Bow dividers

Figure 4-29 Compasses and dividers.

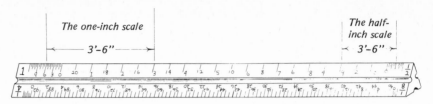

Figure 4-30 Scale rule. The edges that represent the 1-, ¼-, ½-, and ⅛-inch scales are shown.

Pencils and Lead Holders: The weight of a drawn line is determined by the softness or hardness of the lead being used. Leads are letter-graded from B, which is soft and produces a heavy line, to H, which is hard and produces a thin line. 6B is extremely soft and 6H is extremely hard. A wooden drawing pencil of the proper number, or lead, held in a mechanical lead holder may be used. Since the draftsman wishes to produce heavy, medium, and thin lines, a pencil or lead in a lead holder, each of H, 2H and 4H, will give him the necessary variety of line strength.

It is important to keep the lead sharp at all times to produce the proper line strengths and to ensure accuracy of scale. A dull lead can produce a line almost an inch wide on the ½-inch scale. If not controlled, this could completely destroy the accuracy of a page of drawings.

Pens: If it is necessary to ink a drawing, the draftsman can use a standard adjustable architectural ruling pen. These pens are filled by carefully dropping drawing ink between the prongs of the pen. The line strength is adjusted by opening or closing the prongs through turning the adjusting screw on the pen. The prongs of the pen must be kept clean at all times to allow for an even flow of ink. The inking tip on a compass works in the same manner as the ruling pen.

These ruling pens can offer problems to the inexperienced draftsman, however, and he might find one of the technical fountain pens (such as a Rapidograph), a much simpler tool for inking. They are supplied with changeable points for various line strengths, are simple to fill, and supply an even, steady flow of ink. By following the manufacturer's directions for use and care, the draftsman will find them valuable, durable drawing tools.

Paper: If the drawings are to be blueprinted, they must be drawn on a good grade of tracing paper. If tracing paper is used, the draftsman will find it necessary to cover the drawing board first with a piece of opaque drawing paper in order to provide a com-

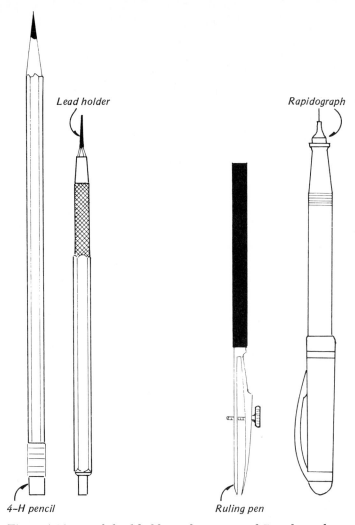

Figure 4-31 Pencil, lead holder, ruling pen, and Rapidograph.

pletely smooth drawing surface and to make the drawing on the tracing paper easier to see.

If the drawings are not going to be blueprinted, they may be done on any medium-weight, white drawing paper approximately the same size as the drawing board.

Accessories: The list of drafting equipment is complete with the addition of a soft pink eraser for removing penciled errors, a sandpaper pad or lead pointer for sharpening pencils and lead, drafting tape for securing the paper to the drawing board, an art gum for cleaning the completed page of drawings, and a soft cloth or paper towel for cleaning pens and dusting instruments.

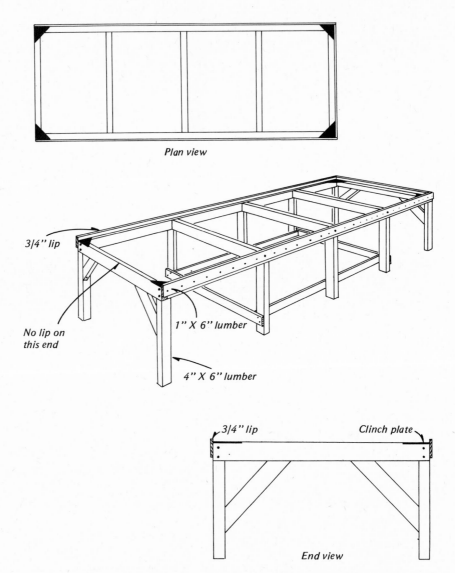

Plan view

3/4" lip

_No lip on
this end_

1" X 6" lumber

4" X 6" lumber

3/4" lip

Clinch plate

End view

Figure 5-1 Template. A workbench for the construction of flats. Some
times the top is covered.

CONSTRUCTING THE SCENERY: GENERAL PRACTICE

CHAPTER 5

1 INTRODUCTION

This chapter, which deals with the general practice of scenery construction, is an introduction to the study of specific problems in Chapter 6. Opening with a discussion of the practical demands of scenery construction, the following sections will consider, in turn, the choice of tools, the selection of building materials, procedures in construction, some methods of joining frames, the general method of covering frames, three systems employed to fasten units of scenery together, and the flameproofing of scenery.

2 PRACTICAL DEMANDS OF SCENERY CONSTRUCTION

Scenery constructed for the stage must fulfill a number of practical requirements.

First, scenery must be designed for easy and rapid construction. The plan of production most frequently adopted by both professional and nonprofessional producing groups allows from three to five weeks only for the complete preparation of a play. Within this brief period the stage designer, the technical director, and his staff and crew must design, draft, build, paint, and fit to the stage usually two or three—frequently more—complete sets of scenery. It is absolutely necessary, therefore, that this scenery be planned for the simplest and quickest possible methods of construction.

Second, scenery must be designed for economical construction. Unless great care is exercised, the item of scenery on the final expense sheet of a production is apt to be a large one. It should be the purpose of the designer and his technical colleagues, therefore, to keep down costs by choosing materials wisely, by adopting efficient methods of building, and, above all, by avoiding waste.

Third, scenery must be designed for quick and silent shifting. That is, it must be constructed in light, well-shaped units that can be handled efficiently by a minimum number of stagehands.

Fourth, scenery must be strong. It must be able to resist considerable strain in the course of being handled by stagehands and actors, especially when it is to be placed in service for performances night after night.

Fifth, scenery must be well assembled. The methods of fastening together the various units must be such that it will be unnecessary to drive a nail during the performance. Nothing sounds more amateurish to the audience during a scene shift than hammering on the stage. The assembling and taking apart of the units should be handled during the shifts quickly and silently.

Sixth, scenery must be designed for easy storage. It must be so planned and constructed that when it is not in use it may be packed away on the stage or in a storeroom in a minimum amount of space. That is, large flat units, such as drops, flats over 5 feet 9 inches wide, and ceilings, must be able to be rolled or folded; three-dimensional frame units, such as platforms, must be collapsible; wide thicknesses on archways and other flats must be removable; and other bulky, awkward units must be made either to be folded or to be taken apart in sections. Scenery that is to be sent on tour and must be planned for storage in a crowded boxcar or truck must be planned to fulfill these requirements especially.

3 WORKSHOP EQUIPMENT

Since the construction of scenery involves standard building procedures primarily, the workshop should be supplied with the various tools that have been designed for specific building purposes and can be purchased at any good hardware store. Following is a list that would equip a shop with the minimum supply of tools necessary for efficient construction:

Hand Tools

Hammers
    Claw hammer
    Rip hammer
    Ball-peen hammer
    Tack hammer
    Staple gun
Saws
    Cross-cut saw
    Rip saw
    Keyhole saw
    Hack saw
    Back saw (for miter box)
Planes
    Block plane
    Smoothing plane
Screw drivers
    Solid screwdriver
    Spiral ratchet screwdriver
Drills
    Brace and various-sized bits
    Push drill
Squares
    Steel framing square
    Combination square
Mat knife
Chisels—various widths
Metal files—flat and triangular
Wood rasp

Clinch plate
Rules
    8-foot steel tape
    6-foot folding rule
    Yardstick
Miter box
Pliers
Crescent wrench
C clamps
Tin shears
Carpenter's vise
Metal vise
Spirit level
Snap line

Power Tools

While a complete set of scenery can be built with the above hand tools, a great deal of time will be saved and a higher degree of accuracy obtained with the addition of certain power tools, such as those that follow.

Radial-arm saw: This power tool, sometimes called a *pull-over* or *swing* saw, is a most valuable addition to a scene shop. It is simple and safe to operate (although caution, of course, must be observed with any power tool) while offering a great deal of flexibility and accuracy. It is used for straight cutting, either cross-grain, rip, or miter. When equipped with attachments, it can be converted into a planer, a router, and various other power tools.

Band saw: This saw, with its long, thin, continuous blade, is used for cutting curved or irregular lines.

Drill press: A heavy-duty drill, the drill press offers control of boring depth and, with speed variation, much more precision than a hand drill. It is useful for both wood and metal drilling and, with attachments, can be converted into other tools such as a sander or router.

These three power tools are heavy pieces of equipment and are usually mounted permanently in the scene shop. There are several portable power tools which, being small and not requiring a large power source, are valuable in the shop and can easily be moved to wherever a power tool is needed.

Skilsaw: This saw, used for straight cutting, can function as a cross-cut saw or as a rip saw. It is not as accurate as the radial-arm saw but is valuable in its portability.

Saber saw: This saw is useful for cutting curves and irregular lines. Because it can cut intricate inside and outside curves, it is more flexible than the band saw and is an invaluable tool in the scene shop.

Electric hand drill: The ⅜-inch electric drill is the most valuable drill for use in the average scene shop. It will accept drill bits from the smallest size up to the ⅜-inch size. With a special gear attachment to reduce its speed and a ratchet screwdriver head, it can also function as an electric screwdriver.

While the above lists would not provide an ideally equipped scene shop, they would provide a shop adequate enough to solve almost any scenic construction problem. Painting equipment and supplies will be discussed in Chapter 7.

One final piece of equipment for securing accuracy and speed and for saving many tired backs in assembling flats, *the template*, should be included in the average shop. The template is a sturdy, open-frame workbench on which flats are built. It is usually waist-high, approximately 6 feet wide and 16 feet long. The actual dimension of the template would be determined by the average size of the flats usually built in a particular shop.

The working part of the bench is a flat, narrow ledge of 4 × 6-inch lumber on edge, extending the length of both sides and the width of each end of the bench. Three 1 × 6-inch strips are fastened to the outside of the ledge on three sides to form a lip that stands ¾-inch above the surface of the ledge. To allow frames with a greater length than that of the bench to lie flat on the ledge, the lip is not fastened to one end of the bench. If the whole bench is made absolutely level and square, scenery may be built on it without having to sight straight sides or test right angles. If the frame of the flat lies well on the ledge and fits snugly against the lip all the way around, the carpenter is assured that the flat is true.

Some templates are made with solid tops and some simply topped with movable boards in order to accommodate flats that are not as wide as the template. Another helpful variation is to have clinch plates set in the four corners of the template flush with the working surfaces.

4 LUMBER MATERIALS

Because all frames must be light and strong, only particular grades of lumber may be used. Requirements of shop and stage demand that the lumber be soft enough for easy working, light enough for easy handling, yet tough enough to stand considerable strain and wear. It must not splinter readily, it must not warp, it must be straight-grained and free from any large blemishes, and it must be well seasoned. By far the best wood for general scenic construction is good-grade Northern or Idaho *white pine*. It is the standard. Sugar pine is the best substitute. Douglas fir, yellow pine, and certain other soft woods also may be substituted; but none of these can approach the efficiency of white pine. (The choice of lumber will depend to a great extent on the section of the country in which the shop is located.)

For ordinary purposes, lumber should be ordered in standard stock-sized strips of from 1×2 inches to 1×12 inches in from 10- to 16-foot lengths depending on the size and type of scenic unit to be built from it. The stock sizes most commonly used in scenery construction are 1×2 inches, 1×3 inches, and 1×4 inches. The stock size of lumber refers to the size of the lumber before it has been dressed—planed and smoothed on all sides—so that a so-called 1×3-inch strip actually measures $3/4 \times 2 5/8$ inches by the time it is delivered from the lumberyard.

For heavier construction such as in platforms, stairs, and so on, a thicker lumber size is needed. Usually 2×4-inch and 2×6-inch stock offers enough strength for platform legs, platform frames, and cross members. It is not necessary for these larger lumber sizes to be of the same high grade as the white pine for flats, but the lumber should be straight and relatively knot free.

Another useful lumber is low-grade 1×4-inch fir to be used for diagonal bracing on tall platforms, battens for hanging lightweight set dressings, and for other utility functions where weight and clear grain are not important.

Molding: Machine-made molding in a great variety of shapes and sizes is available from most lumber dealers. Much time and expense can usually be saved if the dealer's stock is checked to determine the types of molding he has on hand before one settles on a particular molding for a design.

Dowels: The dowel pin, which is usually $1/8$ to 1 inch in diameter and in short lengths, is useful for repairing furniture and for constructing certain detail features of a set.

Larger rounded stock, ranging from 1 to 3 inches in diameter and in long lengths, is useful for making curtain poles, spear handles, and so on. The larger ones can even function as decorative, structural elements of a set.

Lath: Thin ($1/2$-inch thick) strips of lumber of various widths and lengths which are useful in constructing lattice work, columns, trees, and so on.

Plywood: An extremely versatile material for scenery construction, plywood (laminated sheets of veneer) is manufactured in several thicknesses. It comes, usually, in 4×8-foot sheets, and the most practical thicknesses for use in scenery construction are ⅛, ¼, and ¾ inch.

One-eighth-inch plywood is most frequently used as a covering material for objects that will receive hard wear and require a hard surface. It is also excellent for covering objects that are curved or irregular in shape, because it bends easily without breaking and requires minimal structural support.

One-fourth-inch plywood is used primarily for the corner blocks and keystones needed in the construction of a flat. It does, however, prove of value also as a covering material and will provide an extremely hard and durable surface for certain objects. In addition, it is employed to advantage in various kinds of facings, such as risers for steps, groundrows, cutouts, and so on. It should be pointed out, however, that if plywood is used as the surface of a large area, it should be covered with canvas or muslin because, uncovered, it will not take paint evenly and its heavy grain pattern will inevitably show through.

Three-fourths-inch plywood, too heavy to be used as a standard covering material, is employed primarily as material for platform tops and for the construction of irregular outlines in flat and dimensional scenic units.

Composition boards: There are available on the market today many types of compositional material that have proved ideally suited to scenery construction. Composed of various materials, they are usually manufactured in 4×8-foot sheets, are inexpensive and, while not as durable as plywood, are adaptable to many scenic functions.

Upson board is made of laminated paper in sheets of ⅛-inch and ³⁄₁₆-inch thicknesses. While not as strong as plywood, it is less expensive, has a grainless surface, and can be cut with a knife if necessary. Not suitable for structural elements, such as corner blocks and keystones, it is, however, an excellent covering material for cutouts, groundrows, facings, and so forth. It takes paint well without being covered with canvas or muslin. It is wise, however, to paint both sides of a unit built with Upson board to prevent warpage. The use of Upson board in building properties will be discussed in Chapter 10.

Insulation board is a soft material made of compressed pulp and is manufactured under several trade names, for example Celotex. It usually comes in a ½-inch thickness and, being soft and porous, can easily be carved or textured into effective dimensional patterns for use as woodwork or as other detail features of a set.

Its most valuable use, however, is as a padding for platforms. Because it is the same sheet size (4×8 feet) as ¾-inch plywood used for platform tops, it offers the convenience of not requiring cutting and fitting. While it is not as soft a padding as felt or carpeting, it is sufficiently soft to deaden noise. In fact, its relative hardness proves an advantage because it provides a pliant, yet firm surface on which actors move easily and on which scenic units can be shifted readily. It is necessary to cover insulation board with canvas to provide a durable surface. Once it is protected by the canvas cover, it will offer extended, durable service as a platform padding.

Masonite provides an extremely hard, smooth surface of ³⁄₁₆-inch thickness and is valuable as a surfacing material for objects subjected to hard use. It chips rather easily, however, and should be covered with canvas or muslin for protection. Also, its brittleness and density make it difficult to nail through. A small hole drilled through the Masonite before the nail is driven simplifies the process and prevents chipping.

Corrugated cardboard, an inexpensive paper product, is excellent for building lightweight detail features of a set. Strips of it, cut into various shapes and widths and glued together, produce effective molding pieces. Its use in property construction will be discussed in Chapter 10.

As a covering material, the use of cardboard should be limited to those units that will not receive a great deal of hard use.

5 FABRICS

Canvas and muslin: While linen canvas is considered the best fabric for covering scenic units, its cost is prohibitive in most cases and various substitutes have been found. Cotton duck is very serviceable but also expensive. Unbleached muslin, while not as durable as either of the above, has proved to be an effective substitute. Manufactured in various widths and weights, muslin can be used not only to cover framed units of scenery but also to make drops, painted borders, and so on. The wider widths are most convenient, but, if these are unattainable, narrow widths can be carefully seamed together to cover large units or to make drops.

There will be cases in which the designer wishes to have a surface texture other than the relatively smooth surface attainable through the use of canvas or muslin. With experimentation, he will find that almost any material can be used for covering, depending on the effect he desires and the available budget. Following is a list of fairly standard covering fabrics with which the stage designer and carpenter should be familiar and with which, perhaps, they should experiment:

Burlap, rep, and monkscloth: Coarse-textured fabrics useful for hangings, tapestries, and curtains.

Plasterer's burlap: A loosely woven fabric useful for surfacing rocks, mounds, and tree trunks.

Bobbinet: A fine net used for holding together painted, cut foliage borders or cut drops.

Shark's-tooth scrim: A durable, heavy gauze with a smooth side and a ribbed side, suitable for painting when transparent or semi-transparent effects are desired.

Velour: A heavy fabric resembling velvet, used in the making of drapery cycloramas and for covering scenery when a surface with a nap is required.

Duvetyn: A heavy flannel used for draperies or for covering scenery to acquire a nap surface.

Felt: A nonwoven fabric with a nap surface, useful for making cutout details because it does not ravel.

Satin, sateen, and taffeta: Useful in small amounts where a high sheen is desired.

Cheesecloth and tobacco cloth: Thin, soft fabrics useful for soft drapes or hazy effects in foliage borders.

There will often arise a special construction or covering problem for which the above will not offer a solution. A short list of specialized materials follows:

Chicken wire: Useful as a support for cloth or papier-mâché in building up dimensional trees, rocks, and so on.

Pearl screening: Useful as a support for mâché work and also as an effective substitute for glass in windows.

Hardware cloth: Sometimes called "rabbit wire"; useful for mâché support. It holds its shape better than chicken wire but is more difficult to work.

Polyethylene sheets: An excellent substitute for glass in windows. It often needs to be soaped or sprayed to cut down on reflected glare. It is not useful when it is necessary to distinguish shapes through the window.

6   HARDWARE

The following hardware must be ordered from some theatrical supply house:

Lash cleats: Small hooks, on the back of the frame of a flat, around which a lash line is thrown to bind one flat to another.

Lash-line eyes: Metal eyes at the tops of flats through which the lash line is threaded.

Brace cleats: Small plates screwed to the back of a flat into which stage braces may be hooked.

Ceiling plates: Plates for bolting together and hanging ceiling units or any piece of scenery that is to hang parallel to the stage **floor.**

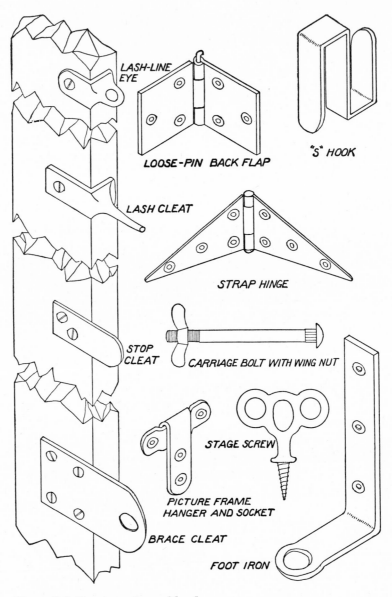

Figure 5-2 Common pieces of hardware.

Hanging irons: Metal straps with a ring in one end for hanging scenery perpendicular to the floor.

Foot irons: Hinged or solid, foot irons are screwed to the bottom of a scenic unit and contain one large hole through which a stage screw may pass to secure the unit to the floor.

Picture hooks and sockets: Hardware used to hang set dressings or otherwise attaching light scenery units to other units.

Tight-pin back-flap hinges: Hinges for fastening two scenic units together permanently.

Loose-pin back-flap hinges: Hinges, from which the pin may be removed, for fastening two scenic units together temporarily.

Stage screws: Large screw with a spiral thread for securing stage braces and foot irons to the sage floor.

Clout nails: Unpointed, wedge-shaped nails for attaching corner blocks and keystones to a flat; 3d (threepenny) clout nails, which are 1¼ inches long, are used primarily.

Scenery nails: ¾-inch-long, coated head nails that can be used in flat construction instead of clout nails. They do not require the use of a clinch plate and are easily removed, but they do not produce as strong a joint as do clout nails.

The following hardware may be secured from a local dealer:

Screws: No. 9 wood screws in ¾- and 1½-inch lengths, and No. 8 wood screws in ¾- and 1½-inch lengths.

Nails: Cement-coated nails in 4-, 6-, and 10d sizes; bright common wire nails in 6-, 8-, and 16d sizes; and bright finishing nails in 2-, 6-, and 10d sizes.

Tacks: Blued upholstering tacks in Nos. 4, 8, and 12 sizes.

Staples: For use with staple gun in ¼- and ½-inch sizes.

Hinges: Strap hinges, butt hinges, and cabinet hinges.

Bolts: Stove bolts of various sizes for bolting metal objects, and carriage bolts of various sizes for bolting wooden objects.

Door knobs and rim locks
Angle irons and corner braces
Pulleys
Screen-door hooks and eyes
Sash cord: No. 8 is used for lash lines and lightweight rigging.
Turnbuckles

7 GLUE

There are certain glues and glue mixtures that are essential to scenery construction.

Ground or flake gelatin glue: The dry particles of this glue must be prepared before use. Place about 1 pound of the particles in a bucket and cover them with water. Place this bucket inside a larger bucket containing a little water and a small block of wood or piece of metal to prevent the smaller bucket from touching bottom. Place both buckets, which now resemble a double boiler, on a hot plate and cook the glue until it is completely melted. Caution must be taken not to let the water in the bottom bucket boil away or the glue will quickly burn. After the glue has been melted, it may be used for mixing paint or for making *dope,* which is the heavy paste used in covering flats.

Dope: To 1 part melted glue add 1 part *Danish whiting,* which is a white, powdered chalk mixed in to prevent the glue from discoloring the canvas. Stir the mixture until it is smooth and free of lumps. The dope should be about the consistency of very heavy cream and can be thinned by the addition of hot water or thickened by the addition of whiting. It will thicken as it cools. If it becomes too thick to brush easily, simply reheat it in the double boiler.

The use of Gelatin glue in the mixing of scene paint will be discussed in Chapter 7.

Casein glue: This powdered glue, which may be mixed with cold water, requires no cooking. It is necessary, however, to follow the manufacturer's directions for mixing it. It is a strong glue with water-resisting qualities and consequently is valuable for outdoor work. It may be used for mixing paint and making dope. Caution must be taken, however, not to let casein glue sit on the skin for long periods, since it will cause irritation.

White polymer glue: This prepared liquid glue, on the market under various trade names such as Elmer's and Scotch, has a wide range of uses in scenery construction, painting, and property construction. Strong, transparent when dry, and water resistant, it is fairly expensive and is best used for small projects.

Wheat paste: Another cold-water glue, wheat paste, while not as strong as any of the above glues, is useful for gluing paper to surfaces or for papier-mâché work.

8 CONSTRUCTION PROCEDURE

With the proper tools and materials, the stage carpenter finds that building for the stage is a simple matter if he organizes a pattern for his work.

a With the working drawings before him, the carpenter is ready to start. He checks them over and decides what materials are required. From stock he selects lumber of the right widths and thicknesses in lengths that will leave the least waste. He examines each piece for straightness and absence of flaws. He sets the best pieces aside for use in parts that require the greatest strength and trueness, such as the stiles of a flat, while he places any slightly blemished pieces in another pile for making toggle rails, cross braces, and so on. Before cutting the lumber, he removes the raw edges (the sharp corners, called appropriately by stagehands the "curse") from each strip with a plane. This eliminates the hazard of splinters. A sixteenth of an inch is all that needs to be shaved off.

b The lumber is now carefully measured, marked, and cut. When several pieces of equal length are to be used, such as the stiles, rails, and corner braces of a series of flats, time as well as accuracy may be gained by cutting one piece for each dimension and using this piece as a model for marking off the rest. After all of one kind have been cut, they may be piled together, as a last check, to make certain that all the pieces are of exactly the same length. This is most important. It is difficult to think of anything more aggravating than the discovery that a handsomely completed flat is just 3½ inches taller or shorter than its fellows.

If pieces of various dimensions must be cut and heaped together, penciled notations should be placed on each to provide ready identification later.

c The next step is the assembling. Each unit, such as the side of a parallel or a window frame, is considered by itself. The various battens that are to compose the frame are laid together in the proper arrangement on either a level floor or the template, the corners of the assemblage are carefully squared, and the parts are secured.

d After the jointing is completed (the procedure for which is presented in the following section), the frame is ready for covering and the application of the necessary hardware.

9 JOINTING

The joint most often used in scenery construction is the simple *butt joint* reinforced with a corner block or keystone. The two pieces of lumber to be joined together are placed with the end of one piece butting against the edge of the other piece at right angles. The corner block or keystone is laid above the joint and secured by either 1¼-inch clout nails, ¾-inch scenery nails, or ¾-inch wood screws.

If clout nails are used, one must place a flat iron, called a *clinch*

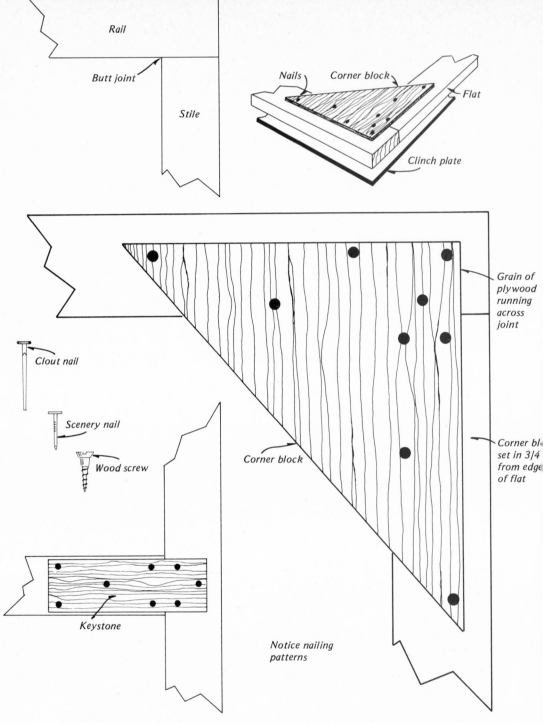

Figure 5-3

Placement of corner blocks and keystones. It is extremely important to set corner blocks and keystones in ¾ inch from the edge of the flat, to have the grain of the plywood running across the joint, and to follow the pictured nailing pattern.

114

plate, under the joint to turn back the point of the nail, which will protrude ¼ inch because the combined thickness of the ¾-inch lumber stock and the ¼-inch playwood corner block totals only 1 inch. The turning back of the clout-nail point produces a strong, durable joint.

If *scenery nails*, which are only ¾ inch long, are used, no clinch plate is required because the nail point will not protrude. This is a quicker joint to make but not as strong as one made with clout nails.

If *wood screws* are used, it becomes necessary to hold the corner block on with small wire brads while the screws are inserted through holes drilled through the corner block.

Whatever method of attaching them is used, corner blocks and keystones must be set in ¾ inch from the outer edge of the piece of scenery being built to allow room for the edges of other pieces of scenery that may later be butted against it from behind. In addition, a stronger joint is achieved if the grain of the plywood corner block or keystone runs *across* the joint rather than parallel with it. Finally, corner blocks and keystones should be cut from ¼-inch plywood with the corner block being a 10 × 10-inch right triangle and the keystone being a rectangle approximately 2⅝ × 6 inches.

There are many times when it is necessary to build flats that can be covered with canvas on both sides. Since the corner blocks and keystones of a regular flat destroy the smoothness of one side of the flat, *double-faced flats* must be built with a different type of joint. A double-faced flat is built with either mortise and tenon joints or halved joints. These joints, however, are practically impossible to cut accurately without the use of power tools.

When special strength is required of certain types of joints, use may be made of glue, a bolt, a small block of wood, an angle iron, a mending plate, or a steel corner brace. Special fastenings and reinforcements will be taken up in their proper places in later sections.

10   COVERING

a   Turn the frame of the flat on its back so that the smooth side is facing up. Place the flat on the template or sawhorses. Lay the canvas or muslin, which has been cut 3 inches larger than the dimensions of the flat, over the frame. Divide the excess canvas evenly so that the cover extends 1½ inches beyond the frame all the way around.

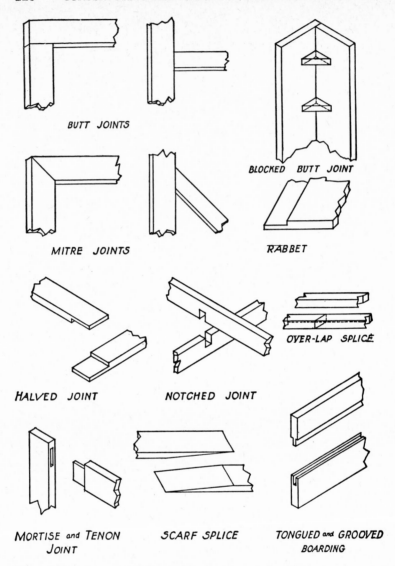

BUTT JOINTS

BLOCKED BUTT JOINT

MITRE JOINTS

RABBET

HALVED JOINT

NOTCHED JOINT

OVER-LAP SPLICE

MORTISE and TENON JOINT

SCARF SPLICE

TONGUED and GROOVED BOARDING

Figure 5-4 Joints commonly used in scenery construction.

b Straighten the canvas so that the weave of the fabric is running parallel to the sides of the frame and perpendicular to the top and bottom. In the middle of either the top, bottom, or side batten, drive a ¼-inch staple with a staple gun through the canvas into the frame ½ inch from the inner edge of the frame. Walk around to the other side and stretch the canvas straight across (two people, each with a staple gun on opposite sides of the flat, speed this process). Set a staple on this side. Repeat the process on the other two sides. Move to the corners and repeat the process. Then

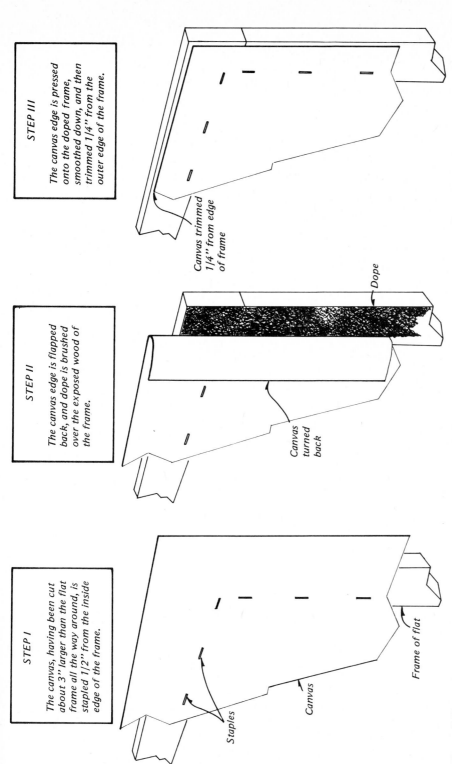

STEP I

The canvas, having been cut about 3" larger than the flat frame all the way around, is stapled 1/2" from the inside edge of the frame.

Staples

Canvas

Frame of flat

STEP II

The canvas edge is flapped back, and dope is brushed over the exposed wood of the frame.

Dope

Canvas turned back

STEP III

The canvas edge is pressed onto the doped frame, smoothed down, and then trimmed 1/4" from the outer edge of the frame.

Canvas trimmed 1/4" from edge of frame

Figure 5-5 Covering the flat. The canvas or muslin should not be stretched too tight or the frame will warp when the flat is painted. Care must be taken not to get dope on the face of the flat.

go around the frame dividing up the space between staples by setting other staples until there is a staple about every 6 inches all the way around the flat. Be certain to pull the canvas evenly and to keep the weave straight. If the canvas is pulled on the bias (with the weave running in a diagonal direction), the surface will pucker. Do not draw the canvas extremely tight, because it will shrink when painted and, if too tight, will warp the flat or pull away from the edges when it does shrink. Do not staple the canvas to the inside braces of the frame.

c Turn back the free flap of canvas all the way around the frame. Coat the exposed wood of the frame with dope (glue and whiting mixture), and then turn the flap of canvas back down onto the dope-covered surface. Using the edge of a small board, go around the flat and smooth the canvas down until it adheres firmly to the frame. Trim the excess off with a sharp mat knife ¼ inch in from the outer edge of the flat.

Caution must be taken not to get dope on the surface of the flat. When it dries, dope has a hard surface that will not take paint as well as canvas and could blemish a finished paint job.

Since many of the compositional materials, such as plywood, Masonite, and so on, do not take scene paint as well as canvas, they should be covered with canvas before they are painted. The process for covering these materials is a simple one: Cut a piece of canvas slightly larger than the area to be covered, apply dope to a small portion of the area and lay the canvas on it, smooth out the canvas on this small area, turn the remaining loose canvas back, coat another small area, and turn the canvas back down onto the doped area and smooth it. Repeat this process until the complete area is covered and then trim off any excess canvas around the edges.

All dope should be completely dry and hard before a flat is painted over, or the canvas will pull away from the surface of the frame.

11 FASTENING THE UNITS TOGETHER

There are three principal ways by which one unit may be fastened to another by (a) a lash line, (b) a loose-pin hinge, and (c) a carriage bolt (Figure 5-6).

a Flat, standing scenery, and occasionally tall built pieces are tied together by the lash-line method. This method uses a piece of No. 8 sash cord, called the lash line, and a series of small metal plates or hooks, called lash cleats, placed parallel to each other near two adjacent edges. The lash line, attached to the upper-right-hand

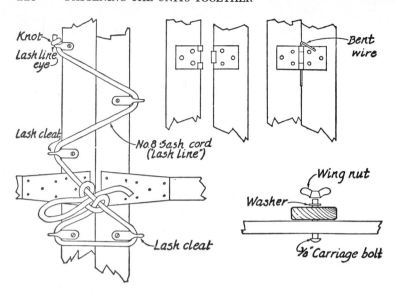

Figure 5-6 Three methods of fastening units together: using the lash line, the loose-pin hinge, and the ⅜-inch carriage bolt with wing nut.

corner of one frame, is tossed over the lash cleat placed a little below it on the other frame, carried over a second cleat lower on the first frame, and so on down, to be tied off on two parallel cleats about 3 feet 6 inches from the floor (Figure 8-1). If the knot is a bow, it may be quickly untied when the scene is struck. This method of lacing two flats or other large units together works very efficiently.

b   Certain small pieces, as well as most of the heavier units, such as platforms and stairs, are fastened to each other by what is commonly called the *loose-pin hinge*. The full title of this humble piece of hardware, however, is a "2-inch loose-pin back flap." One half of the hinge is screwed to the edge of each unit, and fastenings and unfastenings are made simply by inserting or removing the pin (Figure 5-6). As the regular pin fits so snugly that it is sometimes difficult to put in and take out quickly, a short piece of heavy annealed wire (a little smaller than the pin) is commonly used in its place. The top of the wire is bent over to prevent it from falling through.

c   Many structural units, particularly those designed to bear some weight or strain, such as stretchers and temporary braces for platforms and imitation beams, are fastened in place with ⅜-inch carriage bolts put through holes bored in the frames to be joined, and drawn tight with wing nuts over washers (Figure 5-6).

Still another method is occasionally used to join together two pieces of scenery (see Figure 6-22). This involves the use of a large stage picture-frame hook and socket (or an angle iron and a flattened pipe strap). To make the fastening, the hook—attached to one unit—is simply slipped into the socket attached to the other unit. This method, which makes neither a very tight nor a very strong joint, is really only useful for hanging a light piece, such as a false beam or a shelf, on a wall or similar frame.

12   FLAMEPROOFING

Fire regulations in many communities make flameproof scenery necessary. This may be done by painting all frames, before they are covered, with chemicals secured from the Anti-pyros Company in New York or by using canvas already treated. If this is found inconvenient or expensive, scenery may be flameproofed at home by painting both cloth and wood with a 40 percent solution of sodium silicate or a wash made up of the following, stirred well until thoroughly dissolved:

1 pound of borax (sodium tetraborate)
1 pound of sal ammoniac (ammonium chloride)
3 quarts of water

All these chemicals may be secured from a local drugstore. So-called flameproof scenery does not have to be actually 100 percent fireproof. The inspector is usually satisfied if a sample to which a match is applied for a second chars but does not blaze. There should be no live coals.

13   THE USE OF PAPIER-MÂCHÉ AND
    IMPREGNATED FABRICS

Sometimes in making details of scenery (such as simulated carvings) but more often in the construction of properties (such as statues, urns, ornamented platters, and masks), the shop worker will wish to do some molding that cannot be done with either wood or canvas. In these cases he will find papier-mâché very useful.

Papier-mâché is prepared by cutting or tearing long strips of newspaper from ½ to 2 inches wide (depending on the fineness of the molding desired) and soaking these in a mixture of thick *size water* and a little whiting. This mixture is similar to the dope used for gluing down the canvas edges of flats, except that it is a little thinner. In place of this mixture one can use flour paste. The paper strips are torn into easily manageable lengths and pasted on the object to be shaped, one strip crossing the one beneath it to ensure strength. Commonly, three or four layers of paper are required. It will take at least 24 hours for the papier-mâché to dry, and it may take several days.

If the object to be molded is of any considerable size, it should have an armature (interior framework) of wood and chicken wire, worked into a shape approximating the form desired. Unwanted hollows can be filled and desired bulges and projections can be created with twists or clumps of newspaper tied into place. The paper strips are then pasted over all of this.

Such forms as masks cannot have, of course, any underlying framework. They may be made directly on a preliminary molding made of modeling clay (coated with a little Vaseline), allowed to dry, then lifted off. Since the clay itself is moist, however, the coating of paper strips may take a long time to dry. Sometimes it is better first to make a plaster cast of the clay form, to allow this to set and dry, then to cover the inside of it with a thin coating of Vaseline, and to paste the papier-mâché strips in the mold.

Papier-mâché has the advantages of being cheap and easy to work with. It has also certain disadvantages. It is not too strong, it is not waterproof, and when it is stored it is tempting food for rats. A new medium that has none of these disadvantages is an impregnated fabric now being manufactured under several trade names. The best of the products on the market is Celastic, which is extremely rugged, sheds water, and lasts like iron. Celastic may be purchased in sheets of various sizes and various widths. That which is needed is cut off, soaked in a liquid called Celastic Solvent, then applied to the mold and allowed to dry, like papier-mâché. Since Celastic is much stronger than paper, it does not need to be cut into strips pasted one over the other, but it should be applied in small enough pieces to make wrinkling unnecessary. To prevent the Celastic from sticking to the mold, one must coat the mold with Parting Agent before the pieces of the impregnated cloth are put on.

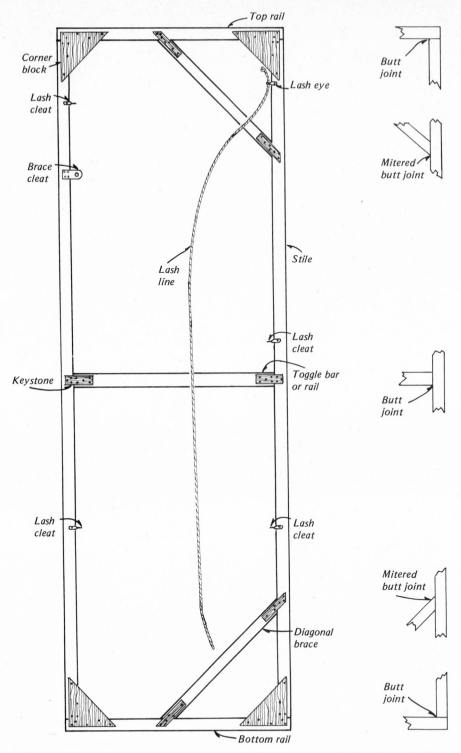

Figure 6-1 Plain flat, rear elevation. Notice the pattern of the lash-cleat placement.

CONSTRUCTING THE SCENERY: SPECIFIC PRACTICE

CHAPTER 6

1 INTRODUCTION

The number of possible scenic units employed in building up stage settings is, as we have said, very large. No attempt will be made in this chapter to describe the construction of all of them. The building plans of the several pieces outlined in the following pages are, however, characteristic of whole groups of others similar in purpose and general structure. Consequently, an understanding of the principles involved in making the units laid out in this chapter should make fairly easy the solution of most of the common problems of construction not specifically analyzed here.

2 SCENERY UNITS

After dramatic and decorative requirements have been considered, scenery must be designed for ease and rapidity of assembling and shifting on the stage. The interest of an audience can be held effectively during a performance only if the time required for changing the scenery is reduced to a minimum. To facilitate the handling and storage of a large set, it is constructed in small unit pieces that can be put together to form the set. Every set of scenery, whether simple or elaborate, is built up of a number of canvas screens, platforms, and other light-frame pieces, which are so designed that they can be assembled or taken apart quickly and easily.

The most common forms of unit scenery may be grouped under five general headings:

Standing Units

Plain flat: A rectangular screen made of wood and covered with canvas, of a standard height, used as a solid wall section (Figure 6-1).

Irregular flat: A flat that is not rectangular but is built in some decorative or descriptive shape (Figure 6-2).

Door flat: A flat with an opening for a door frame (Figure 6-3).

Window flat: A flat with an opening for a window frame (Figure 6-3).

Fireplace flat: A flat with an opening for a fireplace frame (Figure 6-3).

Jog: A narrow flat (Section 6).

Two-fold: Two flats hinged together to fold inward, face to face (Section 6).

Three-fold: Three flats hinged in the same way.

Return: Two flats hinged together to fold outward, back to back.

Door-frame unit: A solid-wood door frame made to fit in a flat designed for it (Figure 6-5).

Window-frame unit: A solid-wood window frame made for a similar purpose (Figure 6-7).

Fireplace unit: A fireplace frame, not always solid, made for a similar purpose (Figure 6-9).

Archway: A flat with an arched opening, usually constructed with a detachable thickness (Figure 6-10).

Hanging Units

Ceiling: A large, horizontal, canvas-covered frame, suspended by a set of lines from the grid, used to close the top of an interior scene (Figures 6-11 and 6-12).

Drop: A large sheet of canvas, partly or fully framed, suspended vertically on a set of lines from the grid, commonly used to represent the sky (Figure 6-13).

Tab: A sheet of canvas or other material, framed or unframed, smaller than a drop but suspended like it, used for a variety of purposes (Figure 6-13).

Border: An abbreviated drop, occasionally used to represent foliage or to mask the flies (Figure 6-14).

Cyclorama: A large curtain of canvas, or other material, hung from a horizontal U-shaped pipe batten suspended by sets of lines from the grid, commonly used to represent the sky in exterior scenes, and for a number of other purposes (Figure 3-9).

Built Units

Platform: A collapsible or rigid frame platform constructed in unit sections (Figure 6-16).

Steps: A light, portable run of steps constructed in unit sections (Figure 6-17).

Column: A light frame or canvas column (Figure 6-18).

Tree: A light frame or canvas trunk (Figure 6-18).

Rock: A light, irregular frame-and-canvas imitation of a rock, made in unit sections (Figure 6-19).

Built-up ground: A similar imitation of a bank of earth.

Set Units

Groundrow: A flat profile of a bank of earth, or a distant mountain, painted on thin three-ply veneer board, cut out, framed behind, and made to stand up independently on the floor (Figure 6-20).

Fence or wall: A frame imitation of a fence or wall, designed to stand up independently of other units on the floor (Figure 6-21).

Set house: Various frame units, designed, like the fence, to stand up independently (Figure 6-22).

Draperies

Under this head may be listed a variety of curtain units, largely unframed.

These units might be called the "standard parts" of scenery. Many nonstandard forms must be designed to meet special demands, but the units listed are used exclusively in most plays.

3 A PLAIN FLAT

A plain flat may be built to any size, depending on the size of the stage and the demands of the set for which the flat is designed. In determining the size of a flat, the designer must take into account ease of construction, handling, and storage. Certain maximum dimensions have been generally accepted. If a flat is greater than 20 feet in height, the lumber for it will probably have to be obtained by special order, because most lumber yards stock only up to 20-foot lengths. The maximum width of a flat has been generally accepted as being 5 feet 9 inches. Retained from the days when there was a great deal of touring, 5 feet 9 inches is the maximum width that will clear a freight-car door. More important, however, is the fact that this width is easy to cover and to handle in scene shifting. Wall sections of a set that are wider than 5 feet 9 inches should be composed of two or more individual flats hinged together on their face, and the hinges and the crack then covered with a strip of canvas called a *dutchman*.

To build a plain flat 12 feet high by 5 feet 9 inches wide, the following procedure is suggested.

a Check the lumber stock to make certain of its exact dimensions. Sometimes variation occurs in the dressing of lumber; it is wise, therefore, to check actual lumber sizes before beginning any construction. The following dimensions of the pieces of a flat are based on the dressed lumber stock's being the standard $3/4 \times 2 5/8$ inches. (See Chapter 5, Section 4 which discusses the dressing of lumber).

b Cut from white pine or other softwood stock the following:

2 battens 1×3 inches by 11 feet $6 3/4$ inches with square ends (stiles)
2 battens 1×3 inches by 5 feet 9 inches with square ends (rails)
1 batten 1×3 inches by 5 feet $3 3/4$ inches with square ends (toggle rail)

2 battens 1×2 inches by 3 feet 6 inches with mitered ends (diagonals)

Place the first four pieces on the template or the floor and put them together in the form of a rectangle, with the two 5-foot-9-inch rails lapping the ends of the two 11-foot-6¾-inch stiles. Making sure that the corners are absolutely square by the use of the template or a framing square, attach the corner blocks as described in Chapter 5, Section 9.

Place the toggle rail between the stiles, centered at 6 feet from the bottom of the flat, and attach the rail to the stiles with keystones. Place the diagonal braces in the upper and lower right-hand corners and attach them with keystones that have one angled end. One end of these keystones should be cut at an angle running parallel to the edge of the frame.

Apply the hardware. Place a lash-line eye in the upper right-hand corner, one lash cleat just above the toggle rail on the same side, and another lash cleat 3 feet 6 inches from the bottom of the flat. On the left-hand side of the flat, place a lash cleat at a point halfway between the lash-line eye and top lash cleat of the right-hand side, and place a lash cleat 3 feet 6 inches from the bottom of the flat. If the flat is over 12 feet tall, of course additional lash cleats are required. If the flat will require the use of a stage brace in order to stand, a brace cleat is attached to the frame. The brace cleat should be placed at a point approximately two thirds of the distance from the bottom of the flat to the top.

Cut a length of No. 8 sash cord long enough to reach from the lash-line eye to within 3 inches of the floor. Knot one end of the lash line and thread the other end through the hole of the lash-line eye. The method of lashing two flats together is described in Chapter 8, Section 4.

After the hardware has been applied, the flat is ready to be covered with canvas. Covering procedures have been discussed in Chapter 5, Section 10.

4 AN IRREGULAR-SHAPED FLAT

Often, flats must be built in shapes other than the rectangle of a plain flat. If a flat is to have, for example, a curved top or an irregularly shaped side, it is, for the most part, constructed in the same manner as a plain flat but a shaped piece of lumber called a *sweep* is substituted for the top rail or a side stile of the flat. The sweep is usually cut from a sheet of ¾-inch plywood or, if small

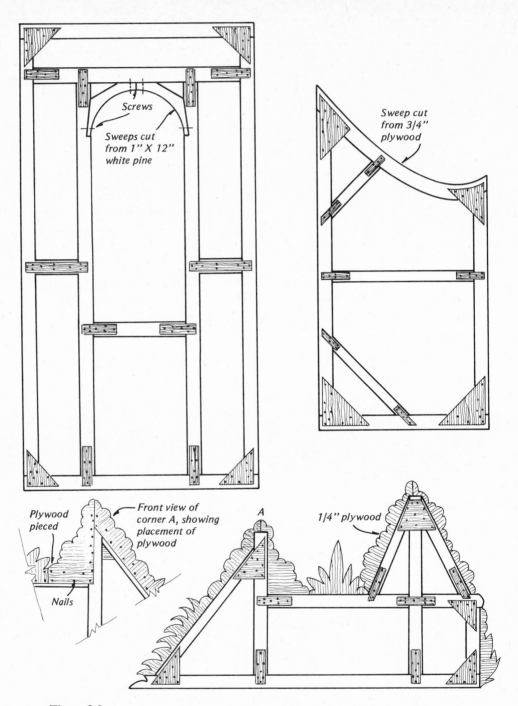

Figure 6-2

Irregular-shaped flats, rear elevation. Notice that the method of construction is essentially the same as that for a regular flat, but irregular-shaped pieces have been substituted for straight pieces where necessary.

enough, from a 1 × 12-inch piece of white pine. It is usually necessary to make a specially shaped corner block with which to join a sweep to the frame of the flat. Corner blocks should be set ¾ inch from the edge of the flat, with their grain running across the joints in the same way as regular corner blocks.

5 A PANELED FLAT

If a wall is to be paneled, a light skeleton is made into the back of each flat to give a footing to the molding strips to be nailed to the face. Two toggle rails may be spaced to catch the upper and lower edges of a panel, while two upright 1 × 2-inch battens are set between these to catch the sides. If the panels are small and the molding light, the vertical battens can be omitted and the molding strips held snugly against the canvas by having them tacked in place through the canvas from behind. If a cornice of any size is to be used, it must be built separately and hung on, or bolted to, the flat or set of flats.

Incidentally, if a picture or mirror is to be hung on a wall, a similar arrangement of batten support may be used. A 2-inch toggle rail is set in the back of the flat high enough to catch the top of the picture. The latter is hung by fastening to it one or two stage picture-frame hooks (which may be secured from any theatrical hardware company) and slipping these into one or two corresponding sockets attached on the face of the flat to the supporting batten. If the bottom edge of the picture leans heavily against the canvas, a second horizontal batten may be used to brace it.

6 A JOG, A TWO-FOLD, AND A RETURN

A jog, a narrow flat, is constructed in the same general way as the larger unit.

A two-fold, a combination of two flats, is hinged so that the members fold face to face. Three or more 2-inch tight-pin back flaps are used to fasten the two frames together, and a 5-inch strip of canvas is glued and tacked carefully over the crack to prevent light from shining between the flats when the two-fold is set up. A three-fold is built in the same way, except that an extra 2-inch batten, called a *tumbler*, must be hinged between No. 2 and No. 3 flats to allow the latter to fold over the edge of No. 1 when the combination is closed and packed away. In this way whole walls are often constructed in one piece.

The return is a two-fold in reverse. It may, if necessary, be made so that it can fold both frontward and backward by using two-way screen-hinges.

7 FLATS FOR A DOOR, A WINDOW, AND A FIREPLACE

One method of treating doors and windows is to construct them of canvas and hinge them to flats. A second method is to build them separately of solid wood, like those found in any real home, and to clamp them, with their frames, into flats when setting the scene. Canvas doors and windows are less expensive, but solid frames are obviously more convincing in appearance. The latter not only give a reassuring impression of substantiality but also add interesting bits of modeling to otherwise flat wall surfaces. By reason of their being set back into the walls 4 or 6 inches they help to suggest that these, too, have thickness—a valuable aid to illusion. The flats illustrated in Figure 6-3 will accommodate either canvas or solid doors and windows.

The construction of these units is almost the same as that of plain flats except that an inner frame is added. In the flat for the door, the toggle is raised to form the top of the opening and two extra uprights are placed between this and the bottom rail. The part of the bottom rail between the uprights is cut away. To prevent the two legs from racking, a *saddle iron,* which is a 5-foot-9-inch piece of $\frac{7}{8} \times \frac{3}{16}$-inch soft steel, drilled and countersunk to accommodate No. 9 wood screws, is fastened to the bottom edge.

In the flat for the window one toggle rail forms the top of the opening, and another one, the bottom. Corner blocks and keystones have been omitted in the diagram (see Figure 6-3) to permit the arrangement of the various joints being shown.

The flat for the fireplace is constructed like that for the door, but with a smaller opening.

In covering each of the three flats described above, the canvas is stretched over the entire flat and tacked, first around the outer edge, then around the opening. The center is finally cut out, and the flaps are pasted and trimmed in the way described in Chapter 5, Section 10.

8 A DOOR-FRAME UNIT

A door-frame unit (Figure 6-4) consists of a solid *shutter* hung in a frame *casing,* built usually of 1×4 to 6-inch white-pine stock and ¼-inch plywood. A section of the casing itself (Figure 6-5) includes a box, or *thickness,* the part that fits into the wall—and a

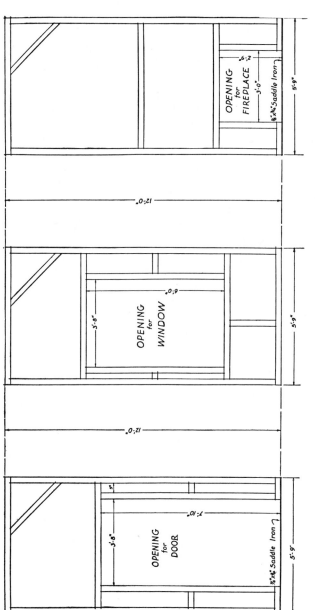

Figure 6-3 Flats for a door, a window, and a fireplace, rear elevation. All joints are reinforced with corner blocks and keystones.

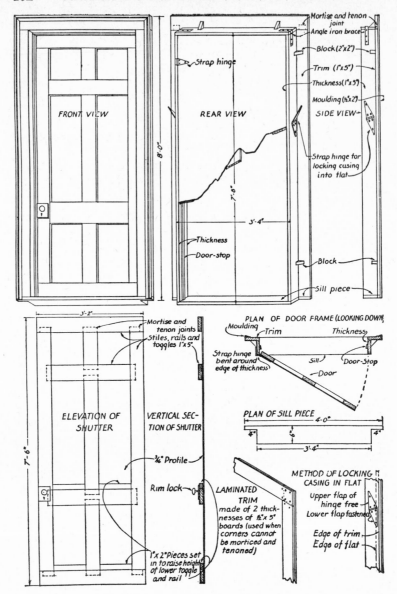

Figure 6-4 Door-frame unit, front, rear, and side views. Section and plan of the casing and shutter.

facing, or *trim*, parallel to the surface of the wall at right angles to the thickness. The door is set back in the casing, so that when the door is closed it shows the thickness; the door is commonly hinged in such a way that when it is opened it swings off- and upstage.

Because the casing can be constructed to fit the shutter more

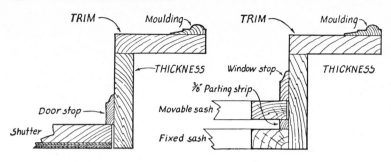

Figure 6-5 Door and window casings. A comparison of the two jambs in cross section.

easily than the shutter can be made to fit the casing, it is wise to build the shutter first. The most common form of door is the paneled one. It is made by fastening (by means of $7/8$-inch No. 9 screws) a sheet of plywood to the back of a light skeleton of 1×4 to 6-inch stock, as illustrated in the drawing. The skeleton that represents the raised framework of the paneling should, if possible, be fastened together by means of mortise-and-tenon joints (glued and nailed without keystones). If tools for making this type of joint are not available, the 1×4 to 6-inch pieces may be attached directly to the plywood. Fasten each piece of the heavier wood to this board with a couple of nails, then turn the door over and secure all the pieces with screws. If the latter method of building

Figure 6-6 Three types of door shutters—rough batten, office, and French.

a shutter is employed, be certain that the sheet of plywood selected for the back is absolutely flat, and heavy enough to keep the shutter hanging true. If a door of any size is to be made this way, it is wise to use plywood of ½-inch thickness, instead of the usual lighter wood. The construction of three other types of door shutters is illustrated in Figure 6-6. Good ready-built shutters can often be picked up quite reasonably at the lumberyard. The only disadvantage of stock doors is that, being built for long wear, they are apt to be heavy.

The casing, as has already been stated, is built in two parts—a thickness and a trim. The thickness, made just large enough to fit the shutter comfortably, is constructed first. Out of 1×4 to 6-inch stock (or heavier if the door unit is to be large), cut three straight pieces for the two sides and the top, and a winged piece for the bottom. The width of the last piece should be that of the others, plus the width of the trim. Put the four pieces together with right-angle box (butt) joints held by 1½-inch No. 9 screws. Wood splits very easily when long screws are driven into it. To prevent this from happening, first make a hole by using a hand drill with a ⅛-inch bit or by driving in and drawing out a sixpenny nail, and then inserting the screw. The head and the sill should lap the edges of the jambs. The sill is attached in such a way that its extra width extends to the front. The trim is fastened with screws to the thickness, at right angles to the latter, all the way around except across the bottom. Its lower edges meet the two narrow wings on the sill. The latter is secured to the former by means of 1¾-inch No. 9 screws put through from below. The sill piece (sometimes called the *saddle*) will sit more steadily on the saddle iron of the flat into which the door frame is placed if a shallow groove is cut in the bottom of the sill.

Use mortise-and-tenon joints, if possible, for fastening together the three members composing the trim. If this cannot be done, build the trim out of two layers of ½-inch stock and lap the corners. That is, cut the three pieces for the first layer so that the two side pieces will extend the full height of the trim and the top piece will fit between them, and cut the three pieces for the second layer so that the top piece will extend the full width and the side pieces will fit below it. Firm corner joints will be obtained if the second layer is bound to the first by a number of screws or by 1¼-inch clout nails driven through and clinched on the under side. For further strengthening, a few 2×2-inch, or larger, rectangular or triangular blocks may be placed in the angle formed by the meeting of the thickness and the trim.

The shutter is hung in the casing by means of two 6-inch strap hinges usually placed on the outside. One flap of each hinge is fastened to the shutter, and the other flap is carried over the edge of the thickness, bent, and attached to the side of the latter. Small strips of $\frac{3}{4} \times \frac{3}{4}$-inch wood, called doorstops, are nailed around the inside of the casing to prevent the door from swinging the wrong way.

The appearance of a door unit is usually very much improved by the addition of a little molding.

Both door and window units are contrived to lock into their respective flats. To make this possible the 6-inch strap hinge is again brought into use. One of these hinges is fastened to the thickness, part way up, on each (Figures 6-4 and 6-7). It is set at an angle, as illustrated, and only the lower flap is screwed to the wood, the upper flap remaining free. In setting the scene the free flaps are raised, the thickness part of the frame is put through the opening in the flat, and the free flaps of the hinges are lowered to bind the door and casing against the 1×3-inch upright battens of the flat that form the sides of the opening. The trim, resting against the surface of the flat on the inside, prevents the frame from falling out.

To permit room for the strap hinges and the little rectangular reinforcement blocks in the angle of the trim and thickness on the casing, and to make it possible to lift door and window frames out and in easily, the openings in the flats should be a little larger than the height and width of the thicknesses. Allow about $2\frac{1}{2}$ inches clearance all the way around. That is, if the overall measurement of the part of the door frame that comes through it is 7 feet 8 inches $\times$ 3 feet 4 inches, the opening in the flat should be 7 feet

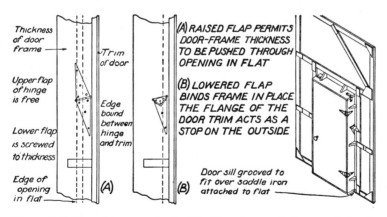

Figure 6-7 Strap-hinge method of locking door, window, and fireplace frames into their flats.

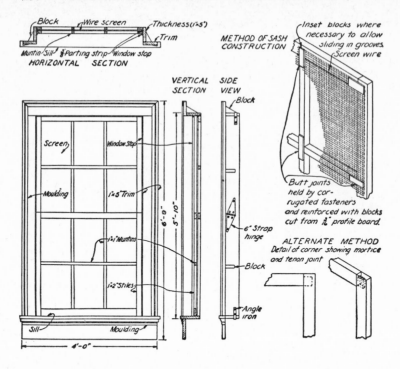

Figure 6-8 Window-frame unit, front and side elevations. Plan and section of a double-hung window.

10½ inches × 3 feet 9 inches. If the little rectangular reinforcement blocks are not used on the casing, a clearance of 1 inch all the way around will be ample.

If a door unit is to be left in a flat through the whole of a performance and set or flied with the flat (as is often done), the door unit may be fastened in place by means of two or four ⅜-inch bolts (put through the trim of the door unit and the frame of the flat) instead of the strap hinges.

A door unit should be well made. If it is loosely put together, it will sag after a little use, and the shutter will bind against the casing. A firmly constructed unit, on the other hand, will last for years.

9 A WINDOW-FRAME UNIT

A typical double-hung window unit (Figure 6-8) consists of two sash frames sliding between ¼ × ¾-inch and ¼ × ¼-inch strips of wood (called a window stop and a parting strip) in a casing similar to that used with the door (see Figures 6-4 and 6-5). The general plan of construction for both units is the same. Sash weights and other hardware are seldom used on windows. If one sash must be raised, it can be held in place temporarily by means of a nail, or some other simple fastening. Because real glass is shattered so easily, it is desirable to use in its place galvanized wire screening (or pearl screening, or translucent plastic sheet) tacked to the back of each sash.

The unit is said to be *practical* if it can be opened, *impractical* if it is permanently closed. The window casing is fastened into its flat by either the strap hinges or the bolt method described in the preceding section.

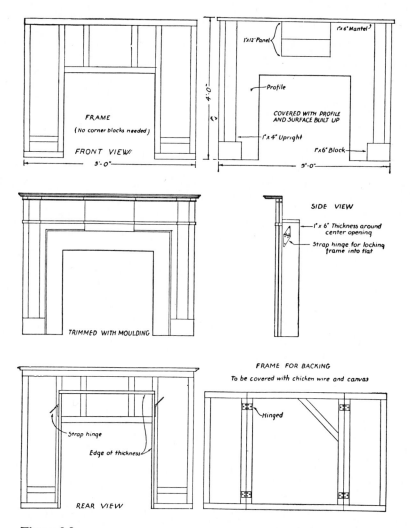

Figure 6-9

Fireplace unit, showing the method of building it up from a flat frame. Also a hinged backing. (The "profile" indicated in the second drawing at the top is plywood.)

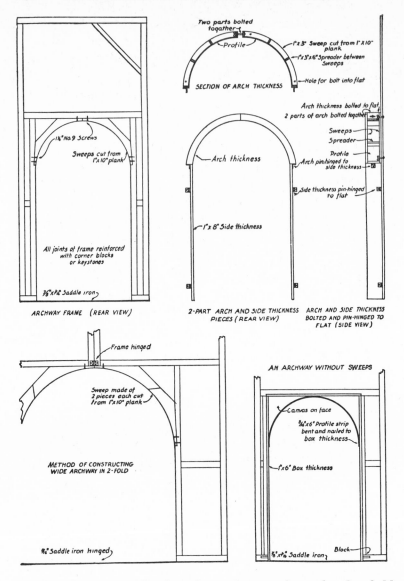

Figure 6-10 Narrow and wide professional-type arches with a detachable thickness, and a homemade arch with a permanent thickness.

Another type of window is the casement window, which hinges at the side. The flat that holds the double-hung type of window is illustrated in Figure 6-3.

10   A FIREPLACE

A fireplace is constructed by nailing or screwing plywood over a light framework of 1 × 3-inch battens (Figure 6-9). After a mantel cut from 1×8 or 10-inch stock is fastened in place, the unit is dressed up with molding and any additional woodwork desired.

The fireplace is used with a flat cut for it (Figure 6-3). If the fireplace is of the type that extends out a few inches from the wall, it will stand safely by itself, especially if its bottom is given a slight rake so that it leans backwards. If it is of the other type, however, such as the one pictured, it is safer to construct it with a 6-inch permanent thickness, and to mount on the outer sides of this two 6-inch strap hinges, to clamp the frame into the flat in the same manner as door and window frames.

A small three-fold screen daubed with gray and black serves as a backing for the opening. If the thickness described above is used, it must be painted to match this.

11   AN ARCHWAY

An archway is made in four parts—a flat, a curved thickness piece, and two side thickness pieces. To build the first, two elements, called *sweeps*, which together form a semicircle, are cut from a wide plank and inserted into the frame of a regular door flat, as illustrated in Figure 6-10. The curved thickness piece (often made in two parts, as illustrated) is made up of two semicircles (or four quarter circles) held apart by light perpendicular blocks of wood. A strip of plywood nailed to the sweeps underneath gives the upper face to the archway. Two 3-inch battens, or wider boards, on edge, make the vertical sides of the opening. To assemble the archway the curved thickness piece is fastened to the flat with 3/8-inch carriage bolts, and the side thickness pieces to both the arched piece and the flat by loose-pin hinges.

A wider arch may be built in a two-fold. In this arrangement the saddle iron, holding the legs of the two flats, should be made to hinge in the middle. If the curved thickness piece is too long for convenient construction or handling, it may be constructed in two or more parts and bolted together.

Without the service of a band saw, cutting accurate sweeps is rather difficult work. A simpler, less "official" arch is illustrated in the lower right-hand corner of Figure 6-10. A square box thickness is fastened to the back of a rectangular opening in the flat, and the curve is created by merely bending and nailing in place a plywood strip (indicated as "profile" in the drawing) of appropriate width. A piece of canvas, on the face of the flat, is tacked to the toggle rail, brought down, and cut and pasted over the edge of the profile. This archway is not always very true, and its thickness cannot be removed in striking, a disadvantage when the scenery

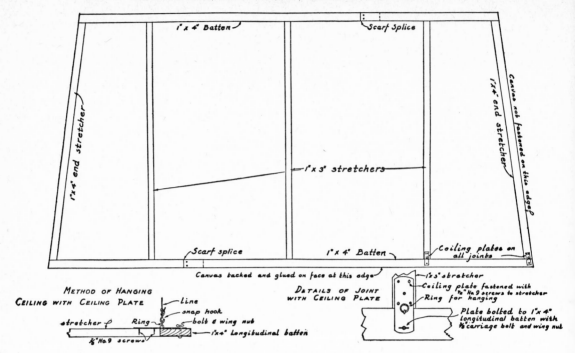

Figure 6-11

Plan for a roll ceiling, looking down from above. When the stretchers are removed, this type of ceiling may be rolled up on the longitudinal battens. Very large or heavy ceilings may be braced on the back with 1×3-inch stiffeners fastened on edge to the stretchers by means of loose-pin hinges.

must be packed; but where accuracy and portability are not so essential, it does well enough.

All solid wood pieces that are to be painted should first be covered with canvas. In covering a sweep, the canvas should be split along the edge and each strip glued down separately in order that the canvas may hug the curve.

12   THE CEILING

In old-fashioned interiors the space over the wings or flats was masked by a series of vertical cloth strips called *borders*. Modern practice, however, uses the more realistic ceiling piece to close in the set above. Attached to two or three sets of lines, it is raised and lowered horizontally.

The more common type for small stages is the *roll ceiling* (Figure 6-11). Its construction is simple. A large sheet of canvas, made by sewing together several widths, with seams running lengthwise, is tacked and glued to two long 1×4-inch battens, one at the upstage edge and one at the down. If the ceiling is to be of any length—over 20 or 22 feet, for instance—each of these battens may be made of two shorter lengths spliced together with a scarf splice (Figure 5-4). Three or more 1×3-inch battens, called *stretchers*, cut the width of the ceiling minus 8 inches (the combined width of the two longitudinal battens), are laid across between the longitudinal battens and bolted to them. A ceiling plate, one half of which is attached to an end of each stretcher by means of ¾-inch No. 9 screws (reinforced with ³⁄₁₆-inch stove bolts if the ceiling is heavy), laps the edge of the longitudinal batten and is fastened to the latter by a ⅜-inch carriage bolt, which passes through a hole in the wood and is drawn up tight with a wing nut above the plate. Stretchers are not attached to the canvas. Therefore, they should be long enough to make a snug fit, and so prevent a sag in the cloth. The outer edge of this canvas at the sides can be fastened temporarily to the last two stretchers by a few tacks driven in part way.

If the ceiling is very wide, two stiffeners (1×3-inch battens on edge) may be pin-hinged across the stretchers to prevent sagging.

To fly the ceiling, two sets of lines with snap hooks are lowered and attached to rings in the plates. When the frame is in use, it is handled in a horizontal position. When it is not in use, one set of lines is detached, and the frame is flied out of the way vertically like a drop. When the ceiling is taken on tour, it is lowered, the stretchers are removed, and the canvas is rolled up on the two long battens.

The *book ceiling*, a type frequently used when the flies are full

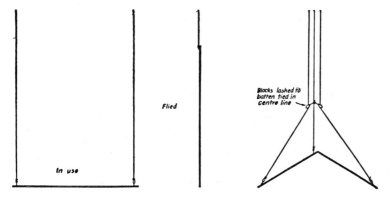

Figure 6-12 Roll and book ceilings, the method by which they are hung and flied. End view.

of hanging scenery and space is consequently precious, is nothing more than a double frame hinged in the middle and suspended on three sets of lines instead of two. If the ceiling is rigged in the manner suggested in Figure 6-12, it may be kept in a closed, vertical position in the flies till it is needed, then dropped and opened out on top of a set by manipulating it from the fly floor alone, without having to lower it to the floor to attach the other set of lines—a distinct advantage when the stage is cluttered with scenery and properties.

Ceilings, both single and double, are often made with sloping sides instead of square in order to fit the shape of the top of the usual interior set. The shorter edge, of course, is upstage. If a ceiling piece is to be taken on the road, it must be so designed that it may be collapsed and packed into a small space, like the two above. If, however, it is to be used on one stage only, it is unnecessary to make its parts detachable. The stretchers can be fastened permanently to the longitudinal battens, the canvas tacked and glued to the outer edges, and any type of simple hanging irons used in place of the more expensive ceiling plates.

Three virtues that should exist in every good ceiling are lightness, tautness, and size sufficient to cover the whole set (except the backings) comfortably.

13   DROPS, BORDERS, AND TABS

If possible, drops (Figure 6-13) should be made of good duck or linen canvas, not muslin, because the material must be strong enough to support itself without the aid of a frame. To prevent wrinkling in hanging, seam the cloth horizontally. Use single straight seams and keep all the selvage edges on the back. Tack the cloth between double 1×3- or 4-inch battens at the top and bottom, taking great care to avoid puckers. The battens are fastened together with $1\frac{1}{2}$-inch No. 9 screws. If the wood strips are not long enough to reach the full width of the drop, they may be spliced with the usual scarf splice, or an overlap splice, but preferably the former (Figure 5-4).

Tapering the drop slightly, that is, making the top 2 feet longer than the bottom, will cause the side edges to hang straighter.

If a drop is cut, it should be backed by a large piece of netting or scrim (depending upon whether a clear or a misty effect is desired) which should extend over the entire open space and support the free branches and bits of foliage (or whatever the elements represent) that compose the silhouette. To attach the netting, turn the drop on its face and glue the netting to the back of the drop

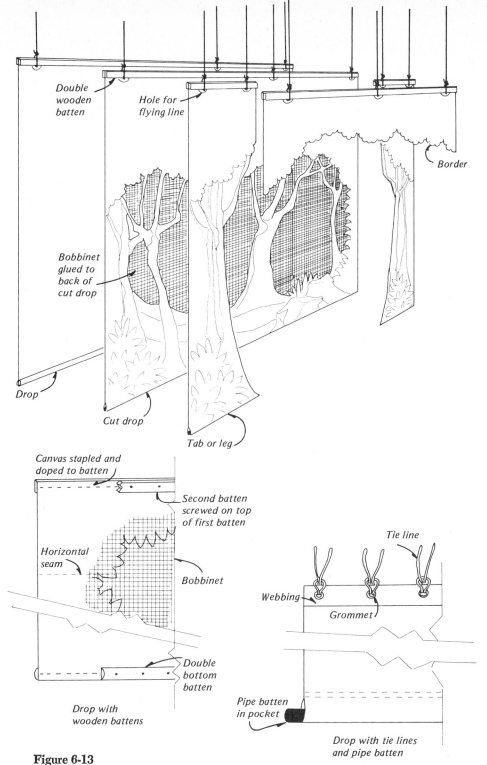

Figure 6-13

Plain and cut drops, a border, and tabs or legs. If a drop is to be rolled up for storage, it should be made with double wooden battens at the top and bottom. If the drop is to be folded, it should have webbing, grommets, and tie lines at the top and a pocket for a pipe batten at the bottom.

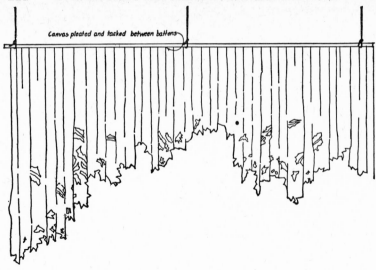

Canvas pleated and tacked between battens

Figure 6-14 Cut and pleated foliage border. Interesting effects can be obtained with this type of foliage piece by draping one or both ends of the canvas.

with some flexible adhesive agent. Rosine, a preparation that is made especially for this purpose and can be secured from any stage hardware company, is generally employed. It is melted for use in the double-boiler arrangement described in Chapter 7, Section 9, and applied with a brush. Some of the cold water pastes are fair substitutes. Whatever the agent is, it should be flexible enough not to crack when the drop is rolled. If the netting used is of the large mesh variety, it will be necessary to attach it to the drop by gluing little strips of cloth over the areas to be fastened.

Stretchers (Section 12) are sometimes used on the back of large drops to make them more rigid.

The border is made in the form of a shallow drop, commonly of only one width of 72-inch canvas, with no battens at the bottom. However, except as an occasional foliage or masking piece, the border is not used very much now.

The tab is made in the form of a narrow drop or border. Drops, borders, and tabs are flied by attaching sets of lines to their upper battens.

14 PLATFORMS

Many times the designer will find it necessary to provide various weight-bearing levels in a set other than the stage floor. Platforms

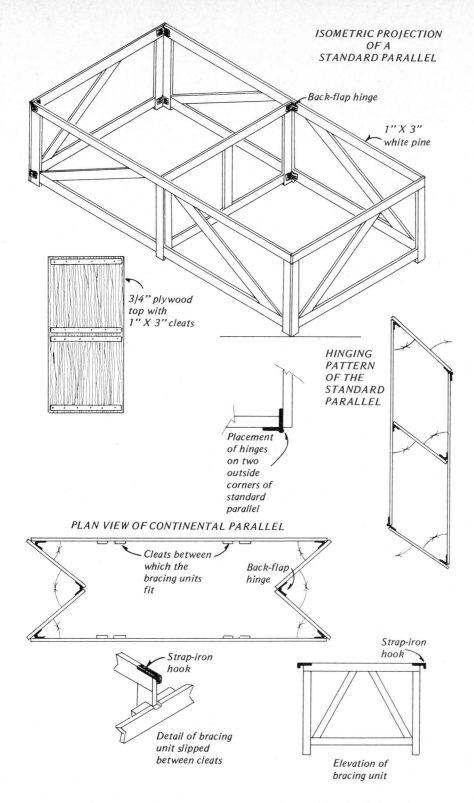

ISOMETRIC PROJECTION OF A STANDARD PARALLEL

Back-flap hinge

1" X 3" white pine

3/4" plywood top with 1" X 3" cleats

HINGING PATTERN OF THE STANDARD PARALLEL

Placement of hinges on two outside corners of standard parallel

PLAN VIEW OF CONTINENTAL PARALLEL

Cleats between which the bracing units fit

Back-flap hinge

Strap-iron hook

Strap-iron hook

Detail of bracing unit slipped between cleats

Elevation of bracing unit

Figure 6-15 Standard parallel and continental parallel. The hinging pattern must be strictly followed or the parallel will not fold.

offer an excellent way to achieve compositional interest in a set while providing the director with a variety of areas at different heights on which to place the action of a play.

Since platforms must be capable of supporting weight, they are of a heavier construction than flat scenery. In addition, they must be built in such a way as to permit their storage for future use. There are several platform types, in either rigid or collapsible forms, that meet the above requirements.

Collapsible Units

The standard parallel: This platform is composed of two parts: the top, which can be made of ¾-inch plywood or tongue-and-grooved stock; and the parallel, which is a supporting frame composed of trestles made of 1×3-inch white pine, with the trestles hinged together to permit folding of the frame. The construction of the parallel is illustrated in Figure 6-15. Each of the five trestle sections is made of 1×3-inch battens with either mortise-and-tenon joints, or butt joints reinforced with corner blocks. The two end trestles overlap the edges of the side trestles and the center trestle fits between the side trestles. The five trestles are fastened together with tight-pin back-flap hinges. *The hinges must be placed in the pattern illustrated in the drawing or the parallel will not fold.*

The top may be made of a sheet of ¾-inch plywood with three 1×3-inch braces screwed to one face of it. These 1×3-inch braces should be set in ¾ inch from the edges of the plywood so that the braces will fit inside the frame when the top is in place. The top should be padded and covered with canvas.

If the top is made of tongue-and-grooved stock, the process is the same.

When this type of parallel is folded up, it is longer than it was when in use. If this causes a storage problem, one can build a continental parallel.

The continental parallel: Similar in construction to the standard parallel, the continental parallel makes use of more pieces and has a different hinging pattern. It provides a sturdier platform than a standard parallel but is a bit more complicated to build.

Each end of this parallel is constructed in two pieces instead of in one piece, and the inside trestles must be removable. Figure 6-15 shows the various necessary pieces and their hinging pattern. Notice that the center trestles slip into a slot made of 1×1-inch strips glued and screwed to the inside face of the vertical uprights of the side trestles. It is necessary to equip the center trestles with countersunk iron hooks, which engage the side trestles and prevent

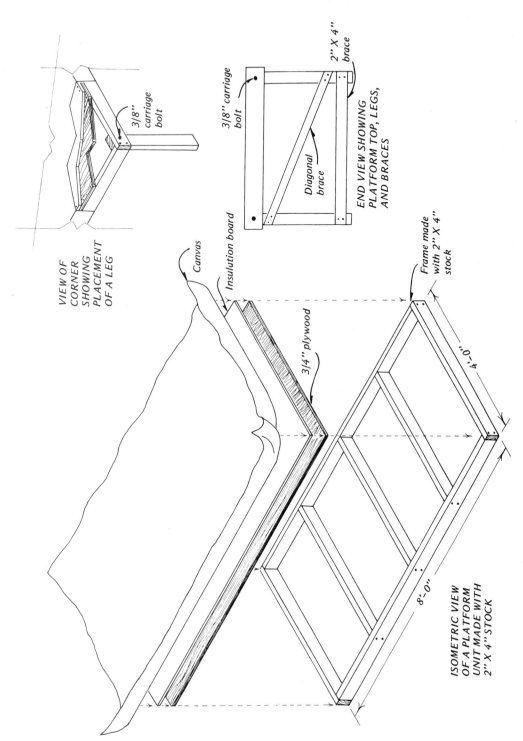

VIEW OF
CORNER
SHOWING
PLACEMENT
OF A LEG

3/8" carriage
bolt

2" X 4"
brace

3/8" carriage
bolt

Diagonal
brace

END VIEW SHOWING
PLATFORM TOP, LEGS,
AND BRACES

Canvas

Insulation board

3/4" plywood

Frame made
with 2" X 4"
stock

4'-0"

8'-0"

ISOMETRIC VIEW
OF A PLATFORM
UNIT MADE WITH
2" X 4" STOCK

Figure 6-16 Rigid platform unit constructed with 2×4-inch stock. The size of this platform is based on the standard-sized 4×8-foot sheets of ¾-inch plywood and insulation board.

them from moving apart. While not as sturdy, the center trestles may be attached to the side trestles with loose-pin hinges.

The top for this type of parallel is built in the same way as one for a standard parallel. In either case, care must be taken to see that the 1×3-inch braces underneath the top will clear the center trestles of the frame when the top is in position.

Both these parallels may be built at almost any height, or one parallel may be stacked on top of another for height. They are not, however, really practical for platformed areas of great height.

For tall platforms, good use can be made of the tubular steel or aluminum scaffolding used in the construction and painting trades. This scaffolding comes in standard-sized units that can be hooked together into practically any size. Expensive to buy and keep in storage, this scaffolding can often be rented inexpensively from a local construction company for use in a particular production.

Some productions require large areas of platforming that do not shift and from which great strength is required. In such a case, the designer will find that a rigid type of platform construction will be more practical than one of the above collapsible types.

Rigid Units

There are no standard methods for building rigid platform units. Methods vary from area to area depending on available material, size of stage, size of shop, storage space, and so on. No matter what method is employed in construction, a platform should provide a strong, padded top, a strong frame, and sturdy legs. The usual practice is to build standard-sized frames and padded and covered platform tops, which can be kept in storage and to which various lengths of legs can be attached as needed.

It is possible to build several types of rigid platforms from standard lumber stock.

a A heavy platform that will offer long service and is easily converted into a wagon. Its various parts are constructed as follows:

1 *Frame:* 2×4-inch stock; butt jointed; nailed with 10d common nails; cross members perpendicular to side rails and evenly spaced.

2 *Top:* 4×8-foot sheet of ¾-inch plywood nailed with 6d coated nails to frame; 4×8-foot sheet of insulation board (felt or carpet could be used), sparsely nailed with 2d coated nails to the plywood; canvas cover pulled over the frame, furnished with boxed corners, stapled and glued to the frame.

3 *Legs:* 2×4-inch legs of any desired length are bolted with ⅜×3½-inch carriage bolts to the inside face of the frame, and

1×3-inch or 1×4-inch diagonal braces are run from leg to leg. It is not necessary for the stock used for diagonal braces to be of the same high grade as that used for flat construction.

b A lightweight platform which, while strong enough for most purposes, is not as flexible as the preceding one. It is constructed as follows:

1 *Frame:* 1×4-inch white-pine stock; butt jointed; joined with 1½-inch No. 8 wood screws; corners reinforced with iron angle irons; three cross members, evenly spaced, and set perpendicular to the sides of the frame. This frame can be made much stronger if white polymer glue is used in addition to the screws in the jointing.

2 *Top:* ¾-inch plywood and insulation board covered with canvas in the same manner as the preceding platform top. A frame made of 1×4-inch stock is usually not heavy enough to be topped with tongue-and-grooved stock.

3 *Legs:* 2×4-inch legs could be used with this frame, but a stronger leg is made by setting the edge of one 1×3-inch white-pine piece of lumber at right angles to the face of another 1×3 inches, making an L-shaped leg. The pieces are joined together with polymer glue and 4d coated nails. The leg is then bolted to the inside face of the frame with 2×⅜-inch carriage bolts. Diagonal braces of 1×3-inch stock nailed (with the head of the nail not driven completely in) from leg to leg provide additional solidity.

c When a large area of playing space is needed under a platform (such as in an Elizabethan inner-below), the frame of the platform must be constructed of a stock heavy enough to support weight without the aid of many legs and diagonal braces.

1 *Frame:* 2×6-inch or, better, 2×8-inch stock should be used. The frame is constructed in the same manner as the 2×4-inch frame except that 16d nails should be used, and the cross members should be spaced, centered every 16 inches along the side rails.

2 *Top:* A platform of this type is stronger if topped with tongue-and-grooved stock, but ¾-inch plywood could be used. The top, of course, should be padded and covered with canvas.

3 *Legs:* 4×4-inch legs bolted inside the frame or set with metal plates under the frame should be used. Another possibility would be the use of lengths of 1½-inch galvanized iron pipe, threaded on both ends, which are screwed into pipe flanges. One flange is attached to the bottom of the platform frame and another flange is attached to the stage floor directly beneath the first flange. One of these pipe legs should be placed at each corner of the platform, or wherever support is needed. This type of platform

usually needs to be braced to the floor with diagonal braces of some sort to keep it from swaying.

A money-saving device in the construction of heavy platform units is to build them of rough-cut lumber. This lumber is not dressed and consequently affords a heavier stock—a 2×4-inch is actually 2×4 inches. Since its surface is rough, it may be covered if necessary, but often its rough surfaces offer an interesting texture for certain designs.

Another economical practice in platform construction is the use of old painted canvas or muslin as the covering. Canvas or muslin, with perhaps three or four coats of paint on it, which has been removed from a re-covered flat is excellent for this purpose. The painted side of the canvas is put facedown on the platform and the canvas is attached in the regular manner. When the top (the unpainted side) is painted, a very strong covering is produced.

Since most platform units are built in a small size to facilitate storage, it is often necessary to attach several of these small units together to produce a larger platformed area. After the platforms have been legged, they may be joined together with ⅜-inch carriage bolts of the proper length. Holes are drilled through the sides and ends of the platforms and carriage bolts inserted which are then tightened with nuts and washers. If the platforms do not shift, they may be simply clamped together with large C clamps.

It is wise to bolt platforms together while they are in the position they will occupy on stage. If this is done, any discrepancy of floor level and leg length may be compensated for while one keeps the tops of the platforms level. After two platforms have been bolted or clamped together, the crack between them should be covered with a dutchman glued down with dope.

There are many methods for facing the visible sides of platforms. Upson board, ¼-inch plywood, and Masonite are convenient facing materials. If these materials are used, however, the facing should be cut approximately ¼ inch less than the height of the platform to ensure that the facing does not extend beyond the top edge of the platform. If these relatively hard materials extend beyond the top edge of a platform, actors could easily trip or, at the least, the edge would get chipped by passing feet during the course of a performance.

Preformed Metal Shapes

There are many factory-formed metal shapes on the market that can be adapted for use in platform construction. Some of them are less expensive than lumber but require the use of metal-working equipment in construction. The standard tee, angle, and channel shapes of structural steel may be easily used as legs for platforms by having holes bored in them at appropriate places for bolts. Their use as framing material, however, almost certainly requires the use of welding equipment.

The Unistrut Corporation has developed various steel shapes with special fixtures that make it possible to construct a frame

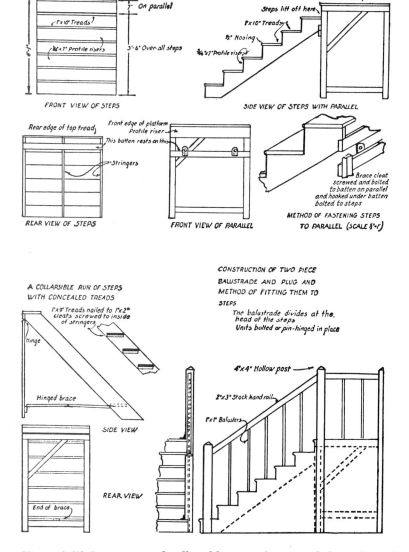

Figure 6-17 Stationary and collapsible runs of steps, a balustrade, and a plug.

and legs for a platform without the necessity of welding. The variously holed and slotted pieces may be put together with bolts and stock fixtures in practically any combination.

15 STEPS AND STAIRS

The principal parts of a simple flight of stairs are the *stringers,* the parallel planks that support the steps; the *treads,* the horizontal boards that form the steps; and the *risers,* the vertical boards that connect the treads.

Figure 6-17 shows a common method of construction. Each step is made by nailing a 1×8- to 12-inch tread across two or more stringers cut from 1×10-inch stock, in such a way as to allow about an inch of the front edge of the tread to overhang the step below. If the step is over 30 inches wide, one or more additional stringers are placed between the outside two. Risers, because they bear no weight, are made of ¼-inch plywood. There is no absolute standard for dimensions of steps. Their height and depth depends on the pitch required of a flight of steps. The amount of 17 inches is frequently employed, however, as a standard overall measurement of a tread and its adjacent riser; that is, if the tread is to be 12 inches deep, the riser will be 5 inches high; if the tread is to be 9 inches deep, the riser will be 8 inches high; and so on.

A flight of stairs, unless it is supported independently, is made to fasten to the platform to which it leads. A 1×4-inch batten is fastened with 1½-inch No. 9 screws across the stringers at the top, under the edge of the last tread, and a similar batten is placed just below its level on the parallel. A couple of brace cleats are screwed to the second batten (on the parallel). To attach the stairs to the platform, the head of the former is lifted and slipped over the cleats of the batten on the parallel. In this position, one batten rests on top of the other. The cleats prevent them from slipping apart. The parallel should be well anchored with stage braces to prevent it from tipping over.

If a long flight of steps is to be constructed, it is planned as a number of unit runs and parallels. When assembled, they are fastened together by 2-inch loose-pin hinges or ⅜-inch carriage bolts. Balustrades, also, are made separately, attached to the edge of 1×10-inch planks, and fastened to the flight of steps with similar hardware. When the side of a staircase is in view of the audience, the entire construction work may be concealed by a triangular flat (*plug*) fastened by loose-pin hinges to the face of the staircase. The balustrade may be constructed as a part of this unit.

A narrow stairway that does not have to reveal its steps from the side may be built without cut stringers. The treads are merely nailed to cleats screwed to the inside of the straight stringers. A small, portable unit, constructed on this plan, is illustrated in the drawing.

Steps should be covered with canvas before being painted.

16   A COLUMN

A column (Figure 6-18) is constructed by nailing wide sheets of ¼-inch plywood around a light cylindrical frame. Wooden discs or rings, each made up of several pieces of 1×6 to 10-inch stock fastened together with corrugated fasteners, form the core of the column. They are spaced at intervals equal to the width of the plywood sheets and held in place by 1×2-inch strips running the length of the unit. The plywood strips are wrapped around this core and nailed to the edge of the discs, or rings, as well as seamed along the strips. The column viewed from one side needs but one good face. In fact, small columns are often made in halves, that is, formed around half discs, called *half-rounds*. This type of column, if it is not held erect by some other structure above, is secured by a brace cleat and stage brace fastened on the blind side (the side away from the spectators). The column should be covered with canvas before it is painted.

Bases and capitals, the use of which is to be avoided if possible because of the nuisance of building them, must generally be made more solidly. Molding may be made flexible enough to bend into a circle by making a series of cuts with a saw on the back or the front of the strip part way through at intervals of ¼ to ½ inch. Ornaments may be molded out of papier-mâché and, when dry, fastened in place with ordinary nails.

Columns are frequently constructed also in the form of simple canvas cylinders stretched between solid bases secured to the floor and wooden discs or frames attached to ropes in the flies. Cloth columns are practicable only, of course, in positions where actors are not likely to lean or brush against them.

17   TREE TRUNKS AND FOLIAGE

The construction of a "solid" tree trunk (Figure 6-18) involves the same principles as those employed in the building of a column, except that a more irregular "core" is often used, and chicken wire and canvas are employed instead of plywood. Irregularities,

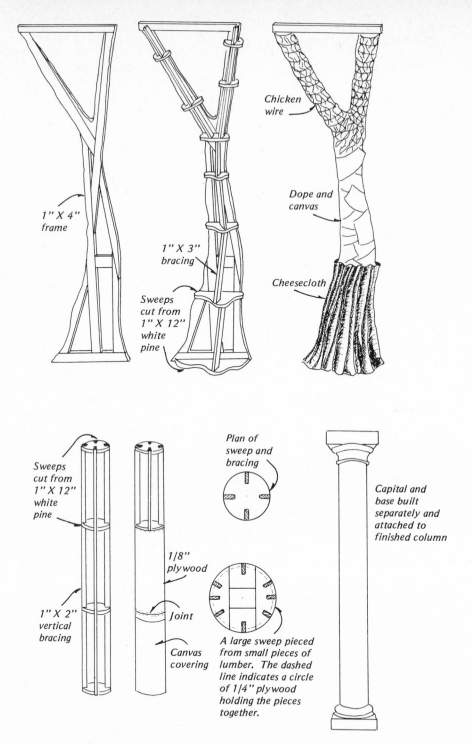

Figure 6-18

Framed tree and framed column. The tree could be covered with papier-mâché instead of canvas if it is not to receive hard use. With the addition of more vertical bracing, the column could be covered with Upson board instead of plywood.

such as knots and excrescences, are built up on the half-cylindrical frame, then chicken wire is tacked over the whole thing with ½-inch staples. Small pieces of scrap canvas are dipped into the hot glue preparation described in Chapter 5, Section 7, and pasted, with their edges lapping, in irregular patterns over the wire. When this dries, a hard, uneven surface remains on which can be painted a suggestion of bark. This type of trunk is held erect with the help of a brace cleat and a stage brace on the blind side.

If the tree trunk called for in the design occupies a position on the stage where the audience cannot scrutinize it too closely and where no actor will brush against it, it is possible to substitute a much more easily built collapsible form for the rather elaborate framed type described above. A wide strip of canvas is tacked in irregular pleats around notched discs at the top and bottom and hung by means of a screw eye to a line in the flies.

Realistic foliage is difficult to create on the stage, except in very expensive ways, and modern scenic artists consequently avoid its use as much as possible. Showing the lower portions of several realistic tree trunks in the foreground, the designer attempts merely to suggest masses of leaves and shrubbery in the background by using well-shadowed cutout drops kept discreetly behind much scrim. Where foliage must be shown downstage, cutout cloth borders can be hung in silhouette. The canvas is frequently gathered or draped, after it is cut, to add to the depth of the foliage (Figure 6-13). The effect secured, especially in fairly dim scenes, is sometimes quite convincing.

Bushes and smaller shrubbery units may be constructed out of actual branches or sticks wired together and shaped up with papier-mâché, in accordance with the artist's design. To this skeleton are attached—by means of short lengths of fine wire—pieces of greenery secured from any concern that makes artificial flowers, or leaf and blossom forms cut from glue-stiffened cloth, crepe paper, or felt. The bush is then painted.

Short lengths of vine and little plants can be made best out of artificial foliage materials bought in the five and ten cent store. At 20 cents a sprig, however, their cost precludes their use for quantitative effects.

18   ROCKS AND BUILT-UP GROUND

Rocks and built-up ground (Figure 6-19) are made by covering light, irregular frames of 1×3-inch stock with chicken wire tacked down with ½-inch staples, and covering the wire, in turn, with

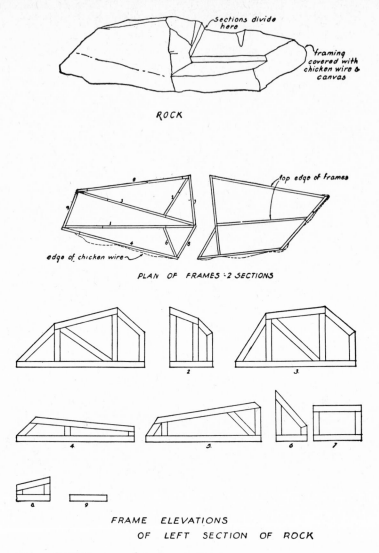

Figure 6-19 Frame rock in two sections.

small pieces of canvas dipped in a mixture of hot glue and whiting, in much the same way as tree trunks are built. If the rock or ground is to be walked on, care must be taken to make the framework strong and rigid. The standard method for building a practical rock is to start with a number of vertical three- or four-sided frames, similar (except that these are irregular) to the sections of a parallel (Section 14). They are of different heights, some straight, some inclined, and some pointed. Placed edge to edge and edge to side, lengthwise, and across, they are fastened together with nails or, better, with 1½-inch No. 9 screws. In the parts of the rock that must be practical, additional battens are nailed at short intervals between sections, and these are covered with pieces of planking arranged in different planes. If the rock is large, it should be made in a number of smaller units and pin-hinged or bolted together. Tufts and folds of brown burlap or felt attached to the surface here and there may be made to suggest patches of earth and knots of grass.

19   GROUNDROWS AND SILHOUETTES

Groundrows and other silhouette pieces (Figure 6-20) are made by nailing ³/₁₆- or ¼-inch plywood over flat frames of 1×3-inch stock, which are put together with corrugated fasteners and reinforced with corner blocks in the usual way. The silhouettes are then painted and the outlines finally cut out with a compass saw. The unit is made to stand up by hinging a triangular brace, called

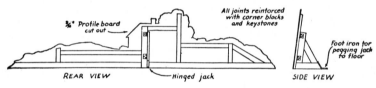

Figure 6-20 Groundrow, rear and side elevations. (What is designated here as cutout "profile board" is ¼-inch plywood.)

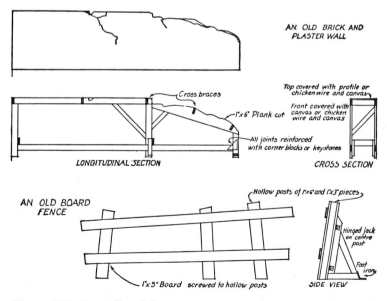

Figure 6-21 Set wall and fence.

a *jack,* to its back. Small units may use an angle iron in place of the jack.

In an emergency, a rather convincing distant mountain can be suggested by pinning a piece of light blue or violet tarlatan to the bottom of the sky drop.

20 WALLS AND FENCES

Walls and fences made as independent units, whatever their design, must be fairly strong as well as lightweight (Figure 6-21). Heavy-appearing parts should be made in skeleton form; that is, brick or stone parts, rails, and posts should be shells only, put together with light lumber and covered (in the case of walls) with plywood, canvas, or chicken wire and canvas. Fence sections are made to stand up by means of jacks.

21 LOG-CABIN WALLS

A simple method of suggesting the solid log walls of a cabin is outlined in Section 19 of Chapter 7.

22 A BEAM

A large beam, or log, seen in three dimensions in a stage setting, is constructed as a light shell of wood, or wood and canvas. If it is small, it is built out of ½-inch planks put together in the form of a long, three-sided trough. If it is large, each of its faces may be made as a narrow batten frame covered with canvas. If it is irregular in shape, it may be modeled by the use of chicken wire and rags dipped in glue. The beam is fastened in its position in the set by means of ⅜-inch carriage bolts and wing nuts or picture-frame hangers and sockets.

23 IRREGULAR THREE-DIMENSIONAL COMBINATIONS

The construction of irregular three-dimensional units, such as dormer windows, alcoves, and perspective set houses—which have to be planned for two-dimensional striking and storage—is always something of a problem. A unit of this type, considered as a combination (often quite complicated) of a number of flat, or semiflat parts, must be analyzed by the designer and carpenter and condensed into its simpler elements. Each part is laid out and built as an independent unit. The various members are then assembled by means of tight-pin hinges, loose-pin hinges, and ⅜-inch carriage bolts and wing nuts in the least involved method possible under the circumstances.

Figure 6-22, by way of illustration, suggests how a small, irregular set house might be laid out. The front and end walls are constructed separately, covered with canvas, and then fastened

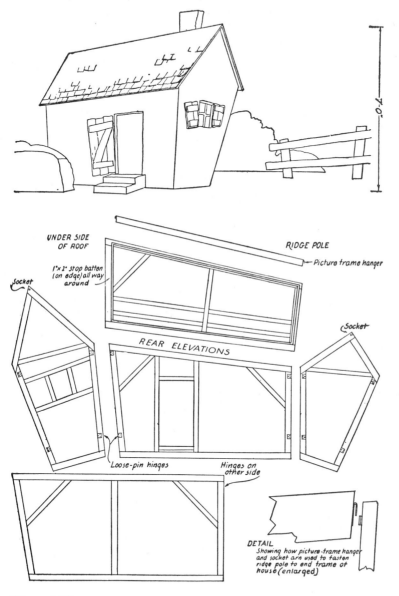

Figure 6-22

Small set house. A set piece of this type may be combined effectively with set walls, fences, and groundrows in the background of various kinds of exterior scenes.

together with tight-pin hinges in such a way that the three frames may be folded up backward like a double return. The rear wall is constructed and covered, and fitted with loose-pin hinges to enable it to be fastened to the end walls (on the inside) when the little house is set up in the wings before the performance. A ridgepole cut to brace the top of the house is fastened to the two end frames by means of picture-frame hangers and sockets or shutter bolts. The roof (only the front half in this case is necessary because the back cannot be seen) is made in the form of a separate lid with a stop batten all the way around on the inside to prevent its slipping up, down, or to the side.

If the roof is carefully made and fastened in place with loose-pin hinges when the house is set up, no additional bracing is necessary.

The chimney, a light box frame covered with light profile board or canvas, may be pin-hinged or bolted to the ridge pole. The door and window in a house of this small size can, if they are not to be "practical," be simply built up on the surface of the walls in which they are supposed to hang. If the roof is supposed to be shingled, it is quite sufficient to use two rows of real wood and to suggest the other rows with paint.

The house just described would be a small one. If a larger "practical" house were required, the walls could be constructed in the same way, but they would have to be either lashed or bolted together, and additional bracing would be required to keep them in position. The roof could still be fastened with loose-pin hinges. Door and window frames would be made separately and fixed in position in the usual way. If it were desirable to bring the house onto the stage in one piece for rapid shifting, it could be flied by means of two piano wires (painted black to make them invisible), each attached to an end frame; the opposite ends of the wires are attached to fly ropes. Or the house might be mounted on a wagon —that is, be bolted or pin-hinged around the outside edge of a wagon built to its shape—with about ½-inch clearance from the floor—and rolled in from the side.

The above description of a knock-down house will suggest some methods of approaching the problems of other irregular three-dimensional pieces of scenery.

24 THE USE OF MOLDING

Decorative woodwork in a setting, such as that around doors, windows, fireplaces, and pilasters, as well as bookcases, cupboards, and other standing properties constructed as scenery, should be dressed with molding. The woodwork never looks quite convincing without it. Molding may be ordered in a wide variety of designs. The most generally useful for elementary construction on the stage is 1-inch panel molding. This is adaptable to many purposes. It can be built up, when desired, by having a lattice strip placed beneath it.

A length of molding can be curved to follow an arched line by making a series of cuts with a saw part way through, about an inch apart, on the edge to be made concave. To fasten the bent molding in place, use 1-inch lath or finishing nails. Place them about 3 inches apart and drive them, not into the strip itself, but into the saw cuts. This will prevent splitting the little segments of wood.

Figure 7-1 Design for *Major Barbara* by Donald Oenslager, reproduced by permission of the designer.

PAINTING THE SCENERY

CHAPTER 7

1 INTRODUCTION

One of the most fascinating and crucial processes in theatrical
production is the painting of the scenery after it is constructed.
No matter how well planned and built, the set that is not effectively painted will be less than successful.

It takes an accomplished artist with a keen eye and experienced
technique to produce a superior paint job, but there are basic

163

techniques that the less experienced may employ to produce effective results. These techniques are useful as a springboard for developing an artist's ability as a painter.

The following pages present many basic materials and some techniques that have been developed by scene painters over the years. They are intended to serve merely as a basis for the personal approach each artist must take as he works out his own distinctive methods.

2 THE APPROACH TO SCENE PAINTING

The first thing that an artist coming freshly to scene painting has to learn is to exaggerate. All painting for the stage must be done in a bold, straightforward way. Effects must be seen from a distance. Fussy details and color are consequently lost upon an audience.

Another thing that must be learned is to paint for stage lighting. The latter can change not only the quality of color, but its intensity as well. Cleon Throckmorton, at one time Art Director for the Provincetown Playhouse in New York, applied brilliant touches of red, green, and blue to the leaves of a real rose vine in a garden set to make the plant look like something more healthy and colorful than the pale weed it appeared to be under stage lighting.

3 PAINT MATERIALS

Ready-mixed scene paints: Casein and latex-based paints are available in either dry, liquid, or pulp form and are used by many scene painters because they are so simple to prepare. They contain a binder and the painter need only add water (to the dry and pulp varieties) to produce scene paint. Since these paints are waterproof when dry, they are useful for outdoor work.

Many painters, however, still prefer to use the older dry pigment and size-water method of mixing paint. They feel that it offers a greater variety of color, is less expensive, and is more flexible to use.

Dry pigment and size water: This type of scene paint is mixed from powdered pigment, glue, and water. The pigment provides the color, glue is the binder, and water is the medium.

Pigment is sold in sixty or more colors. Some of the most serviceable ones are the following:

Light chrome yellow	Magenta
Medium chrome yellow	Venetian red
Hanover green	Raw sienna

Medium chrome green	Yellow ochre
Dark chrome green	Orange mineral
Italian blue	Burnt umber
Ultramarine blue	Drop black

Other useful colors, some of which cost a little more, are lemon yellow, burnt sienna, vermilion, permanent red, purple lake, light Milori yellow, malachite green, and emerald green.

Whiting: By far the most useful pigment for the artist is ordinary bolted whiting. He should estimate that he will use as much of this pigment as all the rest of the pigments put together. Only good-grade whiting should be used. Belgian and Danish whitings are standard.

Common flake glue: Flake gelatin glue is preferable to ground glue, though either may be used. These must be cooked. LePage's, which needs no preparation except thinning with cold water, may be employed in an emergency—only in an emergency, however, because not only is it too expensive for general use, but it has a strong tendency to gray out any pigment mixed with it. Most other cold water glues must be used judiciously.

Casein glue: Casein glue, which may be mixed with cold water, is coming into increasing favor where wearing and water-resisting qualities are desirable, such as on woodwork. It is excellent for outdoor painting. Casein glue, however, is hard on brushes and hands.

Nonrosin white casein: Some artists now use this casein in place of separate whiting and glue for the primary coat. It can be mixed with pigments for secondary coats. A product like Texolite has the advantage of being ready for immediate use without the necessity of adding other glue to it.

4   PAINTING IMPLEMENTS

For painting scenery, three types of brushes are especially serviceable: 8-inch and 6-inch *priming* brushes, for priming and covering surfaces rapidly; 4-inch *laying-in* brushes, for smaller areas; and 2- and 1-inch *lining* brushes, for detail. There are a number of other types, such as round *foliage* brushes and special *liners*, which might be useful. They should all be of the good quality, long-bristle variety used in distempering walls. Brushes deteriorate very rapidly unless they are taken care of. After every painting they should be rinsed, shaken out, and dried in a flat position. Better still, drill a hole in each brush handle and hang the brush up on a nail. Never

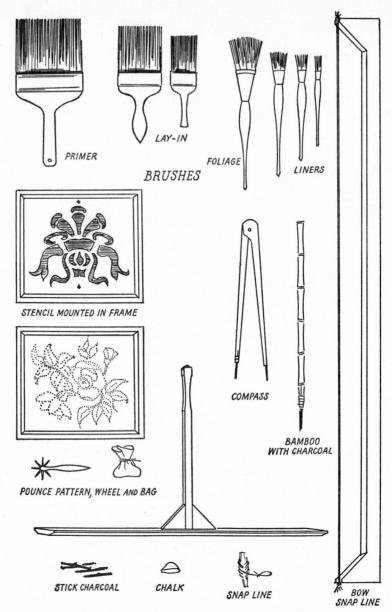

Figure 7-2 Painting implements.

place a brush in boiling water. Other necessary implements for the artist are

A yardstick
Charcoal sticks and chalk
A snap line (about 40 feet of heavy, braided cotton cord)
A bow snap line (for shorter lines)

A pounce wheel (for making holes in a paper over which a pounce
   bag will be patted or rubbed)
A pounce bag (for chalk or charcoal marks)
A straight-edged beveled liner (for ruling short lines)
A 12-foot batten with a perfectly straight edge for ruling long lines
A large wooden compass (for describing circles and arcs)
A feather duster (for removing charcoal and chalk marks)
Stencil paper and frame
Several 2- to 3-gallon pails and smaller pans
Muffin tins (for holding small amounts of different kinds of color)
A gas, electric, or kerosene stove with at least two burners
A spray gun and air compressor

5   THE PAINT FRAME

Another aid to the artist, found in the best-equipped studios, is
the *paint frame*. It is a large, rectangular, wooden skeleton, suspended from a set of ropes or cables and big enough to accommodate a whole drop or set of flats spread out and fastened to it.
Slots are cut in one or more floors to permit raising and lowering
the frame through them and to allow two groups of artists, if
necessary, to work on a large piece of scenery at the same time.
The frame is sometimes counterweighted and operated by means
of a winch or some other manual device, but it is more often
motorized for convenience in handling. Any type of flat scenery can
be painted on this contrivance. This method of painting offers
several advantages over the flat-on-the-floor method: it saves the
artist's back by allowing him to do his work in an upright position,
it spares his having to tramp over the surface of the canvas, and it
gives him the opportunity to step back occasionally and view the
progress of his labor. This is all important, however, only if scenery
must be done in quantity. A university or community theatre
should not worry itself over the problem of investing money in
an expensive paint frame until it already has plenty of room in
its workshop or on the stage and until more important equipment
has been paid for. Flats and drops can be painted very well on a
large floor. Many of the busiest professional studios throughout the
country use this method exclusively.

6   ELEMENTS OF COLOR AND COLOR MIXTURE

Before the scenic artist attempts to go very far into the methods
of painting, he should acquaint himself with the basic principles
of color. He will find that there are many practical modifications

(Section 8) that he will have to make to these theories when he is actually mixing paint, but a knowledge of them will offer him a solid foundation for handling color in the paint room.

The human eye's recognition of color occurs when the eye is stimulated by light being either transmitted or reflected by an object.

We have all noticed that light passing through a prism forms a rainbow spectrum of various colors or hues: violet, blue, green, yellow, orange, and red. The prism allows all the colors of the spectrum to pass through, but most other objects do not permit this. The light passing through a blue stained-glass window appears blue because the glass is transmitting only the blue hue of the light's spectrum. An apple appears red because it is reflecting only the red hue of the light's spectrum. In both cases, absorption by the object of the remaining hues of the spectrum has occurred. The stained glass has absorbed the other hues and transmitted only the blue. The apple has absorbed the other hues and reflected only red. Both the above cases are producing what is called a *subtractive mixture* of color. That is, certain hues of light's spectrum have been subtracted (absorbed) before the eye perceives either the reflected color or the transmitted color, whichever the case may be.

If, however, the blue light transmitted by the stained-glass window is mixed on a white surface with red light from another window, they form magenta or violet-colored light in what is called an *additive mixture*. The eye mixes the two colors of light together as they are reflected.

For a more complete discussion of color as related to stage lighting, the student is referred to *The Essentials of Stage Lighting*, by H. D. Sellman. The scene designer must of course have a complete understanding of the principles of color in stage lighting. Not only will this understanding help him calculate the effect of lighting on his design, but also will show how the same principles may be applied to the mixing of scene paint, because the fundamentals are basic wherever color exists.

In mixing paint, the scenic artist is concerned with subtractive mixing because, when one colored pigment is mixed with another pigment, certain hues are subtracted from each of the pigments, thereby producing the third color. For example, when red pigment is mixed with yellow pigment, all the violet, blue, green, yellow, and red are subtracted (or absorbed), leaving a pigment that will reflect orange.

In the subtractive mixture of paint, magenta (blue red), yellow, and cyan (blue green) are regarded as primary colors. Simply, this means that blue red, yellow, and blue green are the basic colors for pigmentary schemes and that under ideal conditions they may be mixed to make three other colors. Magenta combined with yellow makes red, yellow with blue green makes green, blue green with magenta makes blue. These second three are the secondary colors.

If all these colors are arranged on the circumference of a wheel, such as that indicated in Figure 7-3, one can see other relationships. Colors adjacent to each other, such as yellow, yellow green, and green, are *analogous*. Colors directly opposite each other are *complementaries*. Green is the complement of magenta (blue red), blue is the complement of yellow, and red is the complement of cyan (blue green). In the center of the wheel is gray, the absolutely neutral point. Colors are brightest when they are related to (nearer to) the outside edge of the wheel and dullest when they are related to the center.

When two colors, represented by two points anywhere on the circumference of the wheel, are mixed, they produce a third color. If this were represented in a diagram, the third color, or blend, would be placed somewhere on a straight line drawn between the two original colors. The position of the blend on this line would depend on whether there were more of one of the original colors than the other in its composition. It will be seen that a point on this line (anywhere short of the extremities) is nearer to the hub of the wheel (grayness) than is a point on the circumference. This explains the fact that a mixture is never as intense in tone as a pure pigment. When two colors are combined they lose part of

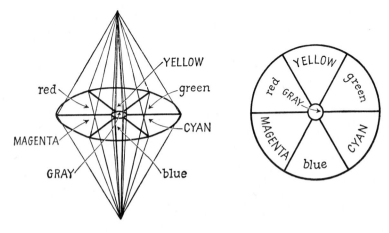

Figure 7-3 Color wheel and color solid.

their intensity (saturation). If pure yellow is combined with pure magenta, for instance, a red is produced which, because it is a mixture, is not quite so intense as a pure red of the same hue. The more widely separated on the color wheel are the colors to be combined, the grayer or more nearly neutral will be the blend. When complementaries (directly opposite colors) are mixed together in correct amounts, they produce a pure gray. This is a useful principle to remember when preparing paint for scenery. A pigment that appears too bright may very easily be toned down or softened (neutralized) by the addition of a little of its complement.

We have just glanced at the color wheel. This, however, is not a complete diagram of the behavior of color. If we place the wheel on edge, we find that it is a cross section of a three-dimensional figure made of two cones with their bases placed together (Figure 7-3). The end points of the two cones represent white and black, respectively, and mark the extremities of the gray line passing through the center of the figure. What happens to a color when it is mixed with white or black can now be seen very clearly. Not only is it grayed but lightened or darkened as well. A cross section of the color solid may be taken at any point, between the extremities, to produce a perfectly proportioned color wheel. The only dissimilarity between a cross section taken near an end and one taken near the center would lie in the fact that the colors on the circumference of the wheel sliced near the end would be less widely differentiated than those on the wheel sliced near the center.

A color, then, has three characteristics, which are determined by its position in this figure. Its *hue* is determined by its position in relation to other colors on the circumference of the wheel—that is, by its redness, yellowness, orangeness, blue greenness, and so on. Its *saturation* is determined by its nearness to the center of the wheel—that is, the amount of gray, or of its complementary, it has in its composition. Its *lightness* is determined by the amount of white or black it has mixed with it. A color of high lightness is called a *tint*, of low lightness, a *shade*.

If we were to list some of the more obvious characteristics of color the following would be included:

Magenta, red, and yellow are warm colors.
Green, cyan, and blue are cool colors.
Analogous colors are harmonious.
Complementary colors offer the greatest contrast.
Colors of high lightness are more "exciting" than those of low
    lightness.

A low degree of lightness gives a greater impression of dignity than a high degree of lightness.

A little bright color outweighs much grayed color.

Mixing colors always lowers saturation. The more widely separated are the hues, the grayer is the result.

The appearance of a color is always influenced by the colors surrounding it.

7   COLOR HARMONY

Harmony is, to a large extent, the result of good proportion.

Almost any color may be placed next to any other color, providing it is used in a correct amount. Two colors that clash when combined equally will usually appear well together in unequal quantities. Proportion involves balance. A little intense (saturated) color, for instance, as we have already noted in Section 6, will hold its own against a considerable amount of neutral (grayed) color. The following suggestions for combining colors are based on principles that operate under most conditions on the stage:

a   Various shades and tints of the same hue may be used together in any proportion.

b   Analogous hues (that is, those adjacent to each other on the color wheel) may be used together in any proportion, if they are used without a third color.

c   Complementaries may be used together in unequal proportion only.

d   Strict neutrals (grays), very light tints, or very dark shades may be used together in their own classes in almost any proportion.

e   Intense (highly saturated) colors may be used with neutral ones in almost any proportion, though balance, especially in the consideration of large designs, generally demands that the neutral colors predominate.

f   A neutral background may be used to tie together smaller masses of bright colors that would otherwise clash.

The greatest encouragement that can be given harmony is to keep the larger areas of the scene fairly neutral, and to sharpen visual interest by building up intensities in certain smaller points only.

8   PRACTICAL MODIFICATIONS

Whatever is said here about color mixtures and color relationships should be regarded as having to do with *principle*. The painter finds in practice that pigments seldom behave just as they should according to the color schemes. The reason for this is that complicating factors that prevent the conditions from being ideal are always present. Theoretically, a mixture of magenta and yellow will make red; practically, it may make a dull, unpleasant brown. What the principle of color mixture (in its simplest form) cannot take into account is the effects of chemical reactions between ingredients, the difference of purity in the pigments, and variations in texture.

The fact that magenta, yellow, and blue green (cyan) are called the three pigment primaries is based on the premise that the pigments being dealt with are transparent. Opaque pigments (such as many of those used in scene painting) tend to behave differently from the others. Since light does not penetrate them, and the effect created by a mixture of two of them depends on the visual blending of tiny spots—color particles of one pigment and color particles of the other—on the outer surface of the painting, the results often fit the *additive* mixture scheme more than they do the *subtractive*.

Backgrounds also influence effects. Painting done on a dark ground tends to be different from one on a light ground. There is a difference also when the pigments are transparent, or when they are applied loosely in splattering or dry-brushing and the ground shows through.

Another complication exists in the nature of surfaces. A shiny surface on one piece of painting may produce an entirely different color effect from a rough one on another, even when the hue, saturation, and lightness in both cases are identical.

Knowledge of how to deal with all these variants comes from practice. Skilled painters use the basic color principles as general guides, but general guides only; they are prepared to adjust proportions and relationships freely in the light of experience.

9 PREPARING THE PAINT

Paint is prepared by mixing pigment with a solution of glue called *size water*, according to the following procedure. Four pounds of flake (or ground) glue are placed in a 3-gallon pail of water, allowed to soak for at least an hour (or better, overnight), and then cooked on a stove. This pail is placed inside a larger one, with a little water and a block of wood or a brick in the bottom of the latter to prevent burning. When completely dissolved, the glue is further diluted to make size water. Four pounds of dry flakes will make from six to eight pails of size water. (This is about the proportion of one cup of glue to a pail.) The more concentrated preparation may be kept as stock to be diluted as it is needed. Because time must be taken to remelt it every time it is used, however, it is wise to make up several buckets of size water at a time to prevent delay in painting. If glue is to be kept on hand for any length of time, a couple of teaspoonfuls of carbolic acid may be put in it to keep if from decomposing.

The glue solution should be warm when it is added to the pigment. Pour the size water slowly into the dry pigment, stirring thoroughly to prevent lumping. It is helpful to stir the pigment vigorously when about half the size water has been added to break up lumps. When the pigment is smooth, add the remaining size water slowly until the paint is the consistency of coffee cream. It is difficult to give any more nearly exact proportions for mixing scene paints, as both glue and pigments vary. Veteran artists judge largely by the "feel" acquired through experience. If too much glue is used, the paint, when dry, will draw and crack on the surface of the canvas; also, the paint will have a tendency to look shiny, and dark stains may appear. If too little glue is used, the paint will powder on a hand rubbed across it. If too much pigment is used, the paint will seem stiff and heavy in brushing, and one stroke will pile up on top of the preceding one. If the mixture is too thin, it will look transparent on the canvas.

The paint, when applied, should be at least slightly warm. The mixture in the bucket should be stirred from time to time to prevent the powder from precipitating. If the pail is set aside for a while and grows cold, it should be thoroughly stirred and returned to the stove briefly before being used again, care being taken that the glue does not burn.

Available on the market now are some new flexible glues, such as glycerin glue, which, though they are a little more expensive than the old flake, make smoother mixtures that attain more desirable results. These glues are generally also more convenient to use.

Certain of the pigments (Prussian blue, ultramarine blue, Van Dyke brown, most of the reds, lampblack, and the anilines) need to be "cut," moistened with a little alcohol, before they are mixed with size water.

10   SOME SUGGESTIONS FOR MIXING PAINTS

It is seldom necessary to use pure colors, except for accents. For most purposes they should be mixed with at least an equal portion of whiting for painting brighter blocks of color, and several times this amount for laying in lighter tones. On the other hand, the use of whiting should be avoided when it is not needed. Whiting exerts a strong influence over other pigments in a mixture; even a small amount dropped by mistake into a pailful of some dark paint (such as burnt umber or black) is apt to destroy its brilliance and make it appear chalky.

The various pigments may be mixed together in any proportion. Only in very unusual circumstances will an artist find just the tone of a color he wants without first blending two or more together.

A word of caution should be given to those experimenting with scene paints for the first time. Water colors invariably look darker when wet than dry, mixtures containing white being especially tricky deceivers in this respect. Those who have trouble estimating in advance the result of a certain mixture would do well to mix their pigments in a dry state before adding any liquid.

It is difficult to match blends. Before painting a sky drop or the walls of a set, therefore, it is wise to mix enough paint to prevent running short at some crucial point. Two 2- or 3-gallon pailfuls will take care of a drop 25×30 feet, or a set of seven flats of standard width and 12 feet high, very nicely.

One of the less attractive qualities of the usual glue-mixed paint is that it may acquire an unpleasant odor after it has been allowed to stand in a warm shop for a day or two. Formaldehyde is a good preservative. Mix 2 quarts of this chemical with 3 gallons of paint. When spraying be careful not to breathe any of the mist. The use of carbolic acid has already been mentioned.

11 THE PRIME COAT

The first coat of paint is called the *prime coat*. Its purpose is to close the pores of the canvas and prepare a working surface for the following coats. Because whiting is the cheapest powder, it is commonly the chief ingredient used, but any other pigment may be employed equally well. Leftover scraps from the previous day's painting may be *boxed* together (poured back and forth into each other) and warmed up to prime the new flats. The tendency in professional studios is to prime a set of scenery with the tint of a color approximating the final tone of the scenery if the effect is to be smooth, and with a complementary to this tone if the effect is to be rough. To prepare a foundation for an open texture the priming is often done with several different colors. The only fixed directions for applying this first coat are to use a large brush and to spread the paint evenly, smoothly, and not too thickly over the canvas.

12 THE FOLLOWING COATS

One coat of paint should be allowed to dry thoroughly before another is applied; otherwise, the damp pigments will mix and produce muddy spots. If the paints are properly applied, one coat will completely hide the preceding one (unless it is in extreme contrast or is mixed with an aniline dye—see Section 29). If it does not, it is probably too thin. If one coat picks up another, the fault lies in one of three possibilities: the fresh paint is too warm, that beneath it is still damp, or the underpaint lacks glue. A little experience will quickly teach one how to avoid such conditions.

13 PAINTING OVER OLD SURFACES

Painting over an old surface often presents some difficulty. Scenic glue deteriorates in time and loses much of its binding quality. The paint on old scenery is often so powdery that it is caught up in the brush strokes and mixed with the new coat—disastrously so if the colors are dissimilar. The surface may be hardened somewhat by first sprinkling it freely with a strong solution of alum.

14 SURFACE TEXTURES

Irregular surfaces on the stage are, when viewed from a distance, more interesting to look at than perfectly smooth ones. For some reason, flatly painted scenery is never quite convincing; its chalky flatness reveals it to be what it really is, color-washed canvas. Even a slightly varied texture, scarcely recognizable as such from the audience, seems to "carry" where the flat one will not. The theory of *broken color*, which maintains that scintillation is secured by breaking up a desired tone into its simpler elements and placing these side by side in little blocks which the eye, at a distance, will blend into one, finds one of its surest proofs on the stage. A plainly tinted wall painted by spattering, one over the other, three coats—one magenta gray, one yellow gray, and one cyan gray—has a suggestion of life that one painted with the same colors mixed together in a pail and applied flatly most clearly has not.

15 PAINTING TECHNIQUES

Following is a list of the most common techniques for applying painted textures to scenery.

Flat base coat: Since the object of this technique is to produce a flat, smooth surface, the scene paint should not be applied in

Figure 7-4 Base coat. The base coat is applied in a figure-eight pattern.

Figure 7-5 Scumbling. Scumbling usually has a "splotchy" appearance before some other texturing technique is applied over it.

parallel strokes, but in overlapping strokes—so as not to produce a discernible pattern. Brushing the paint on in a figure-eight pattern is usually helpful. The paint must be spread over the surface evenly. If some areas are left with thick puddles of paint, these areas will dry darker than areas in which the paint has been spread evenly.

Scumbling: This method makes use of two or more colors of paint applied in irregular areas over the surface. While the areas are still wet, their edges are blended into each other to produce a smooth transition from one color to the next. A good working procedure for this method would be to have a painter for each color. The painters should not interchange brushes from color to color or, eventually, the paints will mix into one dull gray color. In mixing the paint for scumbling, however, it is helpful to intermix small amounts of each color into the others in order to tie all the colors close together in tonal value. Scumbling is useful for producing mottled or rough surfaces. Or, as is so often the case, if it is desirable for the top of a set to be darker than the bottom, dark shades of a color may be scumbled in at the top and lighter ones used as the painter approaches the bottom. Usually other texturing techniques are applied over the scumbled surface. If the freshly scumbled surface has too rough or splotchy a texture (which is commonly true), it may be spattered down with all the colors with which it was scumbled so as to smooth it out.

Spattering: The most generally useful method of texturing, spattering, is accomplished by flicking drops of paint from a large brush onto a surface that has had a base coat and has been placed on the floor. To achieve an even covering of spatter, the painter must load his brush each time with the same amount of paint, change directions of spattering constantly so that there is no discernible pattern, and keep his wrist in tension so that the paint flicks out of the brush rather than pours out. Before starting to spatter each brushful, the inexperienced painter should test himself by spattering on the shop floor or on an extra flat to determine the amount of paint coming out of the brush. Spattering should be done in at least three different colors with each color being allowed to dry before the next one is applied. The simplest combination of colors is two of the component colors of the base coat. In other words, if the base coat is green, blue and yellow would be the first two spatter colors. The third color should be in contrast to the base coat and the other spatter colors—darker, lighter, complementary, warmer, cooler—depending on the effect desired.

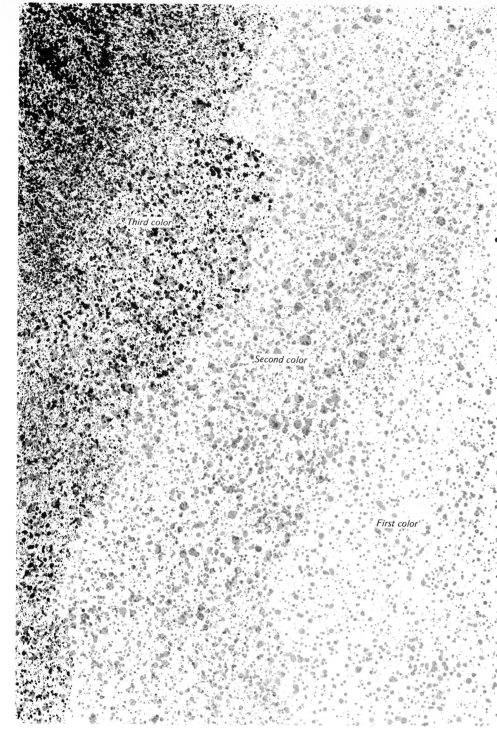

Figure 7-6

Spattering. The illustration shows the steps involved in applying three different colors to a surface. In practice, the entire surface would be spattered with each color, and the specks would be much larger than those in this reduced illustration.

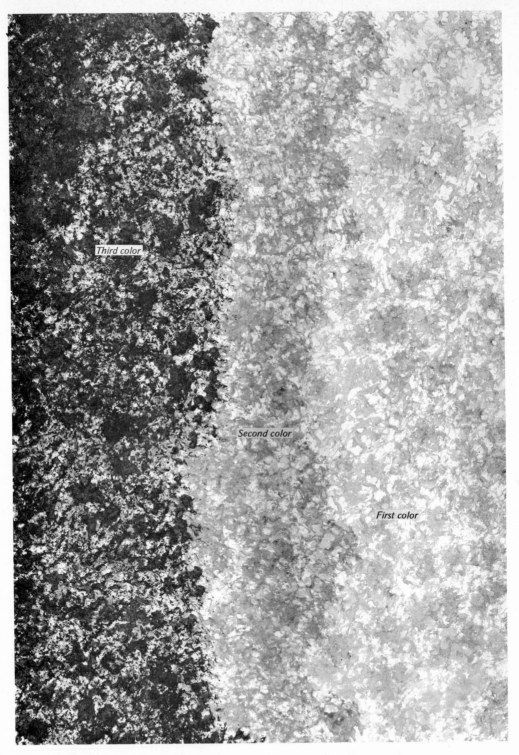

Figure 7-7 Sponging. In practice, the entire surface would be sponged with all three colors, and the texturing would be larger.

To achieve the impression of a smooth plaster wall, the painter should spatter small dots evenly over the surface. For a rougher texture, the painter would apply larger dots in an uneven pattern over the surface.

Sponging: A large natural sponge is dipped into a bucket of paint, squeezed out, and patted gently on the scenery to produce a rough texture similar to stucco. It is necesssary to use a natural sponge. Artificial, cellulose sponges produce too definite a pattern. Also, to avoid a definite pattern, the painter must change directions of the sponge constantly by turning the sponge in his hand and by sponging in overlapping circles. Sponging should be done in two different colors, at least. This technique is useful for texturing small areas after the set is standing.

Stippling: This method, which produces a very fine texture, is impractical for texturing large areas or for use in large theatres. It is done by dipping a brush into the paint, rubbing the brush on the edge of the bucket to remove most of the paint and to separate the bristles, then pushing the bristle ends against the surface, leaving small dots. This technique is useful for texturing small properties, furniture, and scenic units used in arena or thrust-stage presentations.

Rag-rolling: Producing a texture similar to the one produced by sponging, a ragged piece of rolled-up burlap is dipped into the paint, squeezed out, and then rolled over the surface to be textured. Again, change of direction is important.

Drybrushing: Used to simulate wood grain, drybrushing is done with a fairly dry brush that has had most of the liquid taken out of it, and its bristles separated by being drawn across the edge of the paint bucket. The brush is held perpendicular to the surface with the bristles barely touching the surface and then is carefully drawn along the surface leaving thin long lines. Drybrushing should be done in at least three different colors, and it is important to allow one color to dry before applying the next or the colors will mix and become muddy. Effective drybrushing is difficult to do and should be practiced before one attempts to use it in the painting of a set.

Cross-hatching: Producing a woven texture, cross-hatching is done in much the same manner as is drybrushing but, instead of being painted in long lines, it is produced by the arrangement of short, straight lines that cross each other in a woven pattern.

Stenciling: Usually employed to produce a wallpaper pattern, stenciling is done by the application of paint over a cutout stencil. The paint passes through the cutout areas, of course, and not

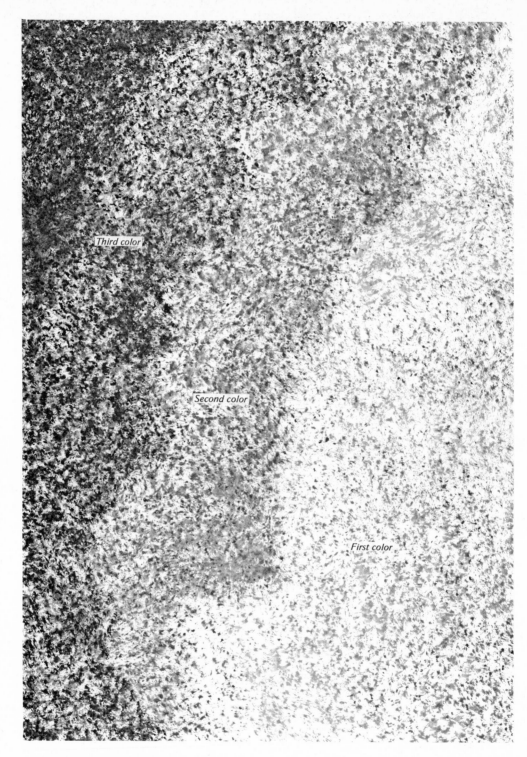

Figure 7-8 Stippling. In practice, the entire surface would be stippled with all three colors, and the texturing would be larger.

Figure 7-9 Rag-rolling. In practice, the entire surface would be rag-rolled with all three colors, and the texturing would be larger.

183

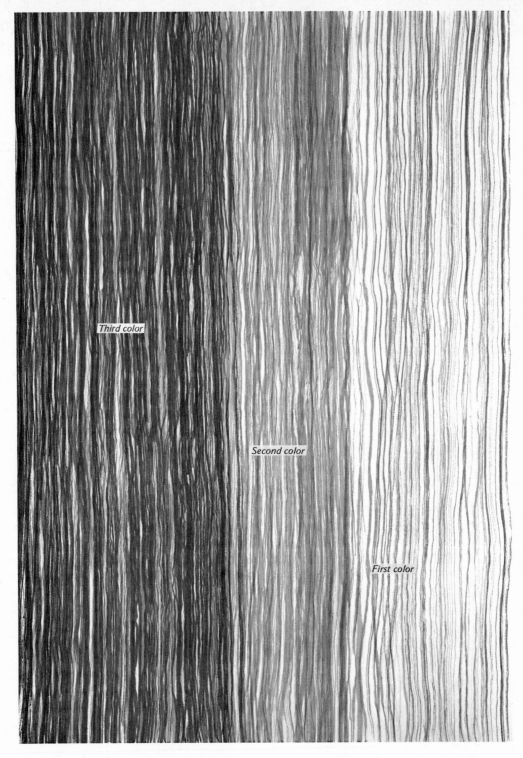

Figure 7-10 Drybrushing. In practice, the entire surface would be drybrushed with all three colors, and the texturing would be larger.

184

Third color

Second color

First color

Figure 7-11 Cross-hatching. In practice, the entire surface would be cross-hatched with all three colors, and the texturing would be larger.

through the solid areas of the stencil. Stencils should be cut from regular stencil paper, but heavy poster board coated with shellac may be used as a substitute. The stencil is lined up on chalk lines that have been snapped on the scenery to keep the pattern straight.

Washing: Used to produce cast shadows or aged spots on scenery, washing makes use of a very thin paint made by thinning regular scene paint with water until the mixture is transparent. The wash is painted on an area that is darkened but whose color and texture still show through the wash. Washing should be done very quickly with a minimum of brushing to avoid muddying the base coat and destroying the texture of the surface.

Spraying: To obtain an even, smooth surface, the painter may make use of an electric compressor and spray gun. Spraying is an excellent method for "softening" harsh corners or areas in a set. It is also helpful in applying base coats, or for stenciling, on large areas. The painter must, however, exert caution in keeping the spray gun clean, or an even flow of paint is impossible. Also, the spray gun used for scene painting should not be used with paints other than water-based paints. If the spray gun, for instance, contains even the smallest amount of oil paint, the scene paint will not flow evenly.

The above techniques of painting—and the ones to follow—should be regarded as simply basic approaches to scene painting and should be modified or disregarded as one discovers better methods. There is probably no area in the theatre that demands more inventiveness and skill than does scene painting. The successful painter is constantly experimenting to discover unique techniques and to improve his painting skill.

16 INTERIOR AND EXTERIOR WALLS

The principles of broken color may be used in developing wall surfaces that are intended to appear either smooth or rough. For the smooth surface, which suits interiors better than it does exteriors, choose two or three colors that are nearly alike, such as blue gray and yellow gray, or light cream, darker cream, and pink. Lay one of the colors on solidly as a ground coat; when it is dry, spatter the second evenly over the first until it nearly conceals it; then spatter over these two the third in the same manner. If the spattering has been properly done, it should present a surface which, from a distance and at first sight, will appear perfectly smooth, but which, upon closer examination, will be seen to have just enough texture to prevent it from looking monotonous and uninteresting. If a hard texture is desired, the spattering should be done on a perfectly dry surface; if a soft texture is desired, a wet surface should be used. Avoid working over a partly wet and a partly dry surface, however, or the result will be uneven.

The use of more widely separated colors in spattering will suggest stucco. If two or more colors are cleverly enough applied by the cloth-rolling method, a very convincing effect of old mottled wallpaper may be produced. If a more pronounced design is desired, simple figures may be cut in oil paper and stenciled onto the wall. In applying the paint through the stencil, use an almost dry brush to keep the paint from running. Avoid any very conspicuous patterns or they will probably refuse to lie at rest on the surface. If the figures appear too vigorous when viewed from a distance, spatter them over lightly with a little of the ground color to tone them back into the rest of the wall. Remember at all times that good scenery acts as an environment and must not detract from the action of the play.

If a warm gray is needed at any point, a serviceable one may be had by mixing together Venetian red and chrome green, plus enough whiting to bring the tint up to the lightness desired. One should never try to get a gray by using just black and white. What results from this mixture is a dull, muddy color.

Old stained plaster, particularly effective for exterior walls, may be suggested by scumbling and blocking in large irregular patches of various light and dark browns, or yellows, reds, and blues, and then spattering over them, while they are still wet, with the same colors. Keep the darker tones near the surface. As dark blue under the prevailing straw and amber lights of the stage looks nearly black, a little of this color may be mixed with a small amount of real black and sprinkled *very lightly* here and there over the plaster, to suggest holes and crevices. Guard against the appearance of large drops or you will give away your secret.

To give interest to highlights and shadows and to produce other interesting qualities through light reflection, in various kinds of textured wall surfaces, use is frequently made of aluminum (silver) powder, which is either mixed directly into the body paints before they are applied, or is made up with size water into a thin wash and spattered over the body coats.

Brick walls should be handled thoughtfully. Rows of regular red rectangles with hard white lines between, seen so often on amateur stages, never look very convincing. Even the most evenly laid walls in actual life show many irregularities and signs of weathering. One good plan to follow in painting is to scumble in first the plaster effect (later to be seen between the bricks) in a full ground coat—not in one tone, but in two or three slightly different ones—

then to lay the bricks in lightly on top of this with a comparatively dry 2- or 3-inch brush. Vary red with a little neutralized orange, brown, and blue. It is well to keep the bricks in fairly straight lines, of course, but do not attempt to paint them too regularly. Knock off a corner here and there and touch occasional edges with darker blue to suggest stains. After the bricks have been laid in, spatter them all over very lightly with the same colors. Keep in mind that an *impression* is what one is trying to create and that fussy details are lost on the audience.

The usual caution may be repeated: Avoid extremes. In developing interiors or exteriors, guard against painting walls either too bright or too dull. They would be conspicuous in both cases.

17   SHADING AND TONING WALLS

In creating wall surfaces an artist must work constantly for variety. He should give special attention to large plain areas. Unless these are well painted, they are apt to appear bare even under the best lighting. It is not enough simply to suggest texture. The artist should work for some difference between illuminated and shadowed areas. The light concentration on a high wall in a night scene, for instance, would naturally be near the bottom where the actors stand and walk in lamplight. In treating such a wall the artist might wisely lay his lightest tints here, and then shade them off gradually into deeper and deeper ones as he proceeds toward the top until the wall appears to melt into darkness. The outer edges of the wall, away from the light source, might likewise be made to fade into the shadows.

Wall surfaces often seem more interesting when they are *toned* (tinted or grayed) with a light scumble or spatter of aniline dye dissolved in size water. One or more tints or shades may be used. A thin wash of silver may be used in the same way. By this kind of silver treatment, dull-looking walls may be given a remarkable sparkle without appreciably changing their color. The dye and silver powders may be mixed in the same bucket, if so desired, and thrown together.

Both shading and toning, if they are to be at all effective, must be done subtly.

18   IMITATING WOODWORK

Woodwork is very difficult to imitate satisfactorily with canvas and paint. When he is preparing a realistic setting, a professional scenic artist likes to use at least some real lumber on the stage. This he can do without great difficulty where frames and moldings are involved; but it is obviously impossible to build a complete wooden interior to represent a shack or a log cabin. Where rough boards must be suggested with paint, lay a ground coat of gray brown, rule the flats with charcoal to indicate positions of the planks, and scumble in each with shades and tints of brown, blue, and gray, using strokes and avoiding making one plank exactly like the next. Alternate a couple of darker boards with a lighter one, and vice versa. Vary the ends, or the middles, of boards. Stain the edges of occasional boards. Now take a little yellow ochre, mixed with white, on an almost dry brush with the bristles spread, and with long sweeps suggest very lightly some pronounced graining here and there. If the pattern of the graining must be made more obvious, mix up a little black aniline dye and sweep it on in the same way with an almost dry brush. If the brown and yellow show up too brightly, reduce their intensity with a little gray or blue. Finally, outline the boards lightly with blue accented with black, draw in a few knots, and drag and spatter a little light gray blue over the entire surface to suggest the rough texture of the wood. A little real lumber seen in beams and supports will complete the general illusion.

In the more pretentious, formal type of interior that must be dressed up with baseboards, dadoes, cornices, wall paneling, and shaped door and window trims, strips of molding may be indicated (when the use of real wood is considered impractical) by laying bands of suitable color and drawing on these, with a 1-inch lining brush, thin lines of highlight and shadow. Wherever the light may be presumed to strike an edge of the molding a line of highlight is ruled. In the hollows below this line (or above—depending on the direction of the light) the lines of shadow are placed. The color for the highlighted strip is commonly prepared by mixing the "local tone" (body color of the molding) with a little white, and the color for the shadows, by mixing the local tone with a little dark blue or blue black. If the lightness of the ground on which the lines of highlight and shadow are to be drawn is extreme, pure white and pure pale blue may be substituted for the mixed colors. The pigment should be applied with a full brush in long, clean strokes, the brush being carried the length of the straightedge once only in each position. If the pigment is scrubbed on, the lines of light and shadow will look fuzzy, heavy, and unconvincing. To rule a crisp, thin line, the broader side of a small brush should be placed against the straightedge; to mark a softer line, the flat side should be turned to the canvas.

19 LOG-CABIN WALLS

To suggest the walls of a log cabin, model the surface of the flats before painting by means of long strips of waste cloth—such as scrap canvas, flour sacks, and any other rags—dipped into a mixture of hot glue and whiting and pasted on to suggest the roughly chopped edges of logs, with clay showing between. The raised portions should be 5 to 7 inches wide, and the spaces between 2 to 3 inches wide. Apply the rags hot, glue them firmly to the canvas, and wrinkle them to suggest the crude longitudinal grain of the wood. As the strips contract considerably in drying, avoid pulling them tightly when putting them on the flats.

Each log should run the full width of a wall. The flats composing a wall must therefore be laid together on the floor and done as a unit, that is, with the strips of cloth carried over the cracks. The flats may be cut apart afterwards. Corners, where two walls meet, must be carefully matched. As the log ends must seem to dovetail, the strips where the two walls join must be arranged in a stagger pattern. If the set is an exterior, the round ends of the wood at each corner should be shown.

When the log strips are dry, drag them in long, irregular streaks and blocks of dark and light grays, browns, and blues; then darken the edges, and put in bits of shadow with dark blue and purple under and above each strip to accentuate the thickness. Suggest clay in the cracks between by blotches of light yellow, blue, and gray. Paint boldly and freely and work for variety and contrast between the wood and the mud.

20 THE SKY

A large drop, high enough and wide enough to back up completely all exterior views, and painted pale blue, is generally used to represent the sky. As it depends chiefly upon lighting for its effect, its own tinting should be very soft. Mix not more than 3 or 4 ounces of Italian blue in a full pail of white, and apply the paint with a large, absolutely clean brush, taking great care not to streak. If it is a big drop, prepare two or three buckets of paint and box them thoroughly (pour them back and forth into each other) before starting. To run short and attempt to match tints in the center of the sky is disastrous. The sky may be given a little texture and a surface that will better reflect different qualities of light that may be thrown on it if it is spattered very carefully and evenly with pale, closely related tints of pink, purple, and blue (a fraction of a degree darker or lighter than the main blue). It may be given added scintillation by mixing into the paint a little aluminum (silver) powder.

The old-fashioned practice of painting a landscape on the sky drop is now frowned upon by the best artists. Besides being difficult to do, it never produces very convincing results and it limits the use of the drop. A simple sky may be used in every set of a play calling for a glimpse of outdoors, whereas a painted landscape fits the locality of just one scene.

If the drop must be rolled up frequently, the paint on its surface should be flexible. If to each 3-gallon pail of paint one adds ½ cup of glycerin, the paint can be prevented from cracking. Or one can use ready-prepared glycerin glue in place of the hard glue.

Sky drops that must be hung close up behind a window or door, or used to back up an exterior setting on a shallow stage, are difficult to light effectively and often have a hard, not very convincing appearance no matter how well they are painted. In such cases it is sometimes advantageous to hang a sheet of gauze just in front of the drop. This may be attached above to the same batten as that which holds the drop.

If a cyclorama is used to represent the sky, it is painted in solid or broken tints of very pale blue (and sometimes other colors) like the drop.

A dome may be painted in the same way.

21 LANDSCAPE PIECES

The character of an outdoor setting is suggested better by a few plastic *set* and *built* pieces, such as groundrows, silhouette hills, rocks, trees, and fences placed in front of the sky, than by anything painted on the drop. The construction of these is described in Chapter 6. When painting them one would do well to keep in mind that, except possibly for the sky on a cloudless day, there are no large masses of flat color in nature. Even a simple tree trunk will show a surprising number of colors—perhaps a dozen or more browns, grays, blues, and greens. Of course it would be impractical to indicate very many of these, but at least two or three tones should be used to indicate that a piece of scenery represents a tree trunk, not a painted post.

Rocks are never a dead gray. For painting the lighted side of a block of granite, use warmer colors—perhaps a dull cream varied with a little rose pink, light brown, and pale blue, whereas, in the shadows, use cooler colors—blue, bluish green, and purple. Green-ish patches of moss may be added. A sandstone wall would be painted in the same way with the addition of a little yellow. Work freely in large blocks of color. Sprinkle the whole piece lightly, when finished, with a small amount of dark and light blue to break up the smooth surfaces and add texture.

Paint mountain rows in light green, blues, and purples, and spatter them well with pale violet (ultramarine blue with a little Venetian red and white) to blend their outlines into the sky. Dis-tant banks of earth may be suggested in much the same way by using burnt umber, ultramarine, and Italian blue. Wherever possi-ble, run a little of the sky color into the faraway objects.

In planning landscapes, keep colors as light as possible, vary the values of tints, and avoid black shadows. Paint objects in the fore-ground in purer, brighter colors than those in the background. The shadow colors should go on first, and the painting proceed step by step from dark to light.

22 FOLIAGE

To repeat the statement made in Chapter 6, Section 17, thoroughly convincing foliage is very difficult to paint. The tendency now is to avoid the use of definite shrubbery and other leafy pieces as much as possible. In out-of-door scenes calling for the presence of trees, an artist generally tries to design his setting in such a way as to draw the main attention to three or four bare, but convincing, solid-looking trunks rising out of sight behind the teaser in the more brightly lighted foreground, while merely *suggesting* masses of leaves, intertwining branches, and silhouettes of other trees (cre-ated by means of dark cutout drops kept discreetly behind much scrim) in the shadows of the background. If a foliage piece, such as a masking border, must be used in the foreground, paint it in blocks to hint at clumps of leaves rather than individual ones; then cut the edges and punch holes in the border (according to the characteristics of the foliage represented), and hang it in silhouette as much as possible. Dark chrome green, leaf green lake, and Hanover green are good foliage colors. They may be modified by mixing white into them. A few touches of neutralized red here and there will add roundness to the blocks of green. Some artists prime their foliage pieces with pure ultramarine and paint over it.

Vines and small bushes are made best out of materials secured at artificial flower shops, or five and ten cent stores. Their cost, however, precludes their use in quantity.

23 MIST AND DISTANCE EFFECTS

Mist effects are created principally by the use of scrim, a dark blue theatrical gauze. One or more thicknesses of it, in the form of a drop, are hung in front of the whole, or part, of a scene. If lights are carefully kept off it, the gauze itself remains invisible but the objects behind it are blurred as though seen through a haze. If two or three small streaks of light are thrown across it, a suggestion of fog is produced. The whole scene back of the scrim may be blocked out by removing the light from behind and bringing it up in front from the side or top. This is the way the famous "transformations" of the old theatre were effected. The atmospheric vapors natural to a landscape contribute much to the impression of distance. Scrim, therefore, is useful for this effect also. With the aid of the right kind of lighting, a deep woods scene can be suggested very simply within a few feet of stage space by hanging, one behind the other, several foliage cutout drops with pieces of scrim glued over the open spaces of each. From the front, each receding silhouette appears dimmer than the one in front of it and consequently the feeling is conveyed that the last group of trees is quite far away.

Certain colors, also, give the impression of distance. Pale blues and violets are especially helpful in this respect. A little very light ultramarine or Italian blue spattered over a row of hills will make them appear ten miles closer to the horizon.

24 PAINTED SHADOWS

A word should be said about shadows. They are never black. They may be brown, green, purple, or almost any color except pure black, which is dead. The ideal plan, of course, is to arrange a set in such a way as to make the shadows fall naturally without painting; but where they must be made artificially, one can use pigments that are neutralized complements to the prevailing colors in the lighting. Where an illuminated area is seen as amber or straw (yellow), the shadows are of blackish, or grayish, blue; where blue green, of red; and so on. "Painted darkness," however, is at best a makeshift device. To be effective at all it must be subtle. It should not appear to have been laid in with a brush. Heavy streaks and blotches are worthless.

25 REPRODUCING FROM SKETCHES

A design for a picture drop or other large piece of scenery must occasionally be copied and enlarged from a small working sketch.

As it is difficult, at close range to his canvas, for an artist to keep the various elements of an extensive composition accurately in proportion, he is compelled to make use of an analytical scheme of reproducing—in other words, to copy the design in small units. The following method is the one generally employed.

The sketch (Figure 7-12), made to a definite scale—generally ½ inch = 1 foot, is ruled off with a pencil in 1-inch squares. The drop, primed with a working surface, is likewise ruled off with charcoal in 2-foot squares. These vertical and horizontal lines are drawn with either a long batten or a *snap line*. The latter is a heavy, braided cotton cord, rubbed with a stick of charcoal, a lump of chalk, or a folded cloth containing a dry pigment, which is held against the canvas and pulled tightly at both ends. When it is lifted in the middle and allowed to snap back onto the cloth, some of the charcoal, chalk, or pigment rubbed along the cord is transferred to the canvas, making a distinct streak.

The design is now transferred from paper to canvas, square by square, chalk or charcoal being used for the outline sketching. The drop is then painted. If any of the black or white lines still show when the painting is completed, they can be dusted out easily with a feather duster or a dry rag.

It is sometimes advisable to work out a difficult detail or a repeat pattern at full size on a piece of wrapping paper first and then transfer this drawing to the canvas. After the drawing has been

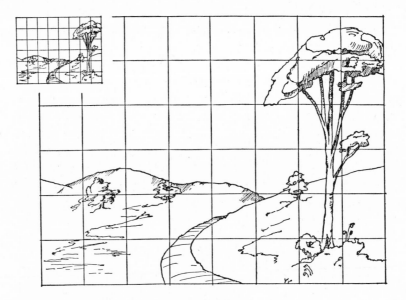

Figure 7-12 Method of enlarging a sketch.

made on the paper, the paper is perforated along the principal lines of the design with a pounce wheel, a small nail, or other pointed object; then the paper is turned over, the burrs are sand-papered off the little holes, the pattern is placed in position on the drop, and a small pounce bag is rubbed or patted over the perforations.

26 GOLD AND SILVER METALLIC PAINTS

Bronze and aluminum powders, which are sold in a number of different tints and shades, are used to represent gold and silver in scene painting. They are mixed with a bronzing liquid for applying to metal, and with a heavy glue size for painting on cloth and wood. Size water in its ordinary strength (½ pound of glue to 3 gallons of water—Section 9) does not bind strongly enough for metallic paints; the proportion of glue for these should be doubled. To prepare the watercolor mixture, first make a thick paste of the metallic powder with a little alcohol and heavy size water used hot, stirring it until it is smooth; then mix in slowly more and more of the size water until the desired consistency is obtained. Place the mixture on the stove and bring it to a boil, stirring it constantly to make certain that it does not burn. If properly prepared, bronze and aluminum paints are thoroughly liquid when warm, and quite stiff when cold. When they are being used they must be kept warm by frequent reheating.

To make these naturally brittle paints a little more flexible for use on drops or other pieces that must be folded or rolled, add about a teaspoonful of glycerin to a pint of liquid, or use a glycerin glue.

If a metallic powder is to be mixed with scene paint it must be prepared separately, according to the directions given above, before it is added to the other pigment; otherwise it will separate out and flake off as soon as the paint is dry.

27 OIL PAINTS

Surfaces on small units, such as door frames and, particularly, furniture pieces, which have to stand constant rubbing from the hands or clothes of actors or must be cleansed now and then with a wet rag, are frequently painted in oil.

Oil paint consists of two parts: the *pigment*, a powder similar to that used in water-color scene paints, but ground more finely; and the *vehicle*, a liquid, the common ingredients of which are linseed oil and turpentine. The best work requires three to five coats. The first, called the prime coat, is composed of much oil and little pigment and turpentine; the intermediate, the body coats, contain more of the second and third elements; whereas the last, the finishing coat, is made up principally of turpentine for a flat surface, or oil for a glossy surface. For the temporary purposes of the stage, one or two coats of the same mixture are usually sufficient. A method very commonly employed in scene painting is to lay in the prime coat with an ordinary watercolor paint made up with a strong size (Section 9), followed by a coat of shellac (Section 28), and to use oil paint in a single, final coat only. Shiny surfaces that reflect light are seldom desired. The most serviceable oil medium, therefore, is ready-mixed, flat, interior paint. It may be thinned, if necessary, with a little turpentine, and made to dry more rapidly by adding a small amount of dryer.

To avoid streaking, oil paint must be applied with considerably more care than scene paint (watercolor). Stir the paint well before using. Break up any lumps in the bottom of the can and see that all the ingredients are thoroughly mixed. Clean the surface to which the paint is to be applied. Brush the paint on with long, straight strokes, evenly, smoothly, and not too thickly. Two thin coats are better than one thick one. Be certain that one coat is thoroughly dry before applying the second.

Oil paint can be laid over a smooth surface of scene paint, but the reverse process is a little more difficult. Scene paint does not stick well to a very smooth surface. Shellacking the surface first, however, will help to make the watercolor coat hold.

Oil brushes must be thoroughly cleaned with linseed oil or turpentine after every use and carefully kept separate from the watercolor brushes.

28 SHELLAC

Shellac, a spirit varnish composed of gum dissolved in alcohol, lends itself to quick and easy methods of imitating surfaced woodwork. A convincing mahogany panel may be created by painting a piece of plywood or framed canvas with white scene paint, graining it with black, and applying over this a couple of coats of orange shellac stained with a little powdered dye of a dark reddish brown color, such as Bismarck brown. If a really nice piece of work is desired, one coat should be allowed to dry thoroughly, and should be sandpapered before the next is applied. In the absence of dye a few teaspoonfuls of burnt umber and Venetian red scene powder may be put into the shellac. Whole interiors are often done in this manner.

Shellac fulfills a number of other paint demands in an excellent manner. One of its best qualities is that of a waterproofing agent. It is sold in two colors, white and orange, is thinned with alcohol, and dries almost instantly.

Brushes used in shellac should be cleaned with alcohol immediately after service and kept separate from watercolor and oil brushes.

29 DYES

Pure aniline dye, or its substitute, the commercial Diamond Dye, employed frequently for toning walls and draperies and occasionally for painting drops that have to be made very light and flexible, is prepared in the following way. Mix 1 ounce of dye with water into a paste, add 1 teaspoonful of salt and 1 quart of water, and bring to a boil. This is the standard method. A shortcut is often taken in scene painting, however, by simply stirring the dye powder into very hot size water. If much painting is to be done with this medium, strong stock solutions of each color may be made up, kept on hand, and diluted with warm size water as needed.

The following colors will be found useful. They may be combined to form a wide variety of intermediate tones. To lighten a dye, dilute it; to darken it, add more stock.

> Brilliant red
> Wine red
> Purple
> Blue
> Green
> Yellow
> Seal brown
> Black

Dye may be applied with an ordinary scene brush. A little dye goes a long way; do not use it heavily. Dye, unlike distemper, is not opaque. One color on the canvas may be modified by brushing another over it; but it cannot be fully blocked out once it is placed. Light areas can be darkened, but dark areas cannot be lightened. It is recommended, therefore, that when the artist is doing any piece of work at all elaborate, he lay in his pale tones first, and proceed from them to his deeper ones.

Anilines are used quite extensively for "toning down" scenery painted in the ordinary way. If the walls of an interior are too lively, for instance, they may be grayed down effectively by spattering them lightly all over with black or blue aniline (Section 17).

In an emergency in regular scene painting, whiting may be tinted with a little dye to take the place of a color that has run short. Seldom very satisfactory, however, the use of this method of mixing pigments is not to be recommended as a regular practice.

Brushes used in dye cannot be thoroughly cleaned by simply being rinsed in water. The bristles, which take up a considerable amount of color, must be "bled" by being soaked for several hours in a pan of whiting and water.

30 THE DRY PALETTE

There are often painting projects that require the use of small amounts of many different colors. To avoid the troublesome and wasteful process of mixing a bucket of paint for each color, the painter may use an artist's palette (or even a piece of Masonite) on which he has placed several small piles of dry pigment. With the pigments, a bucket of size water, and a liner brush, he may mix many colors easily and quickly. By first dipping the brush into the size water and then into the dry pigment—mixing the two until the pigment is completely saturated with size water—he produces a small amount of scene paint. The combination of variously colored pigments on the palette produces any variety of colors. The only two precautions that need to be taken with this process are, first, to make certain that the pigment is saturated with size water, or the paint will not hold to the surface to which it is applied, and, second, to be careful to keep the pigments and mixed paints separated on the palette, or only muddy, dull colors will be produced.

31 DIMENSIONAL TEXTURE IN PAINT

Many interesting effects may be achieved by the mixture of textured materials into scene paint. Sawdust, light sand, excelsior, shredded paper—each may be mixed into the paint to produce rough, dimensional surfaces. It is usually necessary for one to keep the paint well mixed because these materials will quickly settle to the bottom of the bucket. It is also necessary for one to mix the paint with a slightly stronger size water than that used for regular scene paint.

Instead of mixing the textured material directly into the paint, one may sprinkle the material over a wet painted area. An effective rock wall, for example, may be produced by painting small rock-shaped areas and, while the paint is still wet, sprinkling the areas with a lightweight sand or sawdust. The alternation of sand-sprinkled areas with sawdust-sprinkled areas produces rocks of different textures on the same surface. When the unit is dry it should be stood up to allow excess sand and sawdust to fall off. If, for any reason, the material does not hold well, it may be painted over with clear size water to make it adhere.

There is no end to the variety of texturing methods that are adaptable for use in scene painting. The painter simply needs to experiment freely with many materials and methods until he finds those that are most useful for his work.

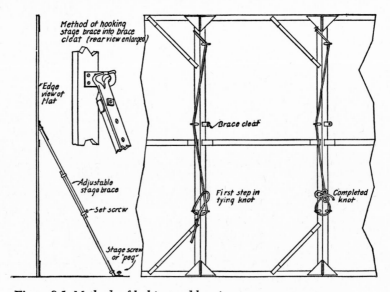

Figure 8-1 Methods of lashing and bracing scenery.

SHIFTING THE SCENERY

CHAPTER 8

1 INTRODUCTION

As has already been stated, one of the requisites of good scenery is that it be designed for easy, silent, and rapid shifting. An audience pays money at the box office for a performance, not for intermissions. The success of a performance is usually determined by its ability to catch an audience's attention and to retain that attention while moving forward with ever-building momentum. Anything in

201

the performance that weakens the momentum is a serious flaw. The most likely place for a performance to lose momentum is between individual scenes or during act breaks. Since there is little to hold the audience's attention during these breaks, they must be as short as possible. Therefore, if a scene shift occurs between scenes or acts of a play, the designer must make certain that his scenery can be shifted quickly enough to avoid breaking the momentum of the performance.

2 PLANNING THE SHIFT

A plan for shifting the scenery must be designed right along with every other aspect of the design. Equally as important as the period, mood, color, and construction of a scenic unit is the method to be employed in moving the unit on and off of the stage. As the designer is developing the floor plan, sketch, or model to picture the scenery as it will appear onstage, he will keep himself aware of how the scenery will be stored offstage and he will develop methods for shifting it. A plan of shifting should be completed before the design is agreed upon by the director and the designer and, certainly, before any piece of the set is constructed.

A helpful device in the planning of a shift is a scaled, unpainted cardboard model of the set containing all the set's individual units. If the designer places this model on a scaled floor plan of the onstage and offstage areas to be used, he may check the shifting methods he has in mind and determine storage patterns. This model can be of value also in explaining the duties of the crew members to be involved in the shift. After each crew member understands the complete shift and storage patterns, he should be assigned specific duties as his part of the complete shift. After the set is finished, the crew should rehearse the shift several times in order to be able to execute it quickly, quietly, and correctly. It is during these rehearsals that any difficulties in shifting will be discovered and corrected—before the set is presented to an audience.

3 TYPES OF SHIFTING

The modern audience's exposure to the rapid, smooth fade-ins and fade-outs of the motion-picture and television media has forced the stage designer to develop techniques of changing stage pictures as smoothly and rapidly as possible without interrupting the action of the play. Several types of shifting arrangements are available to accomplish these ends.

a The masked, or hidden, shift: This type of shift takes place behind the action on stage and is hidden from the audience's view by some sort of masking piece or scenic unit. Frequently, as in many musicals, a scene is played downstage in front of a traveler curtain or a drop while the set for the next scene is being shifted into place behind the curtain or drop. Most musicals, in fact, are written with the shifting problem in mind. Scenes requiring large sets are alternated with "in-one" scenes (taking place downstage in front of a curtain or drop). The designer must calculate the time an "in-one" scene will take to play to determine the length of time available to him for the shift.

b   The blackout shift: To avoid having to open and close a traveler or to fly in drops too often, the designer may choose to do the shifting during blackouts. Shifts of this sort must be short in duration, however, or the audience's attention will be lost. It is often helpful to "cover" these short intervals of darkness with musical "bridges." In this type of shift, the positions of scenic units are usually marked on the floor with luminous paint to enable the crew to find proper locations in the dark. Another helpful trick is for the crew to close their eyes a few seconds before the shift is to be made to allow their eyes to adjust to the darkness.

c   The act-break shift: The shifts that take place during act breaks are usually no problem if the designer has done his job at all well. Usually 10 or 15 minutes is allowed for intermissions and this is sufficient time to shift almost any type of set. The shift should remain quiet, however, and should be completed soon enough to allow time for checking the set and properties before the curtain is raised on the next act.

d   The in-view or "a vista" shift: The in-view shift allows the audience to watch the shifting of the set under complete stage lighting or during the fade from one lighting setup into another. Usually done with mechanical devices such as wagons, revolving stages, flying units, and so on, it becomes a dramatic element of a production if done perfectly smoothly and with a certain magical flair. Crew members should not be visible during this type of shift or most of its effectiveness is lost. Obviously, this type of shift requires a well-equipped stage, well-designed scenic units, a great deal of planning, and several rehearsals to execute it properly.

e   The visible crew or actor shift: Another in-view shift makes use of the theatricality of crew members or actors moving scenic units during the action of the play. This type of shift should be considered as being a part of the action of the play and, often, it is planned and directed by the director in consultation with the designer. If the shift occurs under lighting, the crew is usually costumed or wears some sort of neutral clothing. This type of shift may also be done in silhouette or in some special lighting setup that is used conventionally throughout the production during scene shifts.

f   The area shift: Shifting scenery in one area of the stage while a scene is being played in another area should be considered an in-view shift. Ideally, the area of the stage in which the shift is occurring should be in complete darkness, but it rarely is because of light spilling from the playing area. The crew should wear dark clothing, remain as hidden as possible, and work completely silently or the shift will distract the audience's attention away from the scene being played.

In many of the outdoor theatres, which have no rigging for front curtains, travelers, drops, and so on, the above type of shifting is used almost exclusively. Much of the distraction problem has been solved, however, through the use of a large center stage flanked by two side stages. These playing areas are designed of such size and separation as to minimize the light spill from one area to another. A scene will be played, for instance, on a side stage, while 50 or 60 feet away on the center stage or the other side stage, a set is being shifted in almost total darkness.

In planning the shifting of the scenery, the designer should first decide on which of the above types of shifting lends itself readily to the stage facilities he has available, the manpower he has available, and, most important, to the physical and dramatic requirements of the play and the production.

4   METHODS OF SHIFTING

There are basically three methods by which scenery may be shifted on the stage: hand shifted (called running); suspended (called flying); and castered (called rolling). Usually, in any one shift, some combination of all three methods is employed, but a better knowledge of each individual method is obtained if each is considered separately along with the equipment and hardware peculiar to each. If the designer has a firm understanding of each method, he finds that there is great flexibility in the combinations he may devise for any particular shift.

Running Scenery

This method may be employed to shift any unit of scenery that stands on the stage floor. The equipment involved is used primarily for attaching units together after they have been carried on stage and for bracing and supporting the units while they are standing. The equipment is designed to be detachable or collapsible to facilitate shifting. At best, this type of shifting is more awkward and slow than the other two. It is practically impossible to employ it without the use of the following standard equipment and procedures.

Lashing: Through the use of the standard lashing hardware described in Chapter 5, Sections 6 and 11, two or more flats are bound together by lashing. The lash line, threaded through a lash-line eye in the upper right-hand corner on the back of one flat, is grasped with the right hand, tossed up and over the top lash cleat on the back of the adjoining flat, then brought over a lash cleat a little farther down on the first flat. Directly across from this bottom cleat is a cleat on the adjoining flat. The lash line is looped around this cleat, pulled tight, and then tied with the slip knot shown in Figure 8-4. To loosen the lashing, it is necessary only to pull the free end of the lash line and the knot will become untied.

If it is necessary to lash two flats together to form a straight wall section, the crack between the two flats should be covered by a lip of ¼-inch plywood running the length of one of the flats, beveled on both edges, covered with canvas, and extending beyond the edge of the flat to which it is attached about ½ inch. Better straight wall sections are made by hinging two flats together and covering the crack with a dutchman.

Lashing is an excellent method for securing flats together to form a corner of the set. Stop cleats should be placed on one of the flats to hold the corner securely in position.

Bracing: Scenic units standing on the floor usually require some sort of bracing or support from behind. The two principal methods for providing this support are the use of *the adjustable stage brace* (which must be ordered from a theatrical hardware company) or *the jack* (which may be made in the scene shop). The adjustable stage brace is made of two lengths of 1×1-inch hardwood or aluminum held together by clamps and fitted with a hook at one end, a foot iron at the other end, and a set screw in the center. The two halves of the brace slide so that the length of the brace may be adjusted. To set a stage brace into position, one twists the hook of the brace into the hole of the brace cleat, screws the foot iron to the floor with a stage screw, then loosens the set screw, and, by tightening and loosening the set screw, adjusts the length of the brace until the hook is firmly seated in the brace cleat. Care must be taken to set the stage brace in such a way as to be sturdy without pushing the flat forward or pulling the flat back. Figure 8-1 illustrates the use of the stage brace.

The jack is a wooden triangular-shaped brace that is attached

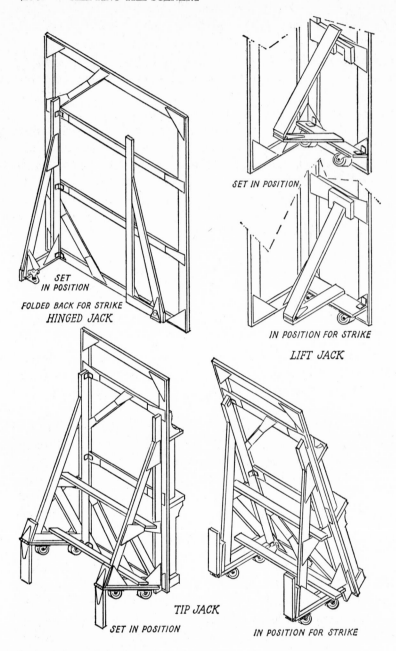

Figure 8-2 Jacks.

to the back of a scenic unit with either tight-pin hinges (if it is to fold against the unit during the shift) or loose pin hinges (if it is to be removed from the unit during the shift). It is equipped with a foot iron on the side that rests on the floor. A stage screw through the hole of the foot iron secures the jack to the floor.

The jack is also an excellent brace to use on stages where one cannot use stage screws. A sandbag, or even a cement block, may be placed across the bottom rail of the jack to hold the jack in position.

The lift jack also is hinged to the scenic unit but in such a way

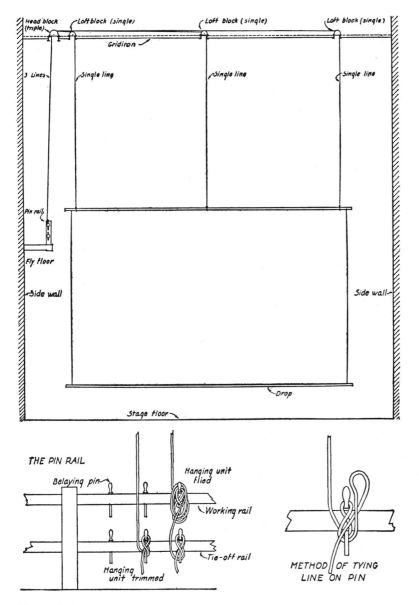

Figure 8-3

Machinery for flying scenery. A general view of the gridiron and the fly floor, and a detailed study of the pinrail showing the method of tying off a line. (Usually there would be three lines together.)

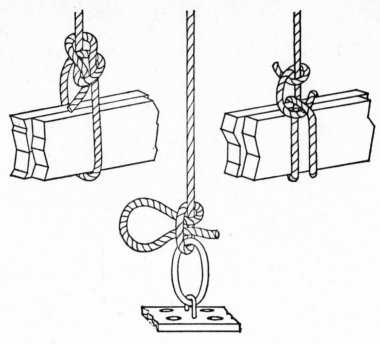

Figure 8-4 Three knots commonly used on hanging scenery. The bowline, left; the clove hitch (plus a half hitch), right; and the slip knot, center.

as to fold up or down. It is used on dimensional, free-standing units and functions more as a shifting device than as a bracing device. Its bottom rail is equipped with casters, and when the jack is pushed down and hooked under a wooden cleat, the wheels touch the floor, lifting the scenic unit slightly. Once the unit is lifted and the jack locked in place, the unit may be rolled offstage.

The tip jack is similar to the lift jack but, instead of lifting the scenic unit, it tips the unit back onto casters at the bottom of the jack. The various types of jacks are shown in Figure 8-2.

Flying Scenery

Before attempting to fly scenery, the designer must have a complete knowledge of the flying system with which his stage is equipped. Standard flying systems are discussed in Chapter 3, Sections 4, 5, and 6.

There are certain principles, techniques, and hardware, however, that are applicable for use with almost any flying system.

General Methods of Flying Scenery

A line is attached to a drop, or other hanging piece, by trying it around the upper batten or into specially attached hanging irons.

The three ropes in a set are called, respectively, the *short, center,* and *long line* as they are fastened to the near end, middle, and far end of the unit of scenery from the point of view of the flyman. The knots (Figure 8-4) used in making the ropes fast to the scenery must be those which combine absolute security with ease in untying. The bowline is commonly used for straight lifts, and the clove hitch for horizontal and bias pulls. If a quick attachment (*temporary* only) is to be made on a light piece of scenery, the slip knot may be employed. This knot, which will not hold well on a batten, is useful only for tying a line into a ring or onto another line.

On units that have no free battens to which the lines can conveniently be attached, hanging irons are used (Figure 8-5). These are fastened vertically, ring end upward, to the back of the unit, near the top, by means of $7/8$-inch (or longer) No. 9 screws. If the weight on each iron exceeds 50 pounds, one or more $3/16$-inch stove bolts should be used with the screws.

The unit to which a set of lines has been attached is flied simply by pulling on the ropes. When it has reached the desired height, the ropes are made fast to a belaying pin. The method for *tying off* is illustrated in Figure 8-3. The ropes are first carried around the lower end of the pin (from left to right), then up, across, and around the upper end (from left to right), down around the lower end and up again, about two and a half times. The set of lines is finally made fast by making a loop, turning it over, bringing it down over the top end of the pin, and pulling it tight, as illustrated. The free ends of the ropes are coiled and hung over the same pin to prevent their getting tangled with other ropes. For

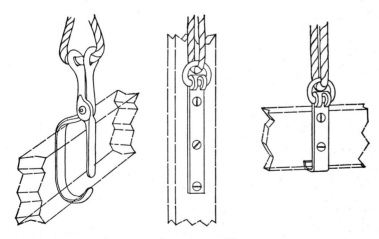

Figure 8-5 Drop hanger and two types of hanging irons.

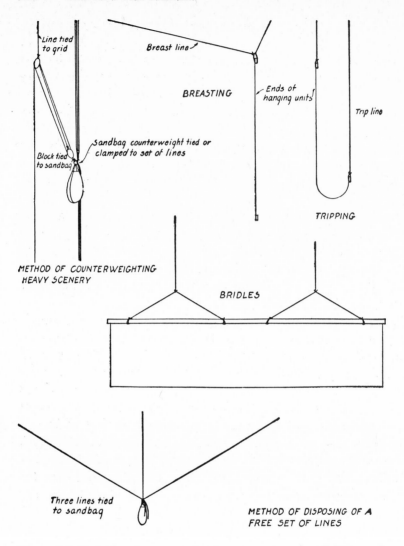

Figure 8-6 Methods of maneuvering hanging scenery with lines and counter-weights.

the sake of clearness in the drawing only one line in each set is shown.

There are two rows of belaying pins on the pinrail: the lower one for tying the drop, or other unit, at *trim*—that is, when it is in position for the set, and the other pin for tying it when it is raised into the flies. This method of using the rail is found serviceable when a piece of scenery must be lifted and lowered during a performance. Trimming takes time, which can be ill afforded during a quick shift. However, by using the two pins, this can be done beforehand. The lower tie remains permanent. When the appropriate scene arrives, the flyman loosens the ropes from the upper pin, lets them slide through his fingers, and when the slack is out he knows the drop or other hanging unit has come automatically to position.

Heavy pieces may be counterweighted by sand bags tied to the lines just below the head blocks (Figure 8-6). A whole rear wall consisting of three or more flats battened together may be balanced this way. A clamp is often used in place of rope for attaching the heavy sandbag to the lines.

A wide piece of scenery, such as a drop, may, in an emergency, be flied on two lines instead of three by using bridles, as illustrated in Figure 8-6.

On a stage equipped with a low grid, a tall drop may be *tripped* out of sight by attaching, from behind, a second, adjacent set of lines to the bottom batten. When both sets of lines are drawn, the drop is folded back and up into a space only half its height (Figure 8-6).

Hanging units may be breasted—that is, pulled slightly forward or backward, or around on a bias—by having upstage or down-stage lines attached to them (Figure 8-6).

A unit is trimmed—that is, straightened so that it will hang squarely and without wrinkles—by having the short, center, or long line drawn up or let out slightly. It is said to be *in trim* when it is in exactly the right position for use on the stage.

A small sandbag should be tied into every set of lines not fastened to scenery to prevent the ropes from being pulled through the blocks when they are drawn up out of the way, and to force them to come down again with their own weight when released.

A word of caution: *Be sure that all hardware and knots used in flying are secure.* Some serious accidents have resulted from pulleys or hanging irons or sandbags that have broken loose during a performance. Examine ropes from time to time for signs of wear.

Specific Methods of Flying Scenery

A drop or a border is flied by tying a set of three or more lines to its upper batten.

A ceiling piece is suspended on two to three sets of lines, and lifted away or lowered to the standing set in the manner explained in Chapter 6, Section 12.

The larger types of cycloramas, unless specially rigged, as is described in Chapter 3, Section 8, are generally too awkward to shift during a performance. All flying of other scenery has to be done inside them. The smaller forms of cyclorama, however, are moved very simply. The rear batten is tied to a full set of lines and the downstage ends of the arms to another set of two lines. If there is no scenery above to foul, the whole thing can be lifted straight up by drawing both sets of lines at the same time. If the cyclorama is of any considerable size, however, this method of handling requires the full stage room, or at least the major part of it. There is another method that permits flying the frame, canvas and all, into a space little larger than that occupied by a drop. Two adjacent sets of lines are employed. The two-line set attached to the downstage ends of the cyc arms is tied on a permanent trim, and the actual flying is done by the rear set alone. When this is drawn, the back, or curve, of the U-shaped frame ascends first, while the arms fall down and back against the body of the cyclorama; then the whole thing is taken up as one flat piece. When the cyclorama is dropped, the permanently tied two-line set, which remained in slack while the piece was in the flies, tightens, and automatically pulls the arms back out into position. If the cyclorama unit is quite heavy, it is important to see that it is adequately rigged. Extra lines may have to be installed for safety.

To speed up the setting and striking of a scene, a complete back wall is frequently hung on a set of lines and flied like a drop. The several flats that compose the wall are first laid flat on the stage, edge to edge, face downwards, and fastened together to make a single rigid panel by placing two or more long battens, called *stiffeners*, across the back. They are fastened to the stiles of the flats by means of long screws or bolts, never nails. Ropes are tied into hanging irons attached at strong points (the center and two ends) to the back of the combination, and the wall is then raised and lowered as a unit. A side wall, also, may be flied in this way by tying to it single lines from an upstage and a downstage set. A whole box interior, with three walls, can, on occasion, be lifted from the stage as one piece by using one full set of lines to support the back, and another set of two to support the two front corners.

Heavy units should be counterweighted by large sandbags tied to each set of lines just below the head block, as illustrated in Figure 8-6. If the wall of an interior that must be placed under the edge of a ceiling is to be balanced in this way, a small auxiliary block and tackle will have to be attached to the sandbag to lift the latter slightly, and so give some slack to the fly ropes when the wall is in position on the floor. Otherwise, the overlapping ceiling will be fouled.

Flying on Small Stages
On small platforms where there is no possibility of constructing a

regular gridiron, a makeshift device can be arranged in the form of a few stout pulleys fastened securely to beams in the ceiling. At a minimum, there should be two sets of pulleys to take care of the front and back edges of the ceiling—one to swing the pipe batten holding the front lighting units, and another to support the sky drop upstage. If the scenery is light, the lines may be tied off on a row of common lash hooks fastened to a board bolted to the wall on the side.

A little more costly, but a stronger and more generally satisfactory substitute for a grid on a small stage may be had by installing a system of light steel I beams and underhang blocks (Figure 8-7). Four beams (about 4-inch), cut long enough to reach the full depth of the stage, are placed against the ceiling and secured to the front and rear walls. One beam extends back from a point above the center of the proscenium opening, two others from points about halfway between that and the sidewalls, and the fourth from a point near the right or left sidewall of the stage. Standard steel underhang blocks with 4-inch sheaves are clamped and bolted to the lower flanges of the I beams in the same general arrangement of parallel "sets" as that employed in the layout of a regular grid. Single blocks are attached to the three beams in the center, and triple blocks to the beam at the side.

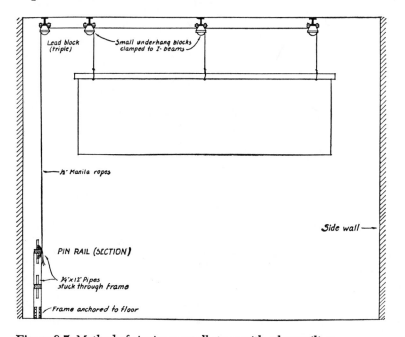

Figure 8-7 Method of rigging a small stage with a low ceiling.

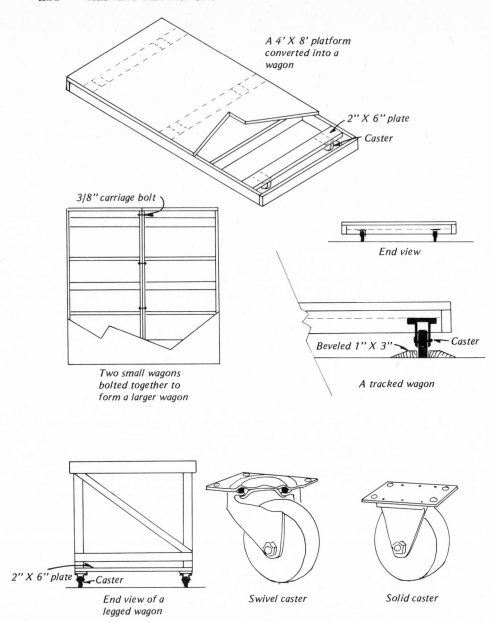

Figure 8-8 Platform converted into a wagon.

A modified pinrail may be constructed by sticking 12-inch lengths of ¾-inch pipe through a 2×4-inch wooden framing anchored securely to the floor. This framing should, of course, be placed directly under the beam carrying the triple blocks.

The lines should be ½-inch Manila ropes. Cotton rope can be trusted only for the lightest of loads.

Rolling Scenery

The use of wheels has become standard practice for shifting dimensional scenic units on the stage floor. Built into wagons, revolving stages, jackknife stages, or shuttle stages, casters have proved invaluable for shifting large sets both quickly and quietly. There are two types of casters that are ordinarily used for moving large units: the swivel caster, for use on units that must move in several directions; and the solid or fixed caster, for use on units that move in a straight line or in a fixed arc. The most suitable casters for stage use are ball-bearing, rubber-tired casters with wheels of at least 3½ inches in diameter. The caster should have a flat plate top with holes in it through which screws or bolts may be inserted. Although the swivel caster is more flexible (being able to move in any direction), it does not run as quietly as does the solid caster.

Some of the major devices by which scenery may be moved by casters are discussed below.

a The wagon: Usually a small unit, the wagon may be easily made by the conversion of a regular 4 × 8-foot platform. The casters are attached to the underside of the platform on wooden plates attached underneath the platform top. The wagon may be equipped with either swivel casters or solid casters, depending on its intended use. When using swivel casters, one must make certain that the caster, when it swivels, will clear the frame of the wagon. Figure 8.8 shows a regular platform converted into a wagon.

b The revolving stage: The revolving stage is a large turntable that revolves to expose sets of scenery placed on various sections of the circle. Some revolving stages have a diameter equal to the width of the proscenium opening. Some revolving stage systems are composed of two or three smaller circles set side by side.

The revolving stage makes use of a fixed pivot point at its center, around which the casters revolve. Revolving stages function best with solid casters that have their axles lined up perpendicular to the pivot point. Placement patterns and construction of some simple revolving stages are shown in Figure 8.9.

c The jackknife stage: This large wagon has a pivot point at one corner instead of in the center as is the case of the revolving stage. It is equipped with solid casters with their axles lined up perpendicular to the pivot point.

To place the jackknife stage on stage, the pivot-point socket is attached to the stage floor as far downstage as possible and slightly offstage, and the pivot point on the wagon is inserted into the socket. If the casters have been lined up correctly, the jack-

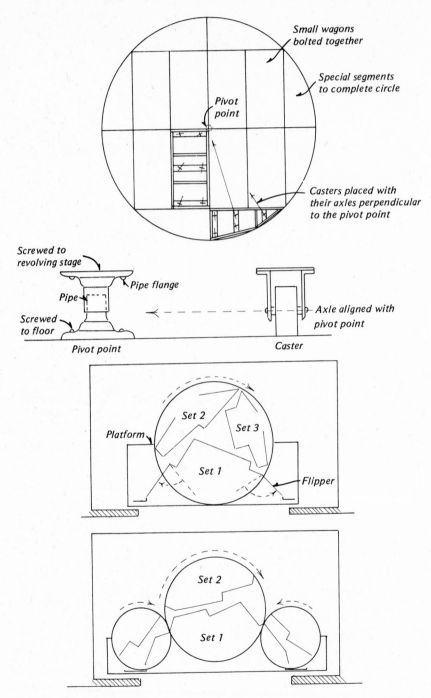

Figure 8-9 Revolving stage. The illustration shows the system of one large revolving stage and the system of three smaller stages.

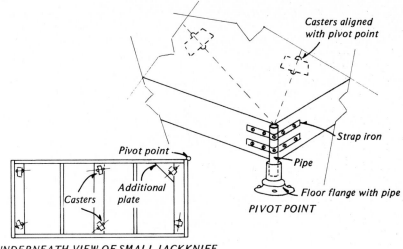

Casters aligned with pivot point

Strap iron

Pipe

Floor flange with pipe

PIVOT POINT

Pivot point

Casters

Additional plate

UNDERNEATH VIEW OF SMALL JACKKNIFE

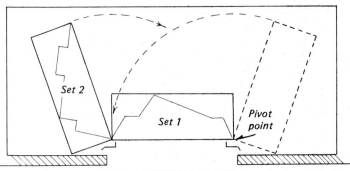

Set 2

Set 1

Pivot point

THE JACKKNIFE STAGE

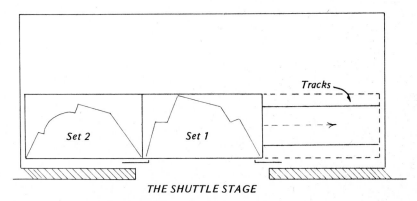

Tracks

Set 2

Set 1

THE SHUTTLE STAGE

Figure 8-10 Jackknife stage and shuttle stage.

218

Figure 8-11 Three settings with interesting uses of materials:
(*Left, above*): *Billy Budd*, designed by Millard MacDonald.
(*Left, below*): *Finian's Rainbow*, designed by Lee Simonson.
(*Above*): *Marat-Sade*, designed by John Sneden, and reproduced
with his permission.

knife stage should roll from an offstage position to an onstage
position in much the same way as a blade in a jackknife swings
open and closes.

If a theatre is equipped with two jackknife stages, one in each
wing, a complete set of scenery may be shifted on one in the wings
while a scene is being played on the other one in the onstage
position. The principle of the jackknife system is shown in Figure
8-10.

d   The shuttle stage: Usually requiring more wing space than
a jackknife stage, the shuttle stages move in a straight line on- and
offstage, which means that the wing space on either side must be
practically equal to the width of the proscenium opening. These
rolling stages make use of solid casters running in, or guided by,
a track to ensure their running in a straight line. The tracks are
either set into the stage floor or mounted on top of it. With two
of these stages, one set may be changed in the wings while another
scene is being played on the other shuttle stage in its onstage
position.

This wagon principle can be used in moving several small sets in a multiset show. Small wagons may be castered, set on tracks, and used practically anywhere onstage to shift small sets or single, heavy scenic units. Arrangements of, and equipment necessary for, shuttle stages are illustrated in Figure 8-11.

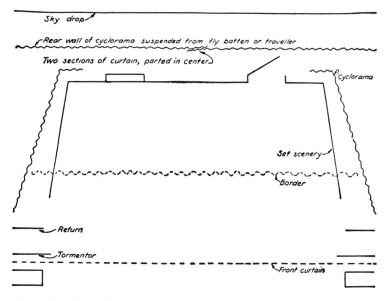

Figure 9-1 Stage layout for minimum scenery.

MINIMUM SCENERY

CHAPTER 9

1 INTRODUCTION

The scenic forms described in the preceding sections of this book are standard. In all essential features they are identical with the forms employed on the stages of New York. They have been planned to meet the requirements of general economy in construction and handling under normal conditions, but they do not take into consideration the abnormal or emergency conditions present in so many of our smaller school and community theatres.

223

"It is all very well," the instructor in stagecraft is reminded, "to talk of standard forms where one has the use of a properly equipped stage and has several hundred dollars to spend on a setting. But what does one do when his resources are limited to a simple platform stage and a budget of, say, twenty-five dollars for a setting? Must he forego all the pleasure of producing plays just because he cannot afford to mount them 'regularly'?" The answer is, obviously, "No." In the following sections are some general hints for designers and technicians forced to work under substandard conditions.

2   THE CYCLORAMA BACKGROUND

A program of special economy in stage settings necessarily involves some form of initial investment. The money saver recommended for purchase or construction by the artist–technician who is required to provide a quantity of scenic environments on a frail allowance is a black cyclorama. Hung around and behind the acting area on the stage, the cyclorama is employed as a neutral background for small screens and other low-cut scenic forms placed in front of it. It is surprising what attractive, dramatically effective, and at the same time inexpensive settings can be produced with this combination of black curtains and painted set pieces—if a person of ingenuity and taste handles the assemblage.

The material out of which the cyclorama indicated is made should be strong—it must stand up under much hard usage. The fabric should be close woven, because the cyclorama must mask efficiently from the view of the audience all still and moving objects offstage. It should also have a rough or woolly surface. Fabrics with smooth surfaces tend to look shiny, and shine is one thing this cyclorama should not do. Cotton velour, with its heavy body and deep nap, is ideal. Duvetyn is more commonly used. It lacks the weight of velour; but it has a good surface and costs about half as much as the other material. Rep is considerably stronger than duvetyn, but it does not absorb light as well, and its price is higher. Where both service and cost must be considered together, good-grade duvetyn is probably the most generally satisfactory cyclorama material obtainable.

The method of constructing and hanging stage draperies is described in Chapter 3, Section 7. In the arrangement suggested here, the sidewalls only are tied to the U-shaped cyclorama frame. For sight-line purposes, the walls are raked outward downstage while the upper corners are turned in and fastened to the transverse batten of the U frame. The frame itself is suspended on two sets of lines (run over stout pulleys securely fastened in the stage ceiling if there is no gridiron).

The two sections comprising the back wall of the cyclorama are hung independently from a fly batten or, better still, from a traveler. Rigged this way, the sections may be lifted as a unit into the flies, or parted right and left, to permit the ready passage of flats and furniture during scene changes. If a sky drop is included in the permanent stage equipment, the rear curtains are planned so that they may open up to a view of the drop.

The question will be asked: Why the choice of black for the cyclorama? The answer is that black is neutral. A black curtain with a soft woolly surface provides the least conspicuous, and therefore the most effective background for other objects on the stage. Black absorbs light. A black cyclorama serves equally well for night and daylight scenes. Brown, blue, cream, and gray draperies reflect light. Their use as background is therefore limited.

Because the cyclorama of black velour, duvetyn, or rep is such an efficient light-absorber, it possesses personally no radiant environmental quality. It should, therefore, never be used alone (except for occasional purely spatial scenes). Black, unrelieved by color, is depressing; an unvaried view of it soon grows tiresome to the spectator. The *feeling* of a cyclorama setting is imparted by the decorative and dramatic shapes placed in front of the cyclorama. Black curtains on the stage should be regarded purely as

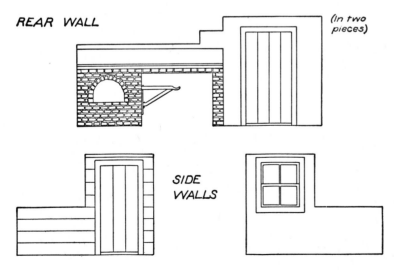

Figure 9-2 Elevations for a set of minimum scenery.

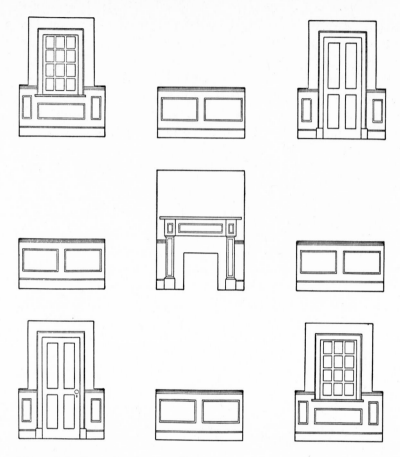

Figure 9-3 General utility set of minimum scenery, designed by Robert Proctor.

contrivances for masking from the audience the sides and top of the stage, and for providing a neutral or spatial background for the scenery proper.

3 THE SCENERY

The minimum type of setting used in front of the cyclorama should be at the same time decorative, dramatically effective, and very simple. The character of its design will be intense and compact; each detail in it—because there are so few details—has to carry a triple load of responsibility for promoting the clarity, beauty, and expressiveness of the whole. Consequently, the composition of suggestive, minimum scenery has to be considered with extraordinary care.

Generally, the most practical approach to the design of this kind of setting is through selection. The artist, viewing on paper or in his mind's eye a full set of ideal scenery, determines what are the most interesting and eloquent features in it and centers his attention on these. Then he proceeds to cut down his original picture by reducing or eliminating the less valuable elements. The cutting begins with the upper, overhead parts of the set. Because the rear plane of the set, however, is naturally, by virtue of its position, more impressive than the sides, he will probably retain in his final design more of this rear part and less of the sides. The area of the back plane may be measurable not only by greater width but also by greater height. Because such architectural forms as doors, windows, and fireplaces tend to capture the audience's eye ahead of flat walls, the artist will let the former dominate the set and draw in just enough of the wall portions, perhaps, to unite the stronger elements and complete the character of the room.

Every detail in the suggestive, cut-down setting is prominent. For this reason the designer must give careful attention not only to scenic elements but also to furniture and other decorative and expressive forms used with them. Even the slightest lack of harmony between properties and scenery will destroy the sense of unity. The forms of the larger furniture pieces especially must be viewed from the standpoint of their effect upon the line and mass composition of the scenery, and the shapes of the two groups of elements—furniture and scenery—must be worked out so that they will complement each other. In the setting for *Stumbling in Dreams* (Figure 9-5), for instance, the piano on stage right is naturally the most prominent object in the room. Because it is used repeatedly through the play, its presence is accentuated by spotlighting. The

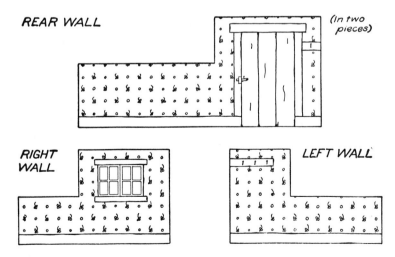

Figure 9-4 Scenery for a small cottage, designed by Wilbur Dorsett.

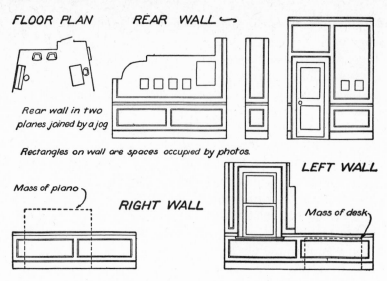

FLOOR PLAN   REAR WALL

Rear wall in two
planes joined by a jog

Rectangles on wall are spaces occupied by photos.

Mass of piano

RIGHT WALL

LEFT WALL

Mass of desk

Figure 9-5 Scenery for a studio room, designed by Samuel Selden.

mass of the low desk on the opposite side of the room is insufficient to balance the form of the piano, so the wall behind the piano is reduced to a minimum and the main weight of the scenery is thrown to the other side.

Color may, and should, be used freely in the cut-down set. Because the overall space occupied by this type of scenery is relatively small in comparison with the expanse of black behind it, all the design elements may be exaggerated somewhat to good effect. This means that all the forms in a suggestive setting—walls, woodwork, furniture, and even costumes—may be a little more highly colored than equivalent forms in a regular realistic setting.

The construction of the scenery discussed in this section follows, more or less, the regular methods outlined in Chapter 5. Light wooden frames are put together with corner blocks and keystones, and then covered with cloth. Because strength in these smaller forms is not of prime importance, a considerable saving in cost can be effected by the use of materials unsuitable for regular scenery. Instead of white pine in 1×3-inch strips, the carpenter can use a cheaper wood (such as common yellow pine) in 1×2-inch strips; and instead of scene linen or duck, he can use a cheap grade of unbleached muslin.

4 LIGHTING MINIMUM SCENERY

If good lighting is necessary for complete scenic forms, it is doubly necessary for reduced forms. To obtain any degree of expressive-

Figure 9-6 Set of minimum scenery used at The University of North Carolina at Chapel Hill.

ness at all out of his settings, the designer of minimum scenery must lean heavily upon an efficient electrical department. It is obvious that the essential qualities of a suggestive setting will reveal themselves rather timidly unless the atmosphere surrounding them is also suggestive. *Suggestive* lighting means *selective* lighting—adequately produced and flexibly controlled. Some stage electrical equipment is absolutely essential—however pinched the designer's budget may be. In fact, the smaller the general budget, the more important it is for the designer to think of that equipment. If he has only $150 with which to rig his stage and prepare his first set of scenery, let him plan to spend at least half of those precious dollars on the lighting.

5 CONCLUSION

Minimum scenery is better than no scenery. Minimum scenery is not better, however, than complete scenery. The half forms described in this chapter represent (except in those plays where many shifts require a strict limitation in each scene) a rather severe compromise not only in size, but also in spirit, with the larger, more completely expressive forms. The artist who is forced to work for the time being under substandard conditions should guard against the temptation to avoid struggle by accepting those conditions as permanent. If he is worth anything as a theatre artist he will strive to improve his production machine until he is able to produce the type of settings he really wants to create. Let him remember constantly the eight requirements of effective scenery discussed in the first chapter of this book and make it his purpose eventually to meet those requirements.

Figure 10-1 Furniture for a production of *Anastasia*.

STAGE PROPERTIES

CHAPTER 10

1 INTRODUCTION

In addition to planning all the scenic units and their shifting patterns, the designer plans the many stage properties needed for a production.

Stage properties are usually of three types: hand properties—small objects handled by the actors (glasses, canes, and lanterns, for example), dress properties—objects used to decorate the set

233

(such as furniture, pictures, and draperies), and set pieces—objects other than furniture on which the actor may stand or sit (tree stumps, rocks, and so on).

In some cases, a person other than the scene designer is assigned the duty of either collecting or constructing the properties for a production. In such a case, however, the work must be done under close consultation with or supervision by the scene designer to ensure that the properties will be compatible with the overall design of the production.

The importance of giving meticulous thought to the properties of a production cannot be overemphasized. They should be planned and executed carefully so that they will contribute to the environment of a production rather than distract from it. Their consideration must not be left until the last hectic moments of the rehearsal period. In fact, they should be finished soon enough so that the actors will have had the opportunity to rehearse with them and get used to them well before performance time.

2 FUNCTIONS OF STAGE PROPERTIES

Stage properties share with the scenery many of the same functions.

a Placing the action: In much the same way as scenery, properties play an important part in describing the locale of the action of a play. The furniture of a set quickly describes the set as representing a living room or a dining room, for example. They also help to describe the historical period and nation in which the action occurs. This latter function often requires a great deal of research on the part of the designer or the property master to ensure that the properties are of the type proper to a particular period or national origin.

b Reinforcing the action: By reflecting a character's personality, financial status, profession, and so on, properties may do a great deal to reinforce the action of a play. Properties may add depth to an actor's performance by supplementing his interpretation. A particular type of umbrella, for example, may reveal a great deal about the person carrying it. The type and condition of the furniture in a setting may indicate the general attitudes of the characters inhabiting the room.

In fulfilling the function of reinforcing the action, properties assume a character of their own. For this reason, they must be chosen carefully to fit properly into the overall scheme of any production.

c Dressing the action: Properties contribute a great deal to dressing the action of a production. Used as color accents, character indications, or to fulfill some functional requirement, properties possess a great deal of attention value because they are more intimately connected to the actor than are the larger scenic units. This attention value must be carefully controlled if a property is to be successful. For example, a too-elaborate property might very well distract from the action by calling too much attention to itself. On the other hand, a too-plain property might seem out of place and thereby become distracting. The designer's responsibility is to place the property in the correct scale of attention so that it fits smoothly into the action, dresses the action, but does not distract from it.

With the growing tendency toward the use of minimal scenery on thrust stages and arena stages, properties assume an even greater role in setting the scene. Since the audience is usually so close to the playing area and solid scenery cannot be used to set the scene, properties receive a greater degree of attention from the audience. Since the property will receive a much closer scrutiny on a thrust or arena stage than it would on a proscenium stage, the designer must consider it carefully down to its smallest detail if it is to be successful. This does not mean that properties for the proscenium stage need not be done with care. They, however, do not require the same minute detail and finish as do properties for the thrust and arena stages.

3 THE LARGE PROPERTIES

a Furniture: By far the best method of obtaining furniture is to purchase it and keep it in storage for future use. By alternating pieces of furniture from stock, by remodeling, refinishing, and reupholstering various pieces, the designer can provide suitable furniture for a wide variety of productions over a long period of time.

Even though plays, so often, require period furniture, it is not necessary to keep a large supply of authentic antiques on hand. In fact, antiques are usually too fragile and distinctive to be of use over a long period. By searching through secondhand stores, the designer will find many inexpensive reproductions of period furniture that are quite usable and attractive. By keen observation of typical period details, he will find furniture that can be altered to resemble authentic period pieces. For example, a 1930's oak dining-room chair with cabriole legs can be made to resemble a quite respectable, mahogany, eighteenth-century occasional chair.

Figure 10-2

Examples of furniture that can be easily made in the scene shop. The fern stand and the Chinese table are made of ¾-inch plywood. The long bench is made of 1×12-inch white pine.

The designer should acquaint himself thoroughly with basic details of various periods of furniture so that he is able to recognize details, in a reproduction, that could be emphasized to suggest an authentic antique. It is not necessary to adhere slavishly to every minute detail of a certain period to suggest that period on the stage.

All the furniture in Figure 10-1 was purchased inexpensively from secondhand stores and remodeled, refinished, and reupholstered to suggest the European environment necessary for the play *Anastasia*.

While it is difficult to build elaborate pieces of furniture in most scene shops, there are many pieces of furniture that can be easily built. If a piece of furniture is based on flat planes with, for example, its few decorative details being scroll work cut with a saw, the piece can usually be built quickly and easily out of ¾-inch plywood or 1 × 12-inch white pine

Many groups, because of lack of storage space or limited budget, find it necessary to borrow furniture for their productions. If this is the case, a few simple procedures should be followed:

1   One person should be responsible for seeing all the people from whom the group may wish to borrow items. This same person should collect all the items and return them.

2   Before accepting the loan of an item, the property master should get a statement of the item's value from the owner.

3   All defects of an item should be noted before it is removed from the owner's premises.

4   Arrangements should be made as to whether the owner wishes program credit or not.

5   No alterations should be made to an item without the owner's permission.

6   Once the item is on stage, it should be protected during shifts, and covered and safely stored after performances.

7   The item should be returned promptly to the owner as soon as it is no longer needed.

8   If the item has been damaged in any way, it should be repaired by someone of the owner's choice with the producing group's paying the bill.

If the above procedures are followed, much misunderstanding, ill will, and expense may be avoided. If a group hopes to be able to consistently borrow properties in a community, that group must establish the reputation of taking businesslike responsibility for the items it borrows.

b   Set pieces: Properties such as rocks and tree stumps must usually be constructed in the scene shop. They are made by the covering of a wooden structure, first, with chicken wire or pearl screening and, second, with canvas that has been dipped into dope. Old painted canvas torn into pieces is excellent for producing a hard, durable surface.

4   SMALL PROPERTIES

a   Dress properties: The many small properties that are used in a decorative manner are varied and extremely important in the creation of an interesting environment for a play. Many of these properties may be borrowed, but, again, the designer may find it simpler in the long run to develop facilities for constructing them. Picture frames made from corrugated cardboard, false book spines cut from Upson board or molded from plastic, and candlesticks made from old balustrade spindles are but a few examples of small, but often important objects that can easily be constructed.

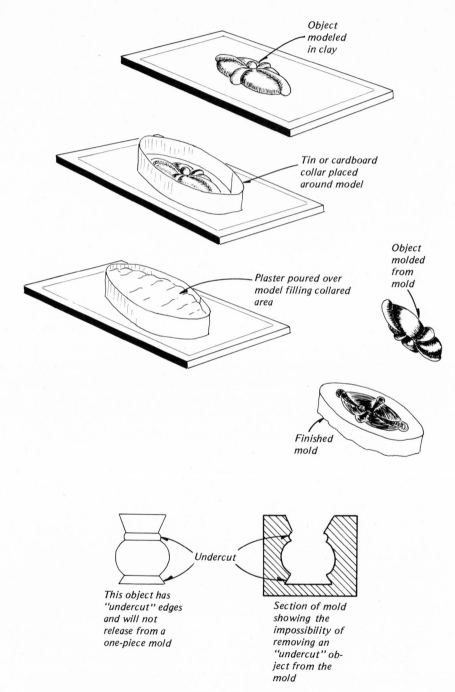

Object modeled in clay

Tin or cardboard collar placed around model

Plaster poured over model filling collared area

Object molded from mold

Finished mold

Undercut

This object has "undercut" edges and will not release from a one-piece mold

Section of mold showing the impossibility of removing an "undercut" object from the mold

Figure 10-3 Process of making a plaster mold.

b Hand properties: Many hand properties must be borrowed or purchased. Most groups, however, attempt to build up a supply of such standard items as dishes, fans, canes, bottles, and so on, to simplify the process of supplying numerous hand properties for many different productions. Special hand properties may be made from standard objects. For example, a teacup that must be broken on stage should be broken beforehand and lightly glued back together. Binoculars may be made by taping two soda-pop bottles together with black plastic tape. Parchment for the inevitable scrolls and letters of period plays can be simulated by white butcher paper coated with orange shellac.

5 MATERIALS FOR PROPERTY CONSTRUCTION

There are many materials available that lend themselves well to property construction. Following is a list of fairly standard materials and suggestions for their use.

a Plaster of Paris: Small objects may be modeled with plaster of Paris, but its weight and fragility do not make it useful for large objects. Its greatest use is for making negative molds from which several copies of an object may be produced. The process for making a plaster mold is as follows. The object to be reproduced is first modeled in clay, partially dried, and coated with some kind of lubricant or parting agent. A collar of light tin or heavy cardboard, wider than the model is deep, is placed in a circle or oval around the model. The collar will contain the plaster and prevent it from running off the model. It also makes it possible to produce a mold that is thick enough to withstand handling. Plaster, mixed with water according to the manufacturer's directions, is poured over the clay model, which should be completely covered with the plaster up to the top edge of the collar. It is a good idea to tap the plaster lightly several times while it is still wet to release any air bubbles it may contain. After the plaster is dry, the collar is removed, the mold turned over, and the clay model removed. The mold now presents a negative impression of the object. One may make several copies of the object by coating the impression with a lubricant and then pressing papier-mâché or Celastic into the impression. When the mâché or Celastic is dry, the positive reproduction of the object may be removed from the mold.

One caution must be observed in the making of the clay model. The model must not have "under-cut" edges or the reproduced object will not come out of the mold when finished. If it is necessary for an object to have "under-cut" edges, a mold of more than one piece must be made. Figure 10-3 shows the various steps involved in making molds.

b Papier-mâché: Papier-mâché is made by the boiling of pieces of soft paper, such as newsprint, in a solution of glue or wheat paste and water. The resulting substance may be used to build up objects on wire armatures or to produce objects from molds. In some cases, instead of boiling the paper and glue, one would glue small strips of paper directly to wire armatures to produce certain objects. This same technique may be used directly over a clay model. The model should be coated with a lubricant before the strips are applied. In the case of a round object—such as the head for a puppet—the dried papier-mâché must be cut off of the model. The two halves of the mâché object may be glued together with additional strips of paper concealing the seams. One can employ the same method, to reproduce objects, using the actual object as the model. For example, to produce a copy of a bottle the craftsman would cover the bottle with aluminum foil and then cover the foil with mâché. The foil prevents the mâché from sticking to the surface of the bottle. When the mâché is dry, the paper shell is cut away from the bottle and the two halves reassembled with glue and paper.

There is a commercially produced "instant papier-mâché," called Celluclay, which is useful for making small objects. Mixed with water according to the manufacturer's instructions, it simplifies considerably the reproduction of objects from molds.

c Celastic: This impregnated fabric is excellent for building strong, lightweight properties. It can be used in all the processes in which papier-mâché is used, while offering much more strength, durability, and water resistance than does mâché. It must be ordered from the manufacturer along with its special solvent and parting agent. The process for its use is simple. A piece of dry Celastic is dipped into the solvent, and, when the piece is completely saturated, it is used to cover wire armatures or to make objects from molds. The mold must be coated with parting agent to prevent the Celastic's sticking to it. Celastic dries rapidly, so it is necessary to work rather quickly with it. Since the solvent is highly inflammable, it must be kept away from an open flame or intense heat.

d Fiber glass: Employed in much the same way as Celastic, fiber glass produces durable, weather-resistant objects. The process involves placing a piece of dry fiber glass over an armature or into a mold that has been coated with a parting agent. The fiber glass is then saturated with a special solvent and hardener. The propor-

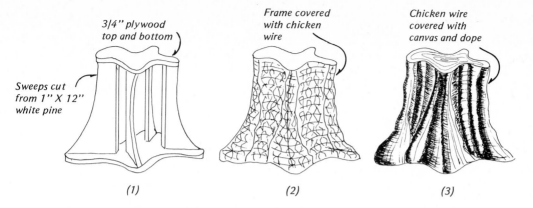

Figure 10-4 Process of making a tree stump.

tion of hardener to solvent determines the hardness of the finished object. The manufacturer's instructions should be followed closely when one is working with fiber glass.

e Canvas and dope: Useful for making large objects such as dimensional rocks, stumps, and so on, these materials are inexpensive, strong, and simple to use. Scraps of old, painted canvas are excellent for this purpose. The scrap of canvas is dipped into the dope and placed over chicken-wire or pearl-screening armatures. To make sure that the doped canvas will hold tightly to a chicken-wire armature, one should push the corners of the canvas through the holes in the chicken wire and press these corners to the back of the piece of canvas, to which the dope will hold them.

f Wool felt: Since felt is not woven but is composed of wool fibers that have been pressed together, it lends itself well to taking various shapes. Since it is expensive, its use should be limited to small objects such as jewelry, armor, and so on. It may be molded over a positive mold or in a negative one. To mold an object from felt, one first covers the mold with aluminum foil and then cuts a piece of felt slightly larger in diameter than the mold. The felt is dipped in glue and lightly squeezed out. It is then stretched and shaped over the contours of the mold until they are completely covered in smooth, sharp relief. Occasionally dipping the fingers in water makes the work easier, but caution must be observed not to keep the felt too wet or it will not mold easily.

6 PAINTING THE PROPERTIES

As a rule, it is desirable for properties to be painted with a water-proof paint. Even the small amount of perspiration on an actor's hands will cause regular scene paint to loosen and rub off. There are several types of paint that offer a suitable finish for property painting.

a Shellac: Shellac, which is available in either white or orange, is an excellent binder when mixed with dry pigment. Paint mixed from dry pigment and shellac produces a hard, rather shiny, waterproof surface. White shellac is most useful because it changes the color of the pigment less than does orange shellac.

Shellac may be used in two ways in combination with scene paint. The shellac may be mixed directly with dry pigment to produce paint, or a thin coat of shellac may be painted over an object that has been painted and textured with regular scene paint.

Shellac does darken the pigment considerably, and the paint does not dry any lighter than it is when wet. It is wise, therefore, to experiment with a small amount of pigment and shellac before attempting to mix a large quantity of paint. In this way, the painter will be assured of producing the color he needs.

If an object is too shiny after being painted with shellac, a light buffing with fine steel wool will eliminate the sheen. If the paint is too thick when mixed, it may be thinned with alcohol. Brushes should be cleaned immediately with alcohol and washed with soap and water.

b Enamel: There is a wide range of enamel paint on the market in a great variety of colors. It may be purchased in cans and applied with a brush or in aerosol cans from which the paint is sprayed. It is available in gloss, semigloss, and flat finishes. If a gloss enamel is used, the finish might reflect too much light. If this is the case, a light buffing with steel wool will reduce the sheen. Brushes used with enamel should be cleaned immediately with turpentine and washed with soap and water.

The spray cans of enamel are rather expensive for use on large projects but are excellent for small objects or for texturing large objects. The manufacturer's instructions for shaking the can and for keeping the spray in working order should be followed.

c Latex: Many of the flat, latex-based wall paints are excellent for property painting. While many of them are available in only light tints, several brands produce colors, generally called "accent colors," which are rich enough in hue for many uses on the stage.

White latex paint may be mixed with scene-paint pigment or aniline dye to produce special tints of colors. To mix dry pigment or dye with latex paint, the painter should pour a small amount of the paint into the dry pigment, mix this into a paste until the pigment is saturated with paint, add a little more paint, stir, and continue this process until the desired color is achieved. The paint may be thinned with water. Here, again, it is wise to experiment with a small amount before attempting to mix a great deal.

Brushes used in latex paint should be cleaned immediately with soap and water. Most of these paints become completely waterproof when they dry and will ruin a brush if allowed to dry on it.

d Metallic paints: Many times on the stage, metal must be simulated from materials such as wood, Celastic, and felt. The success of the simulation usually depends on the way the surface is painted. There are many metallic paints in powder form, premixed in cans or in aerosol cans. The metallic paints that are available in aerosol cans have proved to be the most valuable for painting properties. The aerosol can keeps the metallic powder in solution, the binder does not tarnish the metallic powder, and it is possible to get an even, smooth coat of paint with the spraying action. Also, these paints are available in a wide range of metallic colors from copper to light gold and silver.

There are a few simple techniques that are helpful in the production of a reasonably metallic-looking surface on a nonmetallic surface. Before applying metallic paint to any absorptive surface such as wood, Celastic, and felt, the painter must seal the surface so that it will not absorb the metallic powder on which the paint is based. If the surface does absorb the metallic powder, a dull, unconvincing finish will result. To seal a surface, the painter may coat it with shellac, glue size, or one of the white polymer glues. Particularly absorptive surfaces may require two or three coats before becoming completely sealed.

Another technique that aids in producing a metallic appearance on an object is to use several different metallic colors on one object to create an impression of depth. An object that is painted with only one color will usually appear flat and merely painted. The use of a variety of textures is also helpful. To produce an effective gold object, for example, the painter first seals the surface; second, he sprays the surface with silver paint; third, he stipples the surface with perhaps brown or green; and, fourth, he sprays the edges and depressions with a dark gold paint to tone the object. The complete object may be lightly buffed with a soft cloth to heighten the metallic gleam or, if necessary, lightly rubbed with steel wool to reduce excess sheen.

7   SPECIFIC PROPERTIES

No attempt will be made to discuss all the specific problems a property master may encounter in producing the properties for a pro-

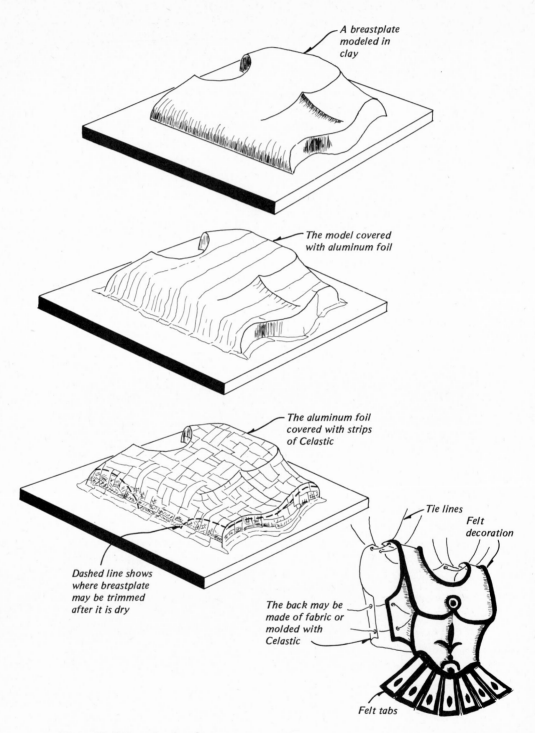

A breastplate
modeled in
clay

The model covered
with aluminum foil

The aluminum foil
covered with strips
of Celastic

Dashed line shows
where breastplate
may be trimmed
after it is dry

Tie lines

Felt
decoration

The back may be
made of fabric or
molded with
Celastic

Felt tabs

Figure 10-5 Process of making armor.

duction, but the discussion of several constructive techniques of some standard properties may prove helpful. These techniques are standard enough to allow their application to many different construction problems.

a Armor: Armor may be made quite easily from either Celastic, fiber glass, or felt. The procedure for producing a piece of armor is simple but time-consuming. The property master first sculpts a life-sized model of the piece of armor in clay. This model should be made carefully to the measurements of the actor who is to wear the armor. A pair of calipers may be necessary to transfer the measurements from the actor's body to the clay model. After the model is finished, it should dry slightly and be covered with aluminum foil, carefully following all the contours of the model. After the foil is in place, the model is covered with the chosen material, which has been made according to the process for that material described in Section 5 of this chapter.

In the case of highly decorated armor, the decoration may be

Figure 10-6

Masks. Masks are made over a clay model in the same way as is armor. The Oriental masks in the photo are made of Celastic. The bird masks are made of papier-mâché.

Figure 10-7

Weapons. The shields are made from Upson board. The small shields are decorated with lash line and upholstering tacks. The halberd is made from Upson board covered with polymer glue. The heads of the spears are sheet tin, the barrels of the pistols are thin-wall conduit, and the stocks are ¾-inch plywood. The broad swords were carved from 1×3-inch white pine and have plywood hilts wrapped with Celastic.

included in the clay model or applied on top of the piece of armor after it is dry. Usually it is simpler to make a "blank" model and to apply the decoration later. This saves considerable time in sculpting the clay model. Texture may be achieved if the decoration is done with a material different from the one used to make the piece of armor. For example, a "blank" Celastic or fiber-glass breastplate may be easily and effectively decorated with felt dipped into glue. The "blank" piece of armor should be fitted on the actor before it is decorated and painted so that adjustments of fit can be made. The decoration and paint may be used to conceal any cutting or piecing that may have been done to acquire a good fit.

Helmets are made in the same way, but they usually require a crown cut from an old felt hat sewn inside the helmet to help keep the helmet on the actor's head.

Masks can be made in the same way, although papier mâché can be used instead of one of the heavier materials. Measurements are particularly important in mask making. The eyeholes in the mask must be placed so that the actor can see, and the bridge of the nose in the mask must be made for the actor's breathing and vocal projection.

Any of the properties worn by actors can be made more comfortable if small pieces of foam rubber are glued to areas of the property that might rub against the actor's body.

b Weapons: The problem of supplying the spears, halberds, swords, shields, and so on, for a production are so varied and complex that the property master finds that he must approach his work with a great deal of ingenuity and ability. Figure 10-7 shows some specific solutions to the production of weapons for the stage.

Figure 10-8 Statues for *Look Homeward Angel*. The large statue uses a department-store manikin as its foundation.

Figure 10-9

Examples of lighting fixtures made from ¾-inch plywood. The small chandelier on the left uses gelatin molds as candle cups and dowel pins as candles. The large chandelier in the center is decorated with prisms cut from a plastic cake box. The chandelier on the right uses inexpensive plastic shades painted with dye.

The principles behind these solutions are varied enough to be applicable to a wide range of problems.

c *Statues:* The problem of producing a large statue of the human figure is easily solved by the use of an old department-store window manikin as the armature for the statue. Most stores have discarded manikins which can be easily obtained. The greatest advantage offered by the manikin is that the proportions of the human body, which are difficult to sculpt and reproduce, are already delineated, as well as a solid structural foundation on which to build.

Various alterations on the manikin may be necessary to produce the desired statue. Arms, hands, legs may be arranged in any attitude. A new head may modeled in clay, reproduced in Celastic or mâché and attached to the body. Body proportions may be changed by the addition of mâché to the body areas to be altered. The statue may be clothed in canvas soaked in dope. The wet canvas is draped and placed in folds over the manikin to achieve the desired style of dress. Sometimes even old clothes or costumes may be used to clothe a statue. A man's old suit, for example, can be soaked in dope and used to dress the statue.

In Figure 10-8, the large statue was constructed with a manikin as the armature. Her arms were arranged by being cut into pieces and then glued into the desired positions. Her dress is made of canvas soaked in dope and arranged in drapes. The wings are made of pieces of corrugated cardboard covered with Celastic feather shapes. Her hair is Celastic and her girdle is a piece of sash line. The base is ¾-inch plywood painted with enamel to simulate marble. Since so many different materials were used, it was necessary to give the complete statue two coats of shellac to seal all surfaces before the final painting and texturing were done.

The small statue in the same picture was made with Celastic and cardboard over a wire armature. The urn is an inexpensive bisque urn decorated with papier-mâché garlands, painted, and spattered.

d Lighting fixtures: Finding real chandeliers, candelabra, or wall sconces to borrow or purchase for use on a setting is usually such a problem that the property master may find it easier to construct his own. These fixtures may be made from strap iron bent to the desired contours or cut from ¾-inch plywood and painted to simulate metal. The use of inexpensive shades painted with dyes, dowel pins for candles, and cut lucite for prisms adds detail for a convincing appearance. These properties may be wired and equipped with candle lamps to further their impression.

8 A SUMMARY

Since producing properties for the stage involves so many different materials and processes, we have attempted in this chapter to present only a few standard materials and procedures that can be applied to specific problems the property master may encounter. In much the same way as scene painting, property construction demands a great deal of ingenuity and experimentation. The property master should, however, possess a general knowledge of period details, have a keen eye constantly on the lookout for the possibilities of altering one object into another one, and, above all, have a strong interest in experimenting with new materials and methods.

GLOSSARY

Acting area: That portion of the stage enclosed by scenery and used by the actors during a performance.

Backing: A flat, a series of flats, a drop, or a tab used to limit the view of the audience through an opening (e.g., a doorway or window) in a set of scenery.

Batten: A length of rigid material, usually wood. Three examples of battens are the 1×3-inch lumber strips used to construct scenery, the strips of wood fastened to the bottom and top of a drop, and the length of wood or pipe on a set of lines, to which scenery is fastened for flying.

Border: An abbreviated drop, used to represent overhead foliage or to mask the flies.

Brace cleat: A small metal plate attached to the frame of a flat. A stage brace is hooked into it to prop up the flat.

Ceiling: A large, horizontal, canvas-covered frame hung on two or three sets of lines, used to close in the top of an interior set.

Ceiling plate: A metal plate with a ring, used in bolting together and flying ceiling frames.

Complementary colors: Colors opposite each other on the color wheel (e.g., purple and yellow). Complementary pigments mixed together produce gray.

Continental parallel: A folding platform unit with removable center bracing units.

Corner block: A piece of ¼-inch plywood, cut in the shape of a triangle and used to reinforce joints in scenery.

Counterweight system: A mechanical system for flying scenery with a counterweight that runs up and down a track at the side of the stage. In contrast to the pinrail system, which is usually operated from the fly floor, the counterweight system is operated from the stage floor.

Curtain line: The line across the stage behind the proscenium that marks the position of the front curtain when it is closed.

Cyclorama: A large drop hung from a U-shaped batten suspended by sets of lines from the gridiron. The cyclorama is generally used to represent the sky.

Door-frame unit: A solid-wood door frame made to fit into an opening in a flat.

Dope: A mixture of glue and whiting with which canvas may be glued to flat frames and with which various objects (e.g., tree stumps) may be covered with canvas.

Downstage: Any position on the stage near the footlights.

Draw curtain: A type of curtain suspended from sliding or rolling carriers running in a track overhead. The curtain is opened by being drawn to the sides.

Drop: A large sheet of canvas, fastened to a batten at top and bottom and hung on a set of lines from the gridiron. It may be used to represent the sky or painted to represent a certain locale.

Dutchman: A strip of canvas doped over the crack and the hinges of a two-fold, or applied to any scenic unit to mask cracks or hardware.

Elevation: A scaled drawing in which an object is pictured as being flattened out with no consideration of depth or thickness.

Fireplace unit: A fireplace frame made to fit into a flat.

Flat: A unit section of flat scenery. A screen made of a wood frame covered with canvas.

Flies: The space above the stage occupied by sets of lines and hanging scenery.

Floor plan: A scaled drawing in which the viewpoint is directly overhead looking down. A floor plan of a set shows the lines that the set would make on the stage floor.

Fly: To lift scenery up above the level of the stage floor (usually out of view of the audience) by means of lines run from the gridiron.

Fly floor: A narrow gallery extending along the sidewall of the stage some distance above the stage floor. The lines used in flying scenery are operated from the fly floor.

Flyman: A man employed to fly scenery.

Foot iron: A piece of hardware used to secure scenery to the floor with a stage screw.

Gridiron or grid: The framework of steel beams above the stage, which supports the rigging employed in flying scenery.

Ground cloth: A large piece of waterproof duck canvas frequently used to cover the stage floor.

Groundrow: A low, flat profile of ground foliage, a bank of earth, or the like, designed to stand up independently on the stage. Generally used to mask the bottom of a drop.

Hanging iron: A piece of hardware attached to the frame of a hanging flat, or other unit, for flying purposes. It has a ring at one end into which the line from the gridiron is tied.

Head block: Three or more sheaves framed together and attached to the gridiron directly above the onstage edge of the fly floor. The lines from the three or more single loft blocks come together at the head block and pass on down together to the pinrail.

Isometric projection: A somewhat distorted-looking, scaled drawing valuable in showing several planes of an object in true proportions.

Jack: A triangular-shaped brace made of wood, which is hinged to the back of a piece of scenery for support. The end of the jack is fastened to the floor by means of a foot iron and a stage screw.

Jackknife stage: A large wagon equipped with casters and with a pivot point on the downstage, onstage corner. It rolls from wings to an onstage position in much the same way as a blade in a jackknife swings.

Keystone: A piece of ¼-inch plywood cut in the shape of a keystone or rectangle and used to reinforce joints in scenery.

Lash cleat: A small metal hook on the back of a flat over which a lash line is thrown to bind the flat to the edge of another flat.

Lash-line eye: The metal eye near the top of a flat through which a lash line is threaded.

Left stage: Any position on the stage to one's left when facing the audience.

Loft block: A sheave (pulley wheel) in a steel frame bolted to the gridiron, through which one line of a set of lines is threaded to fly scenery. There is one loft block for each line in a set of lines.

Masking: A piece of scenery or drapery used to cut off from view of the audience any part of the stage space that should not be seen by the spectators.

Oblique drawing: A scaled drawing in which a complicated face of an object is presented full-front while the sides of the object are projected up to show them in true proportion.

Offstage: Any position on the stage outside the acting area.

Onstage: Any position on the stage within the acting area.

Picture-frame hook and socket: Small pieces of hardware used to hang a lightweight unit of scenery, or a property, on another unit.

Pinrail: The double rail that holds belaying pins on which fly lines are tied. The pinrail is located along the outer edge of the fly floor.

Plywood: Veneer board in three or more plies. It comes in sheets of various thicknesses and is used in constructing flats, properties, and platforms.

Practical: Practicable—capable of being used by the actor. A door with a swinging shutter, or a window with movable sashes, is "practical."

Primary colors: The primary colors in pigment are commonly considered to be blue green, yellow, and magenta.

Proscenium: The wall that divides the stage from the auditorium. The opening through which the audience views the stage is termed the proscenium arch.

Rail: The cross pieces in the frame of a flat. In a standard flat there is a top rail, a toggle rail (in the center of the frame), and a bottom rail.

Ramp: An inclined platform, sloping up from the level of the floor.

Revolving stage: A large circular wagon with a pivot point at its center. Various settings may be mounted on it, and it is rotated as the various sets are to be exposed to the audience.

Right stage: Any position on the stage to one's right when facing the audience.

Saddle iron: A narrow strip of iron placed across the bottom of a door opening in a flat to strengthen the bottom of the flat.

Scale rule: A calibrated ruler used in drafting to reduce the size of an object in a drawing proportionately.

Section drawing: A scaled drawing that shows a view of an object as if the object has been cut through and the cut edges exposed. There are vertical and horizontal sections.

Set: An arrangement of scenery units that suggests a single locale.

Set of lines: A group of ropes hanging from the gridiron, used to fly scenery. There are commonly three or four lines in a set.

Sheave: A grooved pulley wheel.

Shift: To change scenery and properties from one setting to another.

Size water: A thin solution of glue and water that is mixed with dry pigment to make scenery paint.

Solid caster: A wheel mounted on a solid top plate.

Spot line: A single line specifically rigged from the gridiron to fly a piece of scenery that cannot be handled by the regular lines.

Stage brace: An adjustable brace with a forked iron hook on one end which hooks into a brace cleat. The brace has a foot iron at the other end which is secured to the floor by means of a stage screw.

Stage screw: A large, tapered screw with a handle, used to secure foot irons and stage braces to the stage floor.

Standard parallel: A hinged platform unit that can be folded in one piece.

Stile: The long side pieces in the frame of a flat.

Strap hinge: A hinge with long tapered flaps, used primarily for hanging door shutters in their frames and for locking door- and window-frame units into flats.

Strike: To take apart and remove a set of scenery from the acting area after it has been used.

Swivel caster: A wheel mounted on a ball-bearing top plate. The plate turns the wheel in any direction.

Tab curtain: A curtain that opens to the sides and up, creating a draped effect.

Tab or leg: A narrow sheet of painted canvas or other fabric used chiefly to mask the sides of the stage.

Template: A special type of workbench used in the construction of flats.

Toggle rail or bar: The cross piece in the frame of a flat.

Traveler: A slotted steel track used to hang and operate draw curtains.

Trim: To level off a flied piece of scenery at the right height for use during a performance.

Trip: To elevate the bottom of a drop, or other flied scenery, with an auxiliary set of lines in such a way as to make it occupy a space approximately half its height.

Two-fold: Two flats hinged together to fold inward, face to face.

Upstage: Any position on the stage away from the footlights.

Wagon: A low, rolling platform on which a section of a set may be mounted to facilitate scene shifting.

Window-frame unit: A solid-wood window frame made to fit into an opening in a flat.

Wing: The offstage space to the right or left of the acting area.

BIBLIOGRAPHY

Appia, Adolphe, *Adolphe Appia: A Portfolio of Reproductions* (Zurich, Orell-Fussli, 1929).

Ashworth, Bradford, *Notes on Scene Painting*, Donald Oenslager, ed. (New Haven, Whitlock's, 1952).

Birren, Faber, *Color* (New Hyde Park, N.Y., University Books, 1963).

Boyle, W. P., *Central and Flexible Staging* (Berkeley, University of California Press, 1956).

257

Barton, Lucy, *Historic Costumes for the Stage* (Boston, Walter H. Baker Company, 1961).

Burris-Meyer, Elizabeth, *Color and Design in the Decorative Arts* (Englewood Cliffs, N.J., Prentice-Hall, 1935).

Burris-Meyer, Harold, and Cole, E. C., *Scenery for the Theatre* (Boston, Little, Brown, 1972).

Chevreul, M. E., *The Principles of Harmony and Contrast of Colors* (New York, Van Nostrand Reinhold, 1967).

Cornberg, Sol, and Gebauer, E. L., *A Stage Crew Handbook*, 2nd ed. (New York, Harper & Row, 1957).

Craig, E. G., *Scene* (New York, Oxford University Press, 1923).

Evans, R. M., *An Introduction to Color* (New York, Wiley, 1948).

Friederich, W. J., and Fraser, J. H., *Scenery Design for the Amateur Stage* (New York, Macmillan, 1950).

Gillette, A. S., *An Introduction to Scenic Design* (New York, Harper & Row, 1967).

Gillette, A. S., *Stage Scenery* (New York, Harper & Row, 1960).

Heffner, H. C., Selden, Samuel, and Sellman, H. D., *Modern Theatre Practice*, 5th ed. (New York, Appleton-Century-Crofts, 1972).

Jones, Margo, *Theatre-in-the-Round* (New York, Holt, 1951).

Jones, R. E., *The Dramatic Imagination* (New York, Theatre Arts Books, 1941).

MacGowan, Kenneth, *The Theatre of Tomorrow* (New York, Boni & Liveright, 1921).

Mielziner, Jo, *Designing for the Theatre* (New York, Atheneum, 1965).

Miller, J. H., *Freestanding Scenery* (Elmhurst, Ill., The Hub Electric Co., 1969).

Nelms, Henning, *A Primer of Stagecraft* (New York, Dramatists Play Service, 1941).

Oenslager, Donald, *Scenery Then and Now* (New York, Norton, 1936).

Parker O. W., and Smith, H. K., *Scene Design and Stage Lighting*, 2nd ed. (New York, Holt, 1968).

Pendleton, Ralph, ed., *The Theatre of Robert Edmond Jones* (Middleton, Conn., Wesleyan University Press, 1958).

Philippi, Herbert, *Stagecraft and Scene Design* (Boston, Houghton Mifflin, 1953).

Sellman, H. D., *Essentials of Stage Lighting* (New York, Appleton-Century-Crofts, 1972).

Simonson, Lee, *The Art of Scene Design* (New York, Harper & Row, 1950).

Walkup, Fairfax P., *Dressing the Part*, rev. ed. (New York, Appleton-Century-Crofts, 1950).

White, Gwen, *Perspective* (New York, Watson-Guptill, 1968).

INDEX

DATE DUE